BLACK AMERICANS AND THE MISSIONARY MOVEMENT IN AFRICA

Contributions in Afro-American and African Studies
Series Adviser: Hollis R. Lynch

The African Nexus: Black American Perspectives on the
European Partitioning of Africa
Sylvia M. Jacobs

Freedom and Prejudice: The Legacy of Slavery in
the United States and Brazil
Robert Brent Toplin

The World of Black Singles: Changing Patterns of
Male/Female Relations
Robert Staples

Survival and Progress: The Afro-American Experience
Alex L. Swan

Blood and Flesh: Black American and African Identifications
Josephine Moraa Moikobu

From Du Bois to Van Vechten: The Early New Negro Literature,
1903-1926
Chidi Ikonné

About My Father's Business: The Life of Elder Michaux
Lillian Ashcraft Webb

War and Race: The Black Officer in the American Military,
1915-1941
Gerald W. Patton

The Politics of Literary Expression: A Study of Major
Black Writers
Donald B. Gibson

Science, Myth, Reality: The Black Family
in One-Half Century of Research
Eleanor Engram

Index to *The American Slave*
Donald M. Jacobs, editor

BLACK AMERICANS AND THE MISSIONARY MOVEMENT IN AFRICA

EDITED BY SYLVIA M. JACOBS

CONTRIBUTIONS IN AFRO-AMERICAN AND AFRICAN STUDIES,
NUMBER 66

Greenwood Press
WESTPORT, CONNECTICUT • LONDON, ENGLAND

Library of Congress Cataloging in Publication Data
Main entry under title:

Black Americans and the missionary movement in Africa.

(Contributions in Afro-American and African studies, ISSN 0069-9624; no. 66)
    Bibliography: p.
    Includes index.
    1. Afro-American missionaries—Africa—Addresses, essays, lectures.   2. Missionaries—Africa—Addresses, essays, lectures.   3. Missionaries—United States—Addresses, essays, lectures.   4. Missions—Africa—Addresses, essays, lectures.   5. Afro-Americans—Colonization—Africa—Addresses, essays, lectures.   6. Africa—Church history—Addresses, essays, lectures.   7. United States—Church history—19th century—Addresses, essays, lectures.   8. United States—Church history—20th century—Addresses, essays, lectures.
I. Jacobs, Sylvia M., 1946-   . II. Series.
BV3500.B53   266'.023'7306   81-13230
ISBN 0-313-23280-6 (lib. bdg.)   AACR2

Library of Congress Catalog Card Number: 81-13230
ISBN: 0-313-23280-6
ISSN: 0069-9624

First published in 1982

Greenwood Press
A division of Congressional Information Service, Inc.
88 Post Road West, Westport, Connecticut 06881

Printed in the United States of America

10 9 8 7 6 5 4 3 2 1

To my parents,
Charles and Murval Porch

Contents

V. BIBLIOGRAPHICAL ESSAY

Preface

Afro-Americans' historical identification with the continent of Africa is increasingly being seen as one aspect of their survival in the United States. Moreover, their responses to the events occurring on the continent demonstrate a continuing interest in the fate of the homeland. Recently, black Americans and Africans have come to accept the fact that their lives and histories have been intricately linked. Thus, we see a reaffirmation of this kinship bond by Afro-Americans and a concern for a rediscovery of their deep ties to Africa.

This study surveys a topic that has been ignored by most scholars and makes a contribution in an area where there is scarcely any literature. As this examination demonstrates, black Americans were indeed interested in the Christian "redemption" of Africa throughout the years of the American mission movement on the continent. Black Americans actively participated in this movement by supplying financial support to black churches and manpower for both black and white churches. White boards were particularly anxious to send Afro-American missionaries to Africa because certain areas were seen as a "white man's grave" and it was believed that blacks had an immunity to the diseases of tropical Africa. In fact, Afro-Americans accompanied nearly every white missionary pioneer, and in many parts of Africa they were the first American missionaries.

The essays in this collection discuss the role of black Americans in the American Protestant mission movement in Africa before 1960, including the rise of mission sentiment among Afro-Americans and the various types of mission activities in which they were engaged. This anthology lays the foundation for further research in the area of the historical relationship between Africans on the continent and Africans of the diaspora.

I am indebted to two individuals for completion of this study: Arnold Taylor, my mentor and friend, for suggesting this topic to me; and the late Gerald Hartwig for reading the revised manuscript and offering some valuable comments. I extend particular thanks to Helen A. Fuller for retyping the entire manuscript.

INTRODUCTION:
MISSION IDEOLOGY

I

The Historical Role of Afro-Americans in American Missionary Efforts in Africa

1

Sylvia M. Jacobs

The European religious awakening and the evangelical revival in America, which began in the late eighteenth century, brought forth a renewed interest in missionary work. The nineteenth century would become the greatest era of Christian missionary expansion since the early days of Christianity. European and American churches extended their foreign mission activities into Asia, the South Pacific, and Africa. In both Europe and America, the last decade of the eighteenth century and the first decades of the nineteenth century saw a renaissance in the impulse to spread the Christian gospel. This enthusiasm led to the formation of numerous missionary organizations and the sending of missionaries to all parts of the world. The missionary movement gained momentum after 1830, and by the end of the nineteenth century, mission sentiment existed in most churches in the Western world and had a sense of worldwide destiny.[1]

The work of Protestant missionary societies in Africa began in 1737 when George Schmidt, of the Church of the United Brethren or Moravians, went to South Africa as the first Protestant missionary. In the same year, the Moravians began work in West Africa. Other European missionary bodies were soon formed and duplicated these initial efforts in Africa. The earliest of the new foreign missionary societies founded in Europe was the Baptist Missionary Society, which was organized in Great Britain on October 2, 1792, by William Carey. In September 1795, the Missionary Society was established in London (the name

London Missionary Society did not appear in official publications until 1818) and immediately began work in the South Pacific and India. This was followed in April 1799 by the organization of the Church Missionary Society. The Anglican and Free Churchmen, demonstrating interchurch cooperation, united on March 7, 1804, to form the British and Foreign Bible Society.

The London Missionary Society began sending missionaries to Sierra Leone in 1798 and South Africa in 1799. In 1804, the Church Missionary Society sent missionaries to Sierra Leone to begin work among the colonists and indigenous Africans. Although not alone, Great Britain was one of the earliest and strongest European centers of Protestant missionary fervor. But the other various evangelical Protestant bodies of Europe soon joined the missionary movement.[2]

During the first years of the nineteenth century, the most important issue facing European, specifically British, social and religious theorists was the question of human "progress" and "civilization." The theme of conversion—or induced cultural change—was a constant feature of British mission policy during these years. Like many societies, perhaps most, Great Britain overvalued its way of life and undervalued others. This attitude was long-standing in Western culture, and it increased in intensity throughout the nineteenth century. Most Europeans thought that their way of life represented values of universal application. "Barbarians" might acquire "civilization" (of course, that meant "European civilization"), and for some, to carry "civilization" to the "barbarians" was even a "moral duty." This ethical obligation would be accompanied by economic exploitation and commercial profits for the home country. Economic motives were indeed as important as moral proscriptions. By giving the concept a twist, the "civilizing and Christianizing" mission could become an economic mission as well.[3]

The idea that "civilization" meant Westernization enjoyed a special vogue in mid-nineteenth-century missiology. Christianity and "civilization" were inseparable. If it were assumed that Africans were racially inferior, and yet spiritually equal and capable of receiving the Christian message, then the moral duty of the "superior" people was clear. It was to take up the "white man's burden" and exercise a trust over the spiritual and material welfare of people whose racial status was equivalent to that of children. Such people could never attain the heights of Western "civilization"; they might receive all the spiritual blessings of Christianity but still remain within their own inferior culture. Any study of Christianity in Africa since 1800, therefore, must involve an analysis of these alien ideas and philosophies which produced so profound an intervention into African traditional life.[4]

American missionary societies evolved almost directly from British mission bodies, and the idea of foreign missions quickly took root in the United States. American Protestant missionary activity began in the mid-seventeenth century among native Americans. A feature of early nineteenth-century American life was the religious revival, or the Second Great Awakening, which resulted in the rise of the abolitionist movement and led to nineteenth-century mission sentiment. As missionary zeal permeated the American religious community at the beginning of the nineteenth century, white American church boards began to focus on the continent of Africa for possible mission activity.

Thus, beginning in the first decades of the nineteenth century, a number of American church boards began supporting mission work in Africa. By this time, the African arena had already been accepted as a legitimate area for proselytizing; and many American-based churches established missions on the continent. American missionaries helped to spread the dominant theory of white supremacy. Although they may have defended African rights against European exploitation, they, too, regarded Africans as "uncivilized" and "debauched," and they sought financial support from congregations at home by evoking a picture of the ignorant, unclothed, diseased, and generally benighted African.[5]

Five major Protestant denominations in the United States began to send missionaries to Africa in the nineteenth century: Congregationalist, Baptist, Methodist, Episcopalian, and Presbyterian. By 1840, all of these religious sects had organized foreign mission societies and had established mission stations in Africa.

The first American Protestant missionary body, the American Board of Commissioners for Foreign Missions (ABCFM), was

formed in June 1810 and was made up of Congregational, Presbyterian, and Reformed churchmen. This was the first foreign
missionary society in the country, and it was interdenominational. However, with the rise of denominationalism, by the
mid-nineteenth century all the non-Congregationalists had withdrawn and gone their separate ways. The ABCFM was no longer
interdenominational but predominately Congregationalist.

The first ABCFM foreign missionaries were sent to India in
1812. Africa was entered in 1835. In late 1834, the American
Board sent six missionaries to South Africa, hoping to start work
among the Zulus. They subsequently set up the Zulu Mission,
the first American-sponsored mission in South Africa. At the
same time, the American Board was beginning mission activity
in Liberia, opening a station at Cape Palmas. However, in 1843,
as a result of endemic disease, the station at Cape Palmas was
closed and a new station was opened on the banks of the Gabon
River. The ABCFM also chose Bihe as a site of mission activity in
Angola in 1880 and Inhambane in Portuguese East Africa (Mozambique) in 1883. In 1893, the American Board set up a mission
station at Mount Selinda in Rhodesia.

The Congregational Church and the Christian Church merged
into the Congregational Christian Churches in 1931. This group
united with the Evangelical and Reformed Church in 1957 to
form the United Church of Christ, and the union was completed
in July 1961.[6] ABCFM's successor agency was the United Church
of Christ's United Church Board for World Ministries.

In May 1814, the Baptists organized their own separate missionary society, the General Missionary Convention of the Baptist Denomination in the United States of America for Foreign
Missions. The General Missionary Convention was established
because two American Board missionaries in India wanted to
work for a Baptist mission society. For the northern states, this
society was to become the American Baptist Foreign Mission
Society (today, the American Baptist Churches in the United
States). In early 1821, the society sent two blacks, Lott Carey and
Collin Teague, as missionaries to Liberia.

In May 1845, Southern Baptists "seceded" and formed the
Southern Baptist Convention. White Southern Baptists, who had

withdrawn from the General Missionary Convention over the question of slavery and the nature of denominational organization, sent their first three missionaries to Nigeria in 1849—Reverend Thomas J. Bowen, accompanied by Harvey Goodale of Massachusetts and an Afro-American, Robert F. Hill, of Virginia. Hill did not reach Nigeria, however, remaining at a stopover point in Liberia, and Goodale died in Nigeria a few months after he and Bowen arrived. Today the northern and southern branches of the Baptist Church continue to remain separate.

William Colley (who had worked as a missionary in Liberia from 1875 to 1879 for the Southern Baptist Convention) and five other Afro-Americans left Virginia in 1883 for Liberia as the first missionaries of the black Baptist Foreign Mission Convention of the United States, which was constituted in Montgomery, Alabama, in 1880. The convention united with two other black organizations (the American National Baptist Convention, organized in Saint Louis in 1886, and the Baptist National Education Convention, established in Washington, D.C., in 1893) in 1895 in Atlanta, Georgia, to create the black National Baptist Convention of America. In 1915, the group divided over the adoption of a charter and the ownership of a publishing house; two organizations were formed, the National Baptist Convention of America and the National Baptist Convention of the U.S.A., Incorporated. In 1961, as a result of a dispute over procedures in the election of convention officers, the Progressive Baptist Convention, Inc., broke away from the National Baptist Convention of the U.S.A., Inc. Today, the National Baptist Convention of America and the National Baptist Convention of the U.S.A., Inc., maintain mission stations in Africa.[7]

The Methodist Episcopal Church followed the early mission interest of the Congregationalists and Baptists with the formation of the Foreign Mission Board of the Methodist Episcopal Church in 1819 for the work of evangelizing at home and abroad. Its original work was among native Americans. In 1833, Melville B. Cox opened in Liberia the first overseas mission of the Methodist Episcopal Church. However, he died after only four months in the country. In 1885, William Taylor of the Northern Methodist Episcopal Church arrived in Luanda, Angola, with a party of twenty-four missionaries and established a mission station. Later, in the 1890s, the church began work in Rhodesia. In 1908, a station was pioneered in North Africa; by 1914, it had taken possession of some French Catholic churches there and was reaching out to North African Muslims as well.

In 1844, the Methodist Episcopal Church split into two churches—the Methodist Episcopal Church, the northern body, and the Methodist Episcopal Church, South. The Southern Methodist Episcopal Church initiated foreign missionary activity in 1848 when Charles Taylor sailed for China. However, the church did not begin African mission work until 1914, when Walter Russell Lambuth opened the Wembo Niama station in the Congo.[8]

The Methodist Protestant Church of the United States (which withdrew from the Methodist Church in 1830) attempted its first overseas work in 1837 by sending a black missionary to Liberia, but the project proved a failure because only white men were allowed the franchise in the church. The Free Methodist Church also established missions in Africa during the nineteenth century, the first in Portuguese East Africa (Mozambique) in 1885.

In 1939, the Northern Methodist Episcopal Church, the Methodist Episcopal Church, South, and the Methodist Protestant Church were united under a new name, the Methodist Church. In 1968, the Methodist Church merged with the Evangelical United Brethren Church to form the United Methodist Church. The Free Methodist Church has become a world fellowship consisting of three general conferences, in Egypt, Japan, and North America, and continues to maintain foreign missions in Africa.[9]

The second largest Methodist group in the United States today, the black African Methodist Episcopal (AME) Church, began its first mission efforts in 1820, when Daniel Coker, a representative of the American Colonization Society, departed for Africa, later organizing the first foreign branches of the AME Church, in Liberia. In 1891, Bishop Henry McNeal Turner organized AME Conferences in Liberia and Sierra Leone, and in 1898, he consolidated a new branch of the AME Church in South Africa drawn from the Ethiopian movement.

In 1876, the black African Methodist Episcopal Zion (AMEZ)

Church began its foreign missionary activities in Liberia. In that year, Andrew and Rosanna Cartwright of Elizabeth City, North Carolina, arrived in Brewerville, sixty miles in the interior of Liberia. Bishop John Bryan Small, in 1896, became the first missionary bishop assigned to West Africa by the AMEZ Church.[10]

In 1820, at the instigation of the Church Missionary Society, the Domestic and Foreign Missionary Society of the Protestant Episcopal Church in the United States began operation. However, it was not until ten years later that missionaries of the church were sent out: in 1830, two missionaries were dispatched to Greece. The church established its first mission in Africa in 1836 near Cape Palmas, Liberia. In March of that year, two Afro-Americans, Mr. and Mrs. James M. Thompson, started a mission school at Mount Vaughan. Liberia remained the only African field of the Protestant Episcopal Church. In 1967, the general convention adopted the Episcopal Church as an alternative name for the Protestant Episcopal Church in the United States.[11]

Finally, of the larger Protestant churches in Africa, the Presbyterian Church in the U.S.A. organized the Foreign Mission Board of the Presbyterian Church in 1837, after separation from the American Board. The Presbyterian Church had as its pioneer missionary John B. Pinney, who had gone to Liberia in 1833, four years before the establishment of the Mission Board. A black man, James Temple, was sent out in 1833, but he withdrew after only four months. The Presbyterian Church of the U.S.A. began work among Coptic Christians and Muslims of Egypt in 1854 (the first American church to begin work in this area). Thomas McCague and his wife, Henrietta M. Lowes McCague, reached Cairo on November 15, 1854, and were joined by James Barnett of the Damascus mission the next month. The first congregation of the American Presbyterian Church was organized in Cairo in 1865. In the 1880s, it moved into the Cameroons. By the beginning of the twentieth century, northern Presbyterians turned southward from Egypt toward the Sudan. In May 1958, the Presbyterian Church of the U.S.A. merged with the United Presbyterian Church of North America to form the United Presbyterian Church in the United States of America.

In 1861, southern presbyteries formed the General Assembly

of the Presbyterian Church in the Confederate States of America, which was constituted in 1865 into what is now known as the Presbyterian Church in the United States, or the Southern Presbyterians. In 1890, the Southern Presbyterian Church began work in Africa by sending one black minister, William H. Sheppard, and one white minister, Samuel N. Lapsley, to the Congo, thus initiating what was to become one of the largest Presbyterian missions in the country.[12]

Other American Protestant missionary bodies also entered Africa during the height of missionary fervor in the late nineteenth and early twentieth centuries. The Mormons (Church of Jesus Christ of Latter-day Saints) started a mission in South Africa as early as 1836. The Church of the United Brethren in Christ was established in Sierra Leone in 1855 and took over the American Missionary Association's holdings when it withdrew from the country in 1882. The Seventh-day Adventists first sent missionaries to Africa when a station was opened in South Africa in July 1887. In the 1890s, missionaries from the Church of the United Brethren in Christ and the Seventh-day Adventists arrived in Rhodesia. The Watchtower movement (the missionary arm of Jehovah's Witnesses) became active in Nyasaland in 1906-1907. The Christian Church (Disciples of Christ) opened a mission in the Congo in 1899, and it was joined by a number of American churches, including a black group, the Lott Carey Baptist Home and Foreign Mission Convention of the United States, in 1901 and the Assemblies of God (the largest of the Pentecostal bodies) in 1921.[13]

The two greatest Protestant missionary thinkers and administrators of the nineteenth century, whose influence lasted until the middle of the twentieth century, were Henry Venn, general secretary of the Anglican Church Missionary Society (CMS) of London, and Rufus Anderson, corresponding (foreign) secretary of the American Board of Commissioners for Foreign Missions of Boston. These two architects of nineteenth-century missionary policies developed a philosophy for worldwide Protestant mission work.

Henry Venn (1796-1873), secretary of the CMS from 1841 to 1872, was the son of John Venn, a founder of the Church Missionary Society and rector of Clapham in South London who had gathered about him a company of similarly thinking men who came to be nicknamed "the Clapham sect." A financial crisis of the CMS in 1841, the year in which Venn began his work as secretary, served to emphasize the need to review the society's policy toward missions.

Venn's views on missions were firm: "If the elementary principles of self-support and self-government and self-expression be thus sown with the seed of the Gospel, we may hope to see the healthy growth and expansion of the Native Church." In his memorandums of 1851 and 1861, he cautioned that missionaries were to limit themselves to evangelistic work and were not to become involved in church administration once the "native church" was established. He urged missionaries to control their natural desire to stay on as pastors, and he tried to keep them moving to new fields once a congregation had been founded. At this stage, Venn insisted, the missionary would be able to transfer all pastoral work to the "native" congregations under their own pastors and gradually relax his superintendence over the pastors until it "insensibly ceases." Then the missionary and all missionary agencies were to be assigned to new unevangelized regions. As far as the former field was concerned, the missionary had completed his work, and in Venn's words, "the euthanasia of the Mission" had taken place. The "native church" would then be a self-reliant church, including a responsibility for outreach into the non-Christian world around it. Venn's insights were revolutionary for his day.[14]

While Henry Venn was directing the affairs of the Church Missionary Society in London and making his contribution to the principle of missions, the American Congregationalist Rufus Anderson (1796-1880) was performing very similar functions in Boston. These two great mission secretaries had many things in common and continued a warm friendship over many years. They influenced one another's thinking to such an extent that it is not easy to determine which of them first conceived the missionary objective of a "native" church administering, supporting, and propagating itself.

Dr. Anderson is the acknowledged theoretician of the American missionary enterprise. He provided a sound basis for the development of American missions, and nearly all American and Canadian boards and societies adopted most of the fundamental points of his doctrine and professed to follow him, although they did not fully implement all his policies. Andersonian principles continued to provide the foundation of American missions into the 1940s. Mission boards and societies, until the end of World War II, generally stated the aim and goal of their ministry in terms of Rufus Anderson's "three-self" formula, the planting and fostering of churches which would become "self-governing," "self-supporting," and "self-propagating."[15]

After his election to the office of corresponding secretary in 1832, Anderson began an effort to reshape the policy of the American Board and to influence American missions in general. He reacted sharply to what he thought to be wrong objectives and emphases that had been inherited from the earlier missions to native Americans and that prevailed in the foreign work. "Evangelization" and "civilization" had been the key words in American Protestant mission methods. It was believed that both were supplementary and complementary: acceptance of the gospel through "evangelization" brought the desire and incentive to non-Western peoples to attain "Christian," that is, Western "civilization," while if "civilization" were stressed in initial contacts with these people, it produced understanding and acceptance of the gospel. However, Anderson believed that it was a mistake to make the transformation of "civilization" the aim of missionary work.[16]

As a result of the discussions that followed the presentation of the *Report of the Deputation* to India in 1856, the American Board officially incorporated Rufus Anderson's principles into stated doctrine in the celebrated *Outline of a Missionary Policy*, written for the Prudential Committee by Secretary Selah B. Treat and adopted in 1856 as the ultimate and lasting principle. According to Anderson, the missionary movement was "the Christian Church going forth, under its Great Captain, for the subjugation of the world." Similarly, Dr. Anderson believed that "the grand object [of foreign missions] is to plant and multiply self-reliant, efficient churches, composed wholly of native converts, each church complete in itself, with pastors of the same race with the people." While such churches should be self-governing and self-supporting, the fundamental hope was that "they should also be self-propagating from the very first." Rufus Anderson was a pioneer founder of the indigenous church idea and believed that, above all, young congregations were to be churches from the outset and not colonial outposts of Western denominations nor carbon copies of them. Anderson affirmed that "native" pastors would be better able to overcome the obstacles of distance, expense, and climate inherent in a foreign mission.[17]

In practice, there does not seem to have been much difference between the policies of Venn and Anderson. The influence of Rufus Anderson and Henry Venn on each other needs further investigation, as it is obvious that it did exist. There were a number of corresponding factors in the lives of the two secretaries. They were born in the same year, in 1796, and both became foreign corresponding secretaries, Anderson of the largest Protestant society in America and Venn of the largest Protestant group in Europe. Anderson had clearly come to his full position before establishing a personal relationship with Venn, but friendship and discussion of mission principles and problems began with Anderson's visit to London in August 1854. Both leaders declared the tripartite aim of missionary church work—self-government, self-support, and self-propagation. But Anderson's main emphasis was on mission, not church organization, and his order of priorities was first, self-propagating, second, self-governing, and third, self-supporting. This order was exactly the reverse of that given by Venn, who did not, in fact, mention the term "self-propagating" in his first statement of policy. Nevertheless, the genuine desire of these early leaders was to encourage new indigenous churches.[18]

Until at least the 1940s, no American mission agencies or missionaries openly questioned Dr. Anderson's aim for missions, namely, the fostering of self-propagating, self-governing, and self-supporting churches. Within ten years after his death (by 1890), however, American, along with British and continental European, missionaries had caught the "colonial mind" by contagion, and a new emphasis on denominationalism combined with this colonial outlook to stimulate missionary paternalism and imperialism. After this date, the tendency was to make the young churches into ecclesiastical colonial copies of the planting churches. Moreover, after 1880, the idea of conversion declined. In the age of imperialism, racism became dominant in European and American thought. Few believed that the "lower races" could ever reach the heights of Western achievement, though they were entitled, in their "inferiority," to the paternal protection of the Western powers. The idea of trusteeship thus gradually replaced that of conversion.[19]

European and American missionaries went to Africa, and elsewhere, with the certainty that they were obeying the Great Command to go into all the world, baptizing and making disciples of all nations. Above all, missionaries went with an amazing degree of confidence in the supremacy of the Christian and Western social and economic order. Not only that, but these missionaries carried with them an identifiable ideology, characteristic of their age, that undergirded the imperialist expansion of the Western powers in the nineteenth century. This sense of certainty often produced insensitivity to indigenous cultures, and missionaries contended that African traditional religion was not merely the absence of religious truth but was in fact "a positive evil."[20]

During the American Protestant missionary movement in Africa, black Americans assumed a role in the evangelization of the land of their forefathers. Many Afro-Americans accepted the contemporary theory of "manifest destiny" promulgated by whites. They believed they had been brought to America for slavery by "providential design," so that they might be Christianized and "civilized" to return to the "Dark Continent" with the light of "civilization."[21] As one black Methodist clergyman emphasized, "the obligation, my brethren, for African evangelization is . . . upon us—the obligation by racial affinity, by providential preparation, by special adaptation, by divine command, is upon us."[22]

The idea of duty and moral obligation was not the only argument presented for the use of Afro-American missionaries in Africa. Some churchmen voiced the opinion that black Americans were more immune to African fevers than whites. The many diseases of tropical Africa made certain areas of the continent a "white man's grave." White boards believed that black

Americans, because of their African ancestry, had a stronger resistance to the climate and fevers of Africa, and they began to perpetuate the myth that Afro-Americans were better suited than whites for African mission work. Eventually, enough survived to support the idea that blacks had an immunity to the African climate and were more adaptive than whites for African mission work.[23]

Afro-Americans, since their beginnings in America, have felt an ambiguous alliance with Africa. At the same time that they accepted the reality of their African heritage, they endorsed the Western image of Africa as the "Dark Continent." This accounts for the fact that during the latter half of the nineteenth and early twentieth centuries, many blacks supported mission work in Africa and a few even volunteered, believing that this religious and cultural exposure would help make the continent acceptable to the world. Neither the black masses nor their leaders have ever forgotten Africa, and during the height of missionary zeal in Africa they took the natural way to express their interest by sending missionaries there, just as whites were doing. After 1870, black Americans could not resist the call for African missionaries.[24] Although black missionaries were assigned to fields other than Africa by both white and black church boards (the American Episcopal Church, for example, sent blacks to Haiti and the AME Church had missionaries in San Domingo, Barbados, Demarara, the Bahamas, the Virgin Islands, Trinidad, Jamaica, and Haiti), the majority saw their destiny in Africa and volunteered to work there.

Most white American Protestant bodies supporting African missions were anxious to send Afro-American missionaries to the continent and were only limited by the availability of qualified blacks. A very high proportion of the missionaries sent to Liberia by white boards were black. Nearly every white missionary pioneer was accompanied by black assistants, and in many parts of Africa, Afro-Americans were the first American missionaries. As early as the 1820s, black missionaries and bishops of the various church denominations began to write of their experiences in Africa. Although most Afro-Americans had embraced much of the Western religion and culture which portrayed Africa as a "Dark Continent" in need of "Christian enlightenment," and even mouthed similar sentiments, they nevertheless had a very genuine and fairly widespread sense of obligation for Africa and an attitude far less patronizing than whites. At the schools and colleges they attended, many of them sponsored by white churches, black Americans received a strong dose of educational and religious propaganda about their "duty" to the homeland.[25]

The majority of black missionaries who were assigned to Africa were males, although they were usually accompanied by their wives, who shared in the missionary duties. In other cases, single women were assigned to mission work on the continent. Women who went to Africa, either as "missionary wives" or commissioned missionaries, generally aided in upgrading the lives of African women and children, since the mores of the late nineteenth and early twentieth centuries dictated that women missionaries be employed in capacities designated as "woman's work."

American blacks who grew up in the early part of the twentieth century probably first heard about Africa when a minister or missionary appealed for funds to support missions there. The missionaries frequently gave a distorted picture of the African way of life and brought back sensational and ridiculous stories because they either did not understand the culture, wanted to exaggerate their own achievements, hoped to capture and hold their audiences, or were attempting to show the need for continued missionary activity. But whether a black person went to Africa to get away from racist whites in America or to gain the respect of whites and blacks in America, it is practically impossible to imagine the trials and difficulties of climate, disease, loneliness, hostility, and discouragement which all missionaries met when they entered Africa, or for that matter, anywhere else.[26]

The earliest plan contemplated for the use of black American missionaries in Africa was the one proposed by Samuel Hopkins of Newport, Rhode Island, in 1770. Dr. Hopkins, a prominent clergyman of the First Congregational Church of Newport, soon after his installation in 1770, formed a plan that contained both missionary and colonization features. Actually, the missionary tradition had its roots in the colonization movement. Hopkins' plan called for the careful selection and education of American free blacks as Christian ministers who would then emigrate to Africa, settle there, and teach Africans the doctrines and duties of Christianity. His idea was formulated in two circulars issued in August 1773 and April 1776 under the joint signature of himself and Ezra Stiles, pastor of the Second Congregational Church of Newport.[27]

The Missionary Society of Rhode Island administered an African fund of £80 which had been raised by Hopkins for the purpose of sending black missionaries to Africa. Two candidates, both members of the First Congregational Church, were selected to be trained for this purpose. Bristol Yama, a slave, and John Quamine, a free black, both about thirty years old, went to Princeton University to study theology in order to fit themselves as "native" evangelists to their African brethren. Both spoke their indigenous African languages of the Guinea coast.

The interruption of Hopkins's pastoral work at Newport because of the British occupation of the city and other difficulties growing out of the Revolutionary War prevented him from immediately putting his plan into effect. Quamine was killed in the war in a naval battle. In 1789, Reverend Hopkins approached Granville Sharp, principal leader of the fight against slavery in Great Britain, about possible Afro-American migration to Sierra Leone.

In 1791, Hopkins sought to renew his plan, and he made preparations to send Yama and another young black man about twenty years old, Salmur Nubia, a member of the Second Congregational Church of Newport, to Africa. A delegation was sent to Freetown, Sierra Leone, in 1795 to investigate the idea that Hopkins had discussed with Sharp, black emigration, though no one emigrated at this time.

Hopkins died in 1803 before the education of any of his missionaries had been completed and before his missionary dreams were fulfilled. However, it is believed that at least two of his candidates, Nubia and Newport Gardner, later went to Africa under a similar plan of the American Colonization Society (ACS)

in what became Liberia. Eighty-year-old Deacon Newport Gardner and others left the United States on January 7, 1826, with a
contingent of settlers sent out by the ACS.[28]

Other black Americans were involved in early missionary efforts. George Liele was one of the most famous of the early black
Baptist preachers. Liele, a slave, began preaching to other slaves
in his hometown of Savannah, Georgia, during the Revolutionary War, but after the war his master, a Tory, took him to Jamaica. Liele sailed from Savannah in 1783. In Jamaica, he began
what might be styled missionary work and established the Baptist Church among Jamaicans. In 1790, Reverends David George,
Hector Peters, and Sampson Calvert, also black Baptist preachers,
all originally from the United States, sailed from Nova Scotia for
the west coast of Africa where they began proselytizing activities and organized the first Baptist congregation in Sierra Leone.[29]

Before 1900, white American Protestant churches controlled
not only the number of black missionaries in Africa, but also the
areas for their mission work. Needless to say, white Congregationalists, Baptists, Methodists, Episcopalians, and Presbyterians sent Afro-Americans to Africa. But white Americans also
continued to evangelize Africa, and until the post-World War I
period, they dominated the work of missions in East and North
Africa, where the milder climate favored them. In East Africa, a
number of African revolts from 1890 to 1910 also discouraged
the use of black Americans as missionaries.

After 1900, with "Jim Crow," lynchings, and disfranchisement
of blacks prevalent throughout the United States, white mission
boards frequently and spasmodically displayed mistrust and hostility toward black missionaries in Africa, and opposition to them
became widespread. By 1920, the idea of using black missionaries in Africa was all but dead in the white American religious
community. These boards were being pressured to recall black
missionaries stationed in Africa by the European imperialists,
who, by 1920, had occupied all of the continent except the Republic of Liberia and Ethiopia.

One significant reason for the Europeans' negative reaction to
American black missionaries was the reversal of missionary attitudes, aims, and goals in Africa after about 1880, as the empha-

sis of missions changed from conversion to trusteeship. Mission societies insisted that Africans were "naturally" inferior and did not have the qualities needed for pastors and bishops, and that African churches must be ruled by Europeans. For this reason, colonial governments and European churches opposed recognition of AME ordinations and episcopacies and the demand by AME and other black American missionaries of higher education for Africans. Although Protestant missions in other parts of the world, notably in Asia, established school systems from kindergartens to universities, this was not done in Africa, obviously as a response to the policies of the colonial governments there.[30]

Europeans also feared Ethiopianism which became dominant in the late nineteenth century, as well as Marcus Garvey's "Africa for the Africans" campaign after 1916. These colonialists continually attempted to keep potential "troublemakers" out of Africa. They felt that Afro-American missionaries who were Christianizing and educating the Africans would only jeopardize the colonial system. By the early twentieth century, European governments in Africa saw the presence of Afro-American missionaries as threatening. Black missionaries were accused of encouraging political revolts, and colonial governments, believing that these missionaries preached revolution, discouraged their entry.

By the end of World War I, the general consensus of European colonialists was that Afro-American missionaries upset the status quo and caused too many disruptions to warrant their effective use in the "civilizing mission" in Africa. Although there were no legislative restrictions specifically directed against black American missionaries after 1920, most European governments in Africa were strongly opposed to sending them there for mission work. The European imperialists therefore formulated a justification for their exclusion based upon the premise that the Afro-American presence caused unrest and disturbances among the Africans and was dangerous to the maintenance of law and order in Africa.

White American missionary boards doubted whether they could continue to send black missionaries to Africa and accomplish their goal of missionary service. They began to claim that they had been unable to make satisfactory use of Afro-Americans as missionaries. White mission boards in the United States and white missionaries stationed in Africa felt that the time was not right to pressure European governments into accepting black missionaries, and after 1920, they were withdrawn from missionary work on the continent.[31]

During the forty-year period between 1920 and 1960, few black American missionaries not already in Africa were assigned there by white boards. (One notable exception was the establishment of the ABCFM Galangue station in Angola in the early 1920s, manned by Afro-American missionaries.) Black American churches continued to send Afro-American missionaries to Africa, but even they were restricted to certain areas for mission work. By 1945, white boards generally agreed that blacks served better as missionaries in Asia and Latin America. However, after 1960, white boards again used a number of blacks as missionaries to Africa.

One indication of a shift in white American religious interest in the use of black Americans as missionaries in African mission work was the Church Conference on African Affairs held at Otterbein College (Westerville, Ohio) during June 19-25, 1942, under the leadership of Emory Ross. One session of the conference was devoted to "The Contribution of the American Negro to Africa." Participants considered the role black American missionaries had had in Africa after 1920. In light of this discussion, the conference proposed that a larger place be provided for American blacks in missionary service, both as missionaries and as members of mission boards. One recommendation of this group which may have affected American governmental policy was the suggestion that a separate African bureau in the State Department be created. In 1956, the post of assistant secretary of state for African affairs was established.[32]

The impact of missionaries in Africa before 1960 was profound. Missionary accomplishments were in five areas: (1) language translation, (2) education, (3) medical work, (4) industrial and technical training, and (5) social reform. Many major themes of missionary work in the fields of education, medicine, social welfare, and politics still await detailed investigation. Missionaries amassed tremendous knowledge about the African traditional way of life. They spoke the languages of the peoples they missionized and tended to stay in those areas from three to twenty-five years. It was the Christian missionaries who manned and financed most of the first schools in Africa, thus creating an educated elite who went on to form political parties and to become the national leaders upon independence. Missions also established medical clinics and hospitals.[33]

Missionaries were also responsible for less honorable achievements. Missionaries, probably more than any other single group, kept the myth of African "savagery" alive. The image they cast was that of heroes doing battle with the forces of "darkness" —cannibalism, lust, and depravity. It was in the interests of missionaries to debase the condition of African life, and they often denigrated traditional customs and institutions. Protestant missioners also contributed to African religious disunity by spreading the religious ideas of dozens of religious sects throughout the continent.[34]

In the final analysis, when we attempt to assess American Protestant missionary activity in Africa we must recognize, first of all, that American missions and missionaries before 1945 played a minor role in the development of the African church. European, and particularly British, missions took the lead and supplied most of the personnel. European Catholics predominated in French, Belgian, and Portuguese colonies; British and Canadian Protestants in British territories; and German Protestants and Catholics in German colonies before 1920. Nevertheless, the American missions did have an important impact on African education, through their schools. Into the 1950s, missionaries provided most of the primary and secondary education available in Africa south of the Sahara. American missionaries also made a significant contribution to African culture by reducing many African languages to writing.[35]

Equatorial Africa has proved to be a fertile field for American mission work, and presently Americans comprise about one-half of the Protestant missions there. American Protestant missionaries have been active in almost every area of Africa, but only since World War II have they represented the bulk of Protestant missionaries in Africa. Today the most active American Protestant denominations in Africa are the Baptist, Methodist, Presbyterian, and Pentecostal.

In 1900, there were a little over half a million Christians in Africa; by 1960, that figure had grown to almost 35 million and by the early 1980s, almost 130 million.[36] In the early 1980s, Africa was the third most populous continent in the world, after Asia and Europe, with a population of almost 470 million. According to empirical data, by 2000 the total population of Africa will be 768 million, and the continent will have become the second most populous in the world (exceeded only by Asia), with a Christian population of 351 million. By 2000, the Christian community will represent 31.2 percent of the world population. By that date, the center of gravity of the Christian world will have shifted southward, from Europe and North America, to the developing continents of Africa and South America. Africa may well be the home of one of the largest Christian communities in the world.[37]

No general study has been made of the black American as a missionary to Africa. A study of the facts might well reveal that one of the chief problems associated with the use of black Americans was their lack of sufficient preparation, training, education, or experience. In the zeal to send blacks as missionaries to Africa, many times they were sent without adequate qualifications. In addition, some Afro-Americans had less than noble intentions and volunteered for the cause of African missions for escapist reasons.[38]

In the traditional histories of American Christianity and American Protestant religious attempts to evangelize Africa, black American missionaries, as representatives of both white and black denominations, have received little attention. Actually, American missions and missionaries, like the European, had two goals; the primary purpose was evangelistic work, but the secondary one was development in the areas of education, medicine, and agriculture, with the final result being the recreation of Western society in Africa. Afro-American missionaries supported this so-called process of regeneration. As this anthology shows, black American missionaries before 1960 had various motives for African mission work (besides the obvious desire to

Christianize Africans), including a feeling of duty, a chance to combine colonization with missionizing, a desire to prove the black man's capabilities, and an impulse from both individuals and institutions for the educational development of the continent. In fact, one important contribution of Afro-American missionaries stationed in Africa was in the area of education. Their insistence on African education (an issue that blacks emphasized in the United States) eventually resulted in the founding of a number of African schools based on American models. These missionaries were particularly active in Liberia, Sierra Leone, South Africa, the Congo (Zaire), and the Gold Coast (Ghana), while work in Nigeria, Angola, and Nyasaland (Malawi) was sporadic but significant. It is certain, however, that Afro-American missionaries, before their partial exclusion from Africa in the first decades of the twentieth century, were noticeably present and dutifully engaged in mission work. Even after that date, their influence continued to be felt throughout African society.

Notes

1. Philip D. Curtin, *The Image of Africa, British Ideas and Action, 1780-1850* 1 (Madison: University of Wisconsin Press, 1964), pp. 259-260; Clarence Clendenen and Peter Duignan, *Americans in Black Africa Up to 1865* (Stanford, Calif.: Hoover Institution on War, Revolution, and Peace, Stanford University, 1964), p. 45; Clarence Clendenen, Robert Collins, and Peter Duignan, *Americans in Africa, 1865-1900* (Stanford, Calif.: Hoover Institution on War, Revolution and Peace, Stanford University, 1966), p. 20; Ogbu U. Kalu, "Church Presence in Africa: A Historical Analysis of the Evangelization Process," in *African Theology En Route*, ed. Kofi Appiah-Kubi and Sergio Torres (Maryknoll, N.Y.: Orbis Books, 1979), p. 17; and Walter Williams, "Black American Attitudes Toward Africa: The Missionary Movement, 1877-1900" (Ph.D. dissertation, University of North Carolina, 1974), p. 16.

2. Diedrich Westermann, *Africa and Christianity* (London: Oxford University Press, 1937), p. 136; Stephen Charles Neill, *Colonialism and Christian Missions* (New York: McGraw-Hill, 1966), p. 252; and Clendenen and Duignan, *Americans in Black Africa*, pp. 44-45, 62.

3. Paul Bohannan and Philip Curtin, *Africa and Africans*, rev. ed. (Garden City, N.Y.: Natural History Press, 1971), p. 51; and Curtin, *Image of Africa* 1, pp. 259-261 and 2, pp. 415, 420.

4. Stephen Charles Neill, *A History of Christian Missions* (Harmonds-worth: Penguin Books Ltd., 1964), p. 243; Curtin, *Image of Africa* 2, pp. 414, 420, 422; Richard Gray, "Problems of Historical Perspective: The Planting of Christianity in Africa in the Nineteenth and Twentieth Centuries," in *Christianity in Tropical Africa*, ed. C. G. Baëta (London: Oxford University Press, 1968), p. 19; Hugh Stuntz, "Christian Missions and Social Cohesion," *American Journal of Sociology* 50 (November 1944):188; and G. Gordon Brown, "Missions and Cultural Diffusion," *American Journal of Sociology* 50 (November 1944):214.

5. Victor C. Ferkiss, *Africa's Search for Identity* (New York: Braziller, 1966), p. 297; Clendenen, Collins, and Duignan, *Americans in Africa*, p. 61; Clendenen and Duignan, *Americans in Black Africa*, pp. 44-45; and D. L. Leonard, "The Origins of Missions in America," *Missionary Review of the World* (June 1892):423.

6. Kenneth Scott Latourette, *A History of the Expansion of Christianity*, vol. 5: *The Great Century in the Americas, Austral-Asia, and Africa, A.D. 1800-A.D. 1914* (New York: Harper & Brothers Publishers, 1943), p. 360; Charles P. Groves, *The Planting of Christianity in Africa to 1840* 1 (London: Lutterworth Press, 1948), pp. 202-203; Charles Henry Robinson, *History of Christian Missions* (New York: Charles Scribner's Sons, 1920), p. 327; Gustav Warneck, *Outline of a History of Protestant Missions from the Reformation to the Present Time* (New York: Fleming H. Revell, 1901), p. 107; Edward Chester, *Clash of Titans; Africa and U.S. Foreign Policy* (Maryknoll, N.Y.: Orbis Books, 1974), pp. 70-72; Frank S. Mead, *Handbook of Denominations in the United States* (Nashville, Tenn.: Abingdon, 1975), pp. 258-262; and Leonard, "Origins of Missions in America," p. 426.

7. Groves, *The Planting of Christianity in Africa* 1, p. 203; Neill, *History of Christian Missions*, p. 252; Warneck, *Outline of a History of Protestant Missions*, p. 109; Chester, *Clash of Titans*, p. 70; Mead, *Handbook of Denominations*, pp. 43-45; and Leonard, "Origins of Missions in America," p. 433.

8. Thomas B. Neely, *The Methodist Episcopal Church and Its Foreign Missions* (New York: Methodist Book Concern, 1923), p. 71; Johannes Du Plessis, *A History of Christian Missions in South Africa* (London: Longmans, Green & Co., 1911), p. 390; Warneck, *Outline of a History of Protestant Missions*, p. 110; Groves, *The Planting of Christianity in Africa* 1, p. 296; Chester, *Clash of Titans*, pp. 69-71; and Leonard, "Origins of Missions in America," p. 434.

9. Groves, *The Planting of Christianity in Africa* 1, pp. 298-299; Chester, *Clash of Titans*, pp. 71-72; Mead, *Handbook of Denominations*, pp.

188-191, 194-195; and J. Minton Batten, "Henry M. Turner: Negro Bishop Extraordinary," *Church History* 7 (September 1938):231.

10. L. L. Berry, *A Century of Missions of the African Methodist Episcopal Church, 1840-1940* (New York: Gutenberg Printing Co., Inc., 1942), pp. 225-228; William Seraile, "Black American Missionaries in Africa, 1821-1925," *Social Studies* 63 (October 1972):198-199; and Wilbur Christian Harr, "The Negro As an American Protestant Missionary in Africa" (Ph.D. dissertation, Divinity School, University of Chicago, 1946), p. 120.

11. Groves, *The Planting of Christianity in Africa* 1, pp. 297-298; Mead, *Handbook of Denominations*, p. 131; Warneck, *Outline of a History of Protestant Missions*, p. 110; and Leonard, "Origins of Missions in America," pp. 434-435.

12. J. Du Plessis, *The Evangelisation of Pagan Africa, A History of Christian Missions to the Pagan Tribes of Central Africa* (Cape Town: J. C. Juta & Co., Ltd., 1929), p. 99; John Harris, *The Great Commission* (Boston: Gould, Kendall & Lincoln, 1842), pp. 187-188; Andrew Watson, *The American Mission in Egypt* (Pittsburgh: United Presbyterian Board of Publication, 1904), pp. 64-66, 68-70, 97-99; Robinson, *History of Christian Missions*, p. 281; Groves, *The Planting of Christianity in Africa* 1, pp. 204, 297 and 2, p. 298; Warneck, *Outline of a History of Protestant Missions*, p. 111; and Chester, *Clash of Titans*, pp. 69-71.

13. Chester, *Clash of Titans*, pp. 70-72.

14. Max Warren, ed., *To Apply the Gospel, Selections from the Writings of Henry Venn* (Grand Rapids, Mich.: William B. Eerdmans Publishing Co., 1971), pp. 15-34; R. Pierce Beaver, ed., *To Advance the Gospel, Selections from the Writings of Rufus Anderson* (Grand Rapids, Mich.: William B. Eerdmans Publishing Co., 1967), p. 5; Curtin, *Image of Africa* 2, pp. 423-424; and "Henry Venn of the Church Missionary Society," Peter Beyerhaus and Henry Lefever, *The Responsible Church and the Foreign Mission* (London: World Dominion Press, 1964), pp. 25, 27-28, 30.

15. Beaver, ed., *To Advance the Gospel*, pp. 5, 9-10, 37; and "Rufus Anderson of the American Board," Beyerhaus and Lefever, *The Responsible Church and the Foreign Mission*, pp. 30-31.

16. Beaver, ed., *To Advance the Gospel*, p. 13.

17. Ibid., pp. 6, 16, 18, 23, 28, 31, 35.

18. Ibid., pp. 36-37; and "Introduction" and "Rufus Anderson," Beyerhaus and Lefever, *The Responsible Church and the Foreign Mission*, pp. 11, 32-33.

19. Curtin, *Image of Africa* 2, pp. 415, 423; and Beaver, ed., *To Advance the Gospel*, p. 38.

20. Bohannan and Curtin, *Africa and Africans*, p. 54; and Kalu, "Church Presence in Africa," pp. 17-18.

21. Edwin W. Smith, *The Christian Mission in Africa* (London: International Missionary Council, 1926), p. 100; and St. Clair Drake, "Negro Americans and the African Interest," in *The American Negro Reference Book*, ed. John P. Davis (Englewood Cliffs, N.J.: Prentice-Hall, 1966), p. 469.

22. M.C.B. Mason, "Africa in America and Africa Beyond the Seas." This is a lecture given by Mason and can be found in *Solving the Problem* (Mt. Morris, Ill.: Kable Brothers, 1917), p. 138.

23. Tony Martin, "Some Reflections on Evangelical Pan-Africanism" or "Black Missionaries, White Missionaries and the Struggle for African Souls, 1890-1930," *Ufahamu* 1 (Winter 1971):80; Seraile, "Black American Missionaries in Africa," pp. 199-200; and Williams, "Black American Attitudes Toward Africa," pp. 19-20.

24. George Shepperson, "Ethiopianism and African Nationalism," *Phylon* 14 (Spring 1953):14; St. Clair Drake, "The American Negro's Reaction to Africa," *Africa Today* (December 1967):13; and Williams, "Black American Attitudes Toward Africa," p. 23.

25. Clendenen and Duignan, *Americans in Black Africa*, pp. 63-64, 81; Dorothy Porter, "Bibliographic Checklist of American Negro Writers About Africa" in *Africa Seen by American Negroes* (Paris: Présence Africaine, 1958), p. 380; Edwin S. Redkey, "The Meaning of Africa to Afro-Americans, 1890-1914," *Black Academy Review* (Spring-Summer 1972): 56; and Martin, "Evangelical Pan-Africanism," p. 79.

26. Harold Isaacs, *The New World of Negro Americans* (New York: John Day Co., 1963), p. 129; Emory Ross, *Out of Africa* (New York: Friendship Press, 1936), p. 124; and Rayford W. Logan, "The American Negro's View of Africa," in *Africa Seen by American Negroes*, p. 218.

27. Oliver W. Elsbree, *The Rise of the Missionary Spirit in America, 1790-1815* (Williamsport, Pa.: Williamsport Printing and Binding Co., 1928), pp. 66, 109; and Harr, "The Negro As an American Protestant Missionary in Africa," p. 13.

28. Archibald Alexander, *A History of Colonization on the Western Coast of Africa* (Philadelphia: William S. Martien, 1846), pp. 48-59; Christopher Fyfe, *A History of Sierra Leone* (London: Oxford University Press, 1962), p. 112; Elsbree, *The Rise of the Missionary Spirit in America*, pp. 109-110; Clendenen and Duignan, *Americans in Black Africa*, pp. 61-62; Clendenen, Collins, and Duignan, *Americans in Africa*, p. 20; William D. Johnston, "Slavery in Rhode Island, 1755-1776," *Publications of the Rhode*

Island Historical Society 2 (July 1894): 154, 154n, 155, 155n; and Harr, "The Negro As an American Protestant Missionary in Africa," p. 13.

29. Booker T. Washington, *The Story of the Negro, The Rise of the Race from Slavery* 1 (New York: Doubleday, Page & Co., 1909), p. 265; Lewis G. Jordan, *Up the Ladder in Foreign Missions* (Nashville, Tenn.: National Baptist Publishing Board, 1901), pp. 15-17; Edward A. Freeman, *The Epoch of Negro Baptists and the Foreign Mission Board* (Kansas City, Mo.: Central Seminary Press, 1953), p. 107; and Elsbree, *The Rise of the Missionary Spirit in America*, p. 35.

30. Redkey, "The Meaning of Africa to Afro-Americans," p. 21; and Seraile, "Black American Missionaries in Africa," pp. 200-201.

31. Smith, *The Christian Mission in Africa*, pp. 122-123; Seraile, "Black American Missionaries in Africa," p. 201; and "The Negro As a Missionary," *Missionary Review of the World* (December 1903):946.

32. Chester, *Clash of Titans*, p. 73; and "The Contribution of the American Negro to Africa," *Christian Action in Africa*, Report of the Church Conference on African Affairs (New York: Africa Committee of the Foreign Missions Conference of North America, 1942), pp. 140-146, 168.

33. William H.P. Faunce, *The Social Aspects of Foreign Missions* (New York: Missionary Education Movement of the United States and Canada, 1914), p. 104; Jessie Jones, *Education in East Africa* (London: Edinburgh House Press, 1924), pp. 88-89; Chester, *Clash of Titans*, pp. 2, 75; Bohannan and Curtin, *Africa and Africans*, pp. 6, 186; and Gray, "Problems of Historical Perspective," p. 25.

34. Ferkiss, *Africa's Search for Identity*, p. 151; Chester, *Clash of Titans*, p. 75; and Bohannan and Curtin, *Africa and Africans*, pp. 4, 8.

35. Chester, *Clash of Titans*, pp. 74-75.

36. G. C. Oosthuizen, *Post-Christianity in Africa* (Grand Rapids, Mich.: William B. Eerdmans Publishing Co., 1968), pp. 9, 28n; Patrick J. St. G. Johnstone, *World Handbook for the World Christian* (South Pasadena, Calif.: World Christian Book Shelf, 1976), pp. 17-18, 111, 118-119, 122; Robinson, *History of Christian Missions*, p. 280; and David B. Barrett, "AD 2000: 350 Million Christians in Africa," *International Review of Missions* (January 1970):39, 45, 51-52.

37. Annual Table, "Religions of the World," *Britannica Book of the Year, 1981*, p. 606; Chester, *Clash of Titans*, pp. 69-70, 74; and Barrett, "AD 2000," pp. 39, 44-45, 47, 49-52.

38. "Contributions of the American Negro to Africa," pp. 142-143.

The "Black Man's Burden": The Racial Background of Afro-American Missionaries and Africa

2

Donald F. Roth

Nineteenth-century and early twentieth-century American missions in Africa concentrated on more than just spiritual conversion. As the black Methodist Bishop Alexander Camphor put it, "evangelical work alone" was "not enough."[1] Protestant churchmen inevitably saw missions as transmitting a whole system of values—a value structure of which it was hoped Christianity was the centerpiece. But as the nineteenth century progressed, revealing an increasingly urban and secular America, the missionary viewpoint grew more complex. So-called natives certainly needed the uplift of Christianity and civilization. Yet, experience showed that secular transmitters of "civilization" often utilized such interesting lubricants of change as gin or opium. By the early twentieth century, church leaders had become more cautious about the link between civilizing and Christianizing the great unsaved. As one black missionary commented, "along with this form of civilization. . . other things are brought which tend to demoralize rather than civilize."[2]

Even more ambivalent was the situation of the Afro-American churchmen interested in the conversion of Africa. White Protestant church leaders generally held the racial attitudes which were dominant in American society at large. Take, for example, the reaction of the white Presbyterian leader, A. D. Phillips, to William Sheppard's request to become the first Southern Presbyterian missionary to the Congo. Sheppard had attended

Hampton Institute as well as the Presbyterian's own Tuscaloosa Training Institute for Colored Ministers (Stillman College). He had been a diligent and reserved student. Yet, Phillips seriously contended that the sight of half-naked African women would subject Sheppard to irresistible attacks of lust. Phillips's white colleagues agreed that only under the supervision of a white man could a black missionary go to Africa.

A. D. Phillips's low estimate of black character and abilities—estimates unfortunately prevalent among leaders of all the multiracial denominations—delayed Sheppard's tour of Africa until a suitable white overseer could be found to accompany the young Afro-American. (Ironically, Sheppard's companion died soon after arrival, and Sheppard, on his own, survived the threat of lust rather well, remaining in the Congo for twenty years.)[3]

A basic contradiction faced Sheppard and all black missionaries of that day: American Christian civilization, of which they were to be transmitters, retained at its core the idea of black inferiority. In fact, this idea was one prop underlying the prevalent American image of a "Dark Continent" in need of saving. And yet this "Dark Continent" was also the Afro-American's homeland.

Despite such contradictions, the racist nature of American society also acted as a spur to Afro-American interest in African missions. To major black church leaders, like African Methodist Episcopal Bishop Henry McNeal Turner and National Baptist Convention founder William W. Colley, the African mission field was obviously a special "black man's burden." This was work that Afro-Americans were (in Colley's words) "most sacredly called to do."[4] The black American, it seemed, had special abilities to reach the black man in the land of his forefathers. By his success in this sacred project, the Afro-American could prove his own worth and abilities in his American home.

The desire to prove the black man's capabilities by pursuing success in the African mission field was an important motivation behind the black mission movement. One must remember that the all-black churches were the most significant forum independently minded black leaders had. These organizations, separatist in form, were pursuing assimilationist goals in their leaders' desire to create "full-fledged" institutions. Since a strong missionary sector was essential to every nineteenth-century Protestant church, leaders of all-black churches found it imperative that a special black mission movement be founded.[5]

For black leaders working within the multiracial churches, African missions could be an important means for individual advancement in status and prestige. African missions provided a special black arena of activity, within which such persons could prove their worth and abilities. Black missionary bishops of the Methodist and Episcopal churches exemplified this trend.[6] Such churches were reluctant to give black men authority over white congregations through standard episcopacies, but missionary episcopacies allowed these denominations to reward outstanding blacks, while avoiding unwanted integration.

Thus, black church leaders in both the separatist and the multiracial denominations worked in the context of Africa as a special mission field for the black man, and within both types of organizations, black church leaders used this special field as one within which to prove the Afro-American's worth and abilities, either on an institutional or an individual level. But while racist realities served as partial motivation for the black mission movement, racism ultimately undermined its effectiveness.

Even the gentle Bishop Camphor worried that racial strife would mean that the "bloody scenes of the French Revolution" would be "repeated on American soil."[7] Other black mission leaders were milder in their racial commentaries. But the ironies of their position came back to haunt most of these men. By transmitting Christianity in the context of American civilization, these missionaries inevitably were giving away damaged goods. They were in a situation similar to that of numerous Peace Corps volunteers of the early 1960s. Those later, secular missionaries exported the beneficial aspects of technological society; yet, many Peace Corps volunteers were dissatisfied with the form of society which such technology fostered. As noted earlier, nineteenth-century Protestant missionaries, white and black alike, recognized a similar dilemma—that the civilizing process had both Christian and non-Christian results. For the black missionary, the dilemma doubled; Christianity and civilization were reposi-

tories of spiritual and material freedom and yet were also sources
of race prejudice and injustice.

For most of the nineteenth century, black church leaders had
referred to Africa with the "Dark Continent" description familiar
to Americans. But toward the end of that century, emigrationist
leaders like AME Bishop Turner worked to modify the dim view
of Africa common among black churchmen.[8] Using the information which leaders like Turner supplied (as in his *African Letters*),
the Afro-American could begin to look at his prior homeland as
a source of pride and strength.

After 1900, for many black families the evangelical rather than
the emigration publicist became the major source of information
about Africa. (Some men, of course—Turner once again being
the prime example—followed a century-old tradition linking emigration and evangelization.) In their letters to stateside periodicals and in speeches during furloughs, black missionaries increasingly refused to portray the African as "uncivilized" and
"savage"; he was unsaved, perhaps, but not unsound.[9] Men like
Camphor and Sheppard posed the problem in terms of convert-
ing the African soul without changing the African heart. Still,
the problem remained. Black missionary leaders, as well as missionaries of all colors, knew by the end of World War I that an
elite evangelical corps had little chance of protecting African
civilizations from the wholesale intervention brought by the other
legions of the West—military, mercantile, and governmental.

Judged by its own standards, the Afro-American mission movement in Africa certainly failed. The number of missionaries and
their lengths of stay were small, as were the number of converts
they reported. But the interest in Africa was there, and if the
movement ultimately did fail in its own terms, it had major
effects upon the American black man's view of Africa and con-
sequently his own sense of identity. Indeed, the Protestant Church,
with its focus on missionary work, was the primary vehicle of
black American interest in Africa. Missionaries and mission pub-
licists were essential catalysts in forming the Afro-American's
image of his ancestral home.

The most significant factor contributing to the black mission
movement's failure was financing. Foreign mission work was

the most expensive church activity, and black congregations were uniformly poor. For example, while all three of the independent black Methodist churches (the Colored Methodist Episcopal, African Methodist Episcopal, and African Methodist Episcopal Zion) raised funds to send important leaders to Africa early in the twentieth century, none was able to follow up with major mission activity. In each case, enthusiasm and leadership existed in good measure. But the American black man had few extra dollars to expend on Africa's evangelization, and the grandiose schemes of John Wesley Gilbert, William Heard, and Alexander Walters inevitably came to nothing.[10]

Within the multiracial churches, race prejudice, rather than inadequate funding, proved the primary hindrance to the black mission movement. Such churches caught up in the evangelical movement as well, with larger financial resources than the independent black denominations, called upon their black brethren to pursue mission work in the "heart of darkness." Black Baptists, in particular, heard the call from their white co-religionists to join in a "cooperative" venture in Africa. White churches would supply the bulk of the funds and black men the personnel.[11] But as most black Baptist leaders recognized, such offers were not the bargains they seemed. Black missionaries were always denied roles of leadership and, in some cases, even social intercourse with their white colleagues. A case in point: the first black missionary sent to Africa in a cooperative white-black Baptist enterprise came home after five years, having spent the last three in desolate isolation from his racially biased colleagues.[12]

Thus, to finance substantial missions, the black American had either to go to his black brethren who had insufficient means or to join up with his white brothers who refused to treat him on a basis of equality. The inevitable result was that only a handful of black men had successful tenures as African missionaries, despite the constant interest of black church members in such evangelical activity.

But the problem ran deeper. By 1900, only the most naive observer of what some called "aggressive Christianity" could deny that the coming of Christianity and civilization usually spelled the going of African society. Indeed, black missionaries as well as their white counterparts were forced to intercede with other "civilizers" on the Africans' behalf. William Sheppard became an international celebrity when he exposed the atrocities which French and Belgian rubber companies perpetrated upon the Congolese.[13] Yet, ultimately more long-lasting was that more subtle destruction of African mores and customs. The nature of mission work inevitably accelerated this destruction, since concepts of the nonmaterial world were at the core of African civilization. When the black missionary in Africa assisted in the erosion of African society, he was simultaneously destroying his own past. Thus, missions to Africa involved carrying forth American civilization, toward which the Afro-American felt ambivalent, in order to modify African civilizations, about which the American black also had mixed feelings.

The Afro-American movement to evangelize Africa was therefore fraught with psychological as well as financial difficulties. As noted earlier, in terms of the number of missionary years in Africa, the movement barely existed. Yet, this area of black activity was a significant one. Too often, Afro-American interest in Africa has been viewed as historically fragmented; we jump from Henry Turner to Marcus Garvey to the 1950s and African independence. But a continuum of black interest existed between these highpoints of enthusiasm. Never in the history of the organized black church in America—from Richard Allen's day on—was interest in the religious fate of the motherland totally dormant.

Africa, as homeland and as mission field, became a caldron of identity for the black American. When he dealt with his missionary destiny in Africa, the black person examined both the African and the American components of his heritage. The indications are that this examination greatly interested black Americans of this period. When William Sheppard toured the country with Booker T. Washington, Sheppard was able to steal top billing from the founder of Tuskegee in local black newspapers.[14] Alexander Camphor, Henry Turner, the Baptist missionary Clinton Boone, and others visited packed Afro-American churches with lectures on Africa, while their articles and books on the homeland rolled from denominational presses. By the second decade of the twentieth century, the picture these men drew of Africa was no longer painted in dark tones. They brought some tales of cannibalism, but more often of basic kindness and capability. Some, like Sheppard, brought back impressive examples of African artwork. For black men, and indeed for some white men, these were the African experts of the day, men who could speak from actual experiences. Even W. E. B. Du Bois, an early Pan-Africanist who was highly suspicious of Christian missions, called upon Sheppard to be a principal speaker at a 1919 National Association for the Advancement of Colored People (NAACP) symposium on Africa.[15]

The promoters of the Afro-American missionary movement were thus able to contribute to the black man's knowledge of his African heritage. The idea of African missions provided a skeleton upon which to flesh out a view of Africa as homeland, rather than as "Dark Continent." Black churchmen, through the promotion of African missions, became important agents in the transition of Africa's image from "Dark Continent" to the spiritual heartland of the race.

Notes

1. *New Africa* (Monrovia, Liberia) 4 (October and November 1902):301.

2. Southern Presbyterian missionary Henry Hawkins in the *Kassai Herald*, April 1, 1904, p. 1.

3. Donald F. Roth, "'Grace Not Race': Southern Negro Church Leaders, Black Identity, and Missions to West Africa, 1865-1919" (Ph.D. dissertation, University of Texas at Austin, 1975), Chapter 7.

4. W. W. Colley quoted in Lewis G. Jordan, *Negro Baptist History, U.S.A., 1750-1930* (Nashville, Tenn.: Sunday School Publishing Board, 1930?), pp. 154-155.

5. For examples of this attitude, see James A. Handy, *Scraps of African Methodist Episcopal History* (Philadelphia: A.M.E. Book Concern, 1901), pp. 288-289; and the *Voice of Missions* 2 (February 1894):1.

6. For example, see John Wesley Edward Bowen, ed., *An Appeal for Negro Bishops But Not Separation* (New York: Eaton & Mains, 1912), pp. 36-38.

7. *Liberia and West Africa* (Monrovia, Liberia) 6 (May 1904):3.

8. For example, the writings of Turner in his periodical the *Voice of the People*, published in Atlanta for several years after 1900.

9. Examples of such portrayals by William Sheppard can be found in the *Amsterdam News*, May 13, 1911, and the *Missionary* 26 (March and May 1893): 113-114, 168-172. Similar notions are expressed by Camphor in his *Missionary Story Sketches; Folk-Lore from Africa* (1909).

10. Roth, " 'Grace Not Race,' " Epilogue. For some idea of the numerical strength of black missionaries, see James S. Dennis, et al., eds., *World Atlas of Christian Missions* (New York: Student Volunteer Movement for Foreign Missions, 1911). I have a personal statistical file which is somewhat more complete and covers missionaries from 1865 to 1920.

11. Roth, " 'Grace Not Race,' " Chapter 2.

12. Ibid., Chapter 3 for a discussion of C. C. Boone's missionary career.

13. See, for example, Mark Twain's pamphlet *King Leopold's Soliloquy* which deals with Sheppard's revelations.

14. *New York Press*, February 8, 1911.

15. On the NAACP gathering, see Horace M. Kallen and James Weldon Johnson, eds., *Africa in the World Democracy* (New York: National Association for the Advancement of Colored People, 1919). Du Bois treats Sheppard's career in his "Men of the Month" column, *Crisis* 11 (May 1915):15. Du Bois expressed fears of Christian missions in his "Address to the Nations of the World" at the 1901 Pan-African Congress. On this address, see Alexander Walters, "The Pan-African Conference," *A. M. E. Zion Quarterly Review* 11 (April-June 1901):168.

THE MISSION: MOTIVATIONS, OBJECTIVES, AND RESULTS

II

THE MISSION: INTRODUCTION

Thomas C. Howard

Between the Africa of geographical reality and the abstract idea of Africa in the Afro-American's mind there has been a gradual congruence, created by an increasing number of linkages over time. As this collection of essays testifies, one of the earliest and most enduring of these linkages has been the Afro-American missionary enterprise in Africa. The four articles included in this section draw together a number of strands which help to explain the ideas and motivations behind this unique chapter in African and Afro-American histories. The examples discussed here also reveal the extent to which the results of Afro-American activity in Africa could differ from the original aims.

Although the idea of using black American missionaries in Africa can be traced to the very earliest days of modern overseas missionary expansion in the late eighteenth century, it was not until the nineteenth century that a coherent philosophy of mission emerged within various segments of the Afro-American community. When this did happen, it was focused primarily on the settlement of Liberia, and for many years thereafter, Afro-American perceptions of Africa were virtually inseparable from the rivalries and controversies surrounding the Liberian experiment. Only gradually, and concurrent with the changing fate of Afro-Americans at home and the colonial expansion of the European powers in Africa, did a wider African—even Pan-African—stage present itself. Nonetheless, Liberia did remain for some time the centerpiece of Afro-

American rediscovery of the ancestral home, and several themes were destined to persist in one form or another until the present.

Aboard the first ships carrying settlers to Africa was Daniel Coker, a minister of the African Methodist Episcopal Church, the first Afro-American to leave for Africa through the American Colonization Society with a distinct missionary goal, and Lott Carey, an ordained Baptist missionary. Reflecting both the white philanthropic commitment to resolve the American racial dilemma by returning Afro-Americans to Africa and the desire to "redeem" Africa for "Christianity and civilization," missionaries such as Coker and Carey continued to play a crucial role in the future of the settlements of Liberia and Sierra Leone. Among the early settlers there was a general acceptance of Western preconceptions about Africa, as well as an economic dependence on American philanthropy.

These same ideas extend into the next century. By the time Robert R. Moton succeeded Booker T. Washington as president of Tuskegee Institute in 1915, Tuskegee was already the prototype for numerous other American educational institutions for blacks and had come to be viewed as a model for educational experiments throughout colonial Africa. This was in keeping with the educational philosophy popularized by Washington, a philosophy that saw the industrial education promoted by Tuskegee as a universal remedy for the problems of black people. It was as applicable to Africa as to the American South. Not only did Tuskegee become a place of pilgrimage for educators and politicians from throughout the world, but it also developed into a unique training ground for missionaries who desired to share the secrets of Tuskegee with the people of Africa and other portions of the non-Western world.

The scale and scope of Afro-American missionary contact with Africa had grown considerably by 1935 when Moton's term as president of Tuskegee ended, though the underlying motivations had remained remarkably constant. The ideal of religious regeneration remained, just as did the ambition to modernize Africa along Western lines. Unfortunately, most of the Western models available were the products of a society that viewed Africans, wherever they might live, as people in need of long years of tutelage before equality or independence might be achieved.

More optimistically, the vision of a redeemed homeland inevitably led to greater knowledge and intensified contact on both sides of the Atlantic. As Afro-Americans increasingly reevaluated their situation in American society and took action to change it, nationalist movements in colonial Africa did the same. In the end the colonialists got more than they bargained for, because at the same time that American ideas of industrial education were exported to Africa, so were the controversies surrounding it. Traditional missionary ideology which stressed the degeneration of Africa and the need for "redemption" led ultimately to the belief that forces were latent within Africa for self-redemption.

But it was not a simple transition, and at first there were many disappointments. The closer we come to the present in the case studies in this section, the more evidence we have of the complex consequences of missionary ideology. Among the most fascinating aspects of the missionary enterprise has been the inspiration it provided to generations of young Africans to seek higher education in the United States and to foster the development of universities in Africa.

The years from 1900 to 1930 witnessed an increasing flow of Africans to the United States, often as a result of contact with Afro-American missionaries or with other Africans who had benefited from an American education. Many of the Africans who came to the United States were inspired initially by the Tuskegee ideal and received support from American philanthropic organizations.

Nnamdi Azikiwe was encouraged to travel to the United States in the 1920s by James Aggrey, a prominent African educator who had earlier traveled from Africa under the sponsorship of a missionary of the African Methodist Episcopal Zion Church. Aggrey, and later Azikiwe, had lofty ambitions for their homeland and did what they could to reinterpret the traditional missionary ideals of redemption and civilization into the realities of twentieth-century educational ideology. Both were influenced by the industrial educational concept promoted by Tuskegee, though in separate ways both broke with it. Unfortunately, the ideas that were substituted for it frequently were only slightly less incompatible with the African environment. Rather than "Tuskegees-in-Africa," the new ideal was to establish universities on African soil, but modeled on American.concepts.

The later ideals of African nationalists, Azikiwe among them, were grandiose and clearly promised too much. Despite the rhetoric about the ideal of new departures for African education and the need for the creation of a truly African university adapted to the needs of the people, the clash between alien traditions was more often the reality. The new missionaries were governmental and philanthropic agencies aiming at their own version of African "redemption." It was a curious legacy of those early Afro-American missionaries in Liberia. But there were other legacies also, not the least of which has been the rediscovery of Africa by Afro-Americans and the promise of greater understanding and cooperation in the future.

Rhetoric and Reality: Colonization and Afro-American Missionaries in Early Nineteenth-Century Liberia

3

Tom W. Shick

The return of Afro-Americans to West Africa during the nineteenth century was carried out with the rhetoric of achieving "African redemption" through the spread of "civilization and Christianity" on the continent. It was used to justify the establishment of an Afro-American settler colony in 1822, which twenty-five years later became the Republic of Liberia. The nature of the immigration made all settlers missionaries in the land of their forefathers. Although exiled from America, they consciously created a society that reflected their American background and that stood in sharp contrast to traditional African culture. Their experience shaped attitudes among settler descendants that persisted into the twentieth century and became a significant part of the Liberian national ethos.

The American Colonization Society was formed in 1816 as a national organization to "ameliorate" the condition of "Free People of Color" in America. The founding members, all influential Euro-American citizens, included many who were clergymen. In fact, the concept of colonization had evolved from the criticism of slavery within the church establishment. Between con-

This chapter is adapted from Tom W. Shick, *Behold the Promised Land: A History of Afro-American Settlers in Nineteenth-Century Liberia* (Baltimore: Johns Hopkins University Press, 1980). Copyright 1980 by Johns Hopkins University Press. Reprinted by permission. The research for this chapter was made possible by a grant from the Social Science Research Council.

doning continued bondage on the one hand and demanding unconditional emancipation on the other, colonization was a moderate alternative for religious leaders disturbed by the moral implications of slavery.[1] Typical of their ranks was the Reverend Robert S. Finley, a Presbyterian minister from Basking Ridge, New Jersey. He saw colonization as an opportunity to use Christian charity in addressing a social issue of national importance. "Could not the rich and benevolent devise means to form a colony on some part of the Coast of Africa, similar to the one at Sierra Leone, which might gradually induce many free blacks to go there and settle, devising for them the means of getting there, and of protection and support till they were established?" To Reverend Finley, Africa was the ideal place for such a colony because of three distinct benefits that might accrue: "We should be cleared of them; we should send to Africa a population partially civilized and christianized for its benefits; our blacks themselves would be put in better condition."

The American Colonization Society had an additional goal. Once a colony was planted in Africa, the colonization supporters believed that slaveholders would be encouraged to emancipate slaves for removal there. Charles Fenton Mercer, a Virginia congressman, became a founding member of the American Colonization Society on this very basis. He had earlier reminded the Virginia Assembly that "many thousand individuals in our Native State. . . are restrained from manumitting their slaves. . . by the melancholy conviction that they cannot yield to the suggestions of humanity without manifest injury to their country."[2] Ultimately, the society's founders hoped to remove the entire Afro-American population, both slave and free, with the support of the federal government. Thus, a commitment to resolve America's racial dilemma by exiling Afro-Americans was interfaced with a mixture of professed benevolence towards the stigmatized Afro-Americans and Christian missionary zeal towards Africa.

For the men and women who went to West Africa under the auspices of the American Colonization Society, emigration fused a growing race consciousness with a missionary impulse that coincided with the society's spirit. They were convinced that the degradation of the African race would never end until those who were able demonstrated the capacity for social and political elevation. Emigration, more than their escape, was perceived as their duty in order to establish a strong, independent "Negro Republic."[3] It was in those terms that Liberia's most distinguished nineteenth-century citizen, Edward Wilmot Blyden, appealed to Afro-Americans to return to Africa. Blyden, an ordained Presbyterian minister, outlined their task as "rolling back the appalling cloud of ignorance and superstition which overspreads the land, and to rear on those shores an asylum of liberty for the downtrodden sons of Africa wherever found." He argued that such emigration had a direct mandate from God. Their sojourn in slavery was providential, according to Blyden, in that it prepared them to return to Africa and spread "Christianity and civilization" among their African kin. Thus, Blyden ascribed deep religious overtones to the nineteenth-century call for emigration to Liberia.[4] The motive behind the settlement of Afro-Americans in Liberia was destined to involve emigrants in conflicts as they struggled to maintain Western standards in the midst of a traditional African cultural environment.

Once the American Colonization Society was formed in Washington, its leadership tried to persuade the federal government to aid their declared program. The earlier abolition of the slave trade and one of its consequences gave the society a way of approaching its objective. In 1807, a federal law had been passed making illegal the further importation of African slaves to the United States. The American Naval Squadron then began to stop vessels in the Atlantic Ocean and seized slave cargoes when they were discovered.[5] Once these "Recaptured Africans" were in custody the problem then was what should be done with them. Charles Fenton Mercer proposed a federal bill in 1818 that would "transfer the responsibility for disposing of rescued Africans from the state to the federal government."[6] His legislative proposal called for the establishment of a government agency in West Africa where rescued Africans would be resettled. The president would be authorized to make all necessary arrangements while Congress was to appropriate $100,000 for the project. On March 3, 1819, the bill became law as "an Act in addition

to the acts prohibiting the Slave Trade."[7] The American Colonization Society encouraged James Monroe, as president, to interpret his mandate liberally. They hoped he would use his authority
to purchase territory for a colony. Such a colony could then
receive Afro-Americans as well as newly Recaptured Africans.

Monroe discussed the idea of forming a colony in Africa with
his Cabinet advisers. Legal questions were raised about the constitutionality of the United States buying territory in foreign
lands. The reservations of his advisers forced Monroe to move
cautiously. He finally agreed to start the program only after the
American Colonization Society indicated a willingness to assume
the direct responsibility for purchasing land. With this technical
distinction clear, James Monroe considered the government role
only as facilitating the resettlement of Recaptured Africans. In
1819, he announced that two federal agents and a representative
of the American Colonization Society were being sent to West
Africa. The officials, along with a company of laborers and artisans, had orders to establish a government station on the African coast.[8] Thus, the first step towards creating a colony to
receive Afro-Americans was accomplished with federal assistance.
The assistance, however, was based on solving the special problem of resettling Recaptured Africans and remained limited in
scope. Nevertheless, the American Colonization Society had the
start it had hoped for and eventually honored James Monroe for
his efforts by naming the first settlement of the colony after him,
Monrovia.

On January 31, 1820, the ship *Elizabeth* sailed from New York
City with a company organized by Samuel Bacon, the appointed
government agent. His assistant was John P. Bankson, and the
American Colonization Society representative was Samuel Crozer.
The most important members of the company, however, were
eighty-six Afro-Americans. The government chose to view these
individuals as workers required to construct the government
station. They were in fact the first settlers to emigrate to Africa
under the auspices of the American Colonization Society. All
were free Afro-American volunteers from New York City, Philadelphia, Washington, D.C., Baltimore, and Petersburg, Virginia. More than half of the company were women and children,

which made their classification as purely workers questionable. Samuel Bacon offered the explanation to the secretary of the navy that the men refused to go without their families. The males in the company were laborers, farmers, and artisans with the notable exception of Daniel Coker. Coker was a school teacher and minister of the African Methodist Episcopal Church. He represented the first Afro-American to leave for Africa through the American Colonization Society program with a clear missionary purpose.[9]

The sailing of the *Elizabeth* was marked by an elaborate ceremony in New York City. Hundreds of well-wishers assembled at a local Afro-American church. After an impressive religious program, a procession was formed to accompany the adventurers to the point of embarkation.[10] The voyage began with high spirits among both the settlers and their Euro-American companions. The harmonious start was short-lived because tensions surfaced over who should exercise authority. In his diary Daniel Coker made note of disturbances that resulted when the ship's captain and the agents tried to enforce their authority. Coker found himself in the role of mediator during one tense situation that threatened to explode into open rebellion. One of the settlers and the ship's captain became embroiled in a fight in which pistols were almost used. Coker described the events that followed:

After things had little subsided, Mr. Bacon came to me as I was waiting by the cabin door, bathed in tears, said to me, "Brother Coker, this is an awful judgment upon us; come, let us go below and have religious worship." We did so, with the emigrants. He said much to the purpose; after he was done, I spoke with them in his absence for about a half hour; I felt that it was not labor lost—it was a weeping time.[11]

As the days passed during the voyage, Reverend Coker was pressured to assume a direct leadership position by the other settlers. They were influenced by his opinions and seemed willing to support him. Despite his growing popularity among the Afro-Americans, Coker refused to lead a challenge against Bacon, Bankson, and Crozer, He believed that it was "the height of ingratitude to manifest any distrust of the sincerity of the Agents, after such proof and the comforts of a civilized life."[12] Coker's reluctance to challenge the agents estranged him from many of the settlers.

After a passage of only thirty days, the ship *Elizabeth* landed in Sierra Leone and then proceeded to Sherbro Island where the station was to be built. The company was met by John Kizell who recommended that they accept temporary shelter in Campelar, a place that Samuel Bacon described as "a village of about twenty houses built in the native style, situated on nearly the east end of Sherbro Island."[13] The location was unfortunate and almost destroyed the entire company. Campelar was unhealthy because of the absence of fresh water and the low, swampy condition of the land. By May 1820, just five months after leaving New York City, all three agents as well as twelve settlers died.[14]

As disease took its toll on the company, the issue of authority once again flared with even greater intensity. Many of the surviving settlers refused to accept any authority but their own. Before Samuel Crozer died, he formally transferred to Daniel Coker his own responsibility as the American Colonization Society agent. Coker accepted only in the interest of preventing the total collapse of the company's concerted effort. His hesitancy was in part motivated by the knowledge that several settlers wanted Kizell to assume control over the group. Coker decided to return to Freetown, Sierra Leone, with all of the survivors who would follow. Once back in Freetown, the demoralized company was allowed to stay at Fourah Bay by the British authorities there. They awaited additional supplies and manpower from America. The first attempt to "plant the colony" was disastrous, but the survivors still hoped to secure a permanent site for the settlement.

Daniel Coker continued to keep his diary while living at Fourah Bay. He gave considerable thought to his religious beliefs and the goals of colonization. The distinct possibility of dying before the colony was formed led Coker to confide in his diary that "Moses was I think permitted to see the promised land but not to enter in. I think it likely that I shall not be permitted to see our expected earthly Canaan. But this will be of but small moment so that some thousand of Africa's children are safely landed."[15]

Coker was also able to observe the dynamics of more immediate matters that reflected religious differences within the company. He saw that the settlers tended to isolate themselves from each other on the basis of their particular Protestant denomination. He tried to be optimistic, however, and hoped that "notwithstanding this...we shall get along in harmony."[16]

By March 8, 1821, supplies and reinforcements reached the settlers when the brig *Nautilus* arrived in Freetown. Among the new settlers on the *Nautilus* was the Reverend Lott Carey, leader of the Baptists in the new company. Carey was born a slave on a plantation in Charles City County, Virginia. He was baptized in 1807 by Elder John Courtney, pastor of the First Baptist Church in Richmond. In 1813, Carey bought his freedom and that of his two children. In a public statement before emigrating to Africa, Lott Carey declared his intentions:

I am about to leave you; and expect to see your faces no more. I long to preach to the poor Africans the way of life and salvation. I dont [*sic*] know what may befal me, or whether I may find a grave in the ocean, or among the savage men, or more savage wild beasts, on the Coast of Africa; nor am I anxious what may become [of] me. I feel it my duty to go.[17]

Prior to his departure, both Lott Carey and Collin Teague were ordained and accepted as missionaries by the Baptist Board of Foreign Missions on May 1, 1819. Baptist members of the *Nautilus* company agreed to form a church congregation before departing and elected Lott Carey as their pastor. The constitution of this church was modeled after the Samson Street Church of Philadelphia, and the congregation worshipped together during their journey to Africa.[18]

The pattern of forming church congregations before leaving America became a significant characteristic of immigration to Liberia. It contributed to the formation of competing groups among the settlers as well as providing potential leadership for the larger community. Even while at Fourah Bay, Daniel Coker was aware of conflict between different denominational groups. The Reverend Joseph R. Andrus and Christian Wiltberger were sent out by the American Colonization Society to replace the deceased Samuel Crozer. Ephraim Bacon and Jonathan B. Winn also arrived to become the new government agents. Coker reported that when Andrus called a religious meeting of the settlers, some of them refused to attend and instead organized a separate meeting. In frustration, Coker wrote:

O Bigotry thou art no friend to religion or colonizing. I cannot see why such pains should be taken to oppose the Episcopal Church. I fear that no good will result from this great and important undertaking. I feel it to be a duty to enter this on this journal and bear testimony against the spirit. I wish to see every one enjoy the privilege of worshipping God according to the dictates of their own conscience. But this spirit and conduct I must condemn.[19]

As soon as Andrus and Bacon arrived in Freetown, they set out along the coast in search of a new site for the settlement. On April 12, 1821, they signed a treaty agreement for land with King Jack Ben of Grand Bassa. The American Colonization Society received the treaty but refused to ratify it because of an article that prohibited interference with the slave trade.[20] The society, in reaction to the treaty, dispatched Dr. Eli Ayres to relieve Reverend Andrus as principal agent. He arrived in November 1821 to find only Wiltberger awaiting him in Sierra Leone. Both Andrus and Winn had died, while Bacon was on his way to America by way of the West Indies in extremely poor health. Agent Ayres, finding the Fourah Bay situation deteriorating, was determined to find a suitable location for an independent colony. He was able to get the assistance of Lieutenant Robert F. Stockton, commander of the USS *Alligator*. Finally, Ayres and Stockton negotiated an agreement with King Peter and his associates for land on Cape Mesurado.[21] The formal possession of the Cape on April 25, 1822, took place on Providence Island and marks the beginning of the Liberian colony.

As the American Colonization Society sent out new emigrants to their fledgling colony, they encouraged religious groups to establish missionary programs among both the settler and African populations. The first ordained Methodist missionary to Liberia was the Reverend Melville B. Cox who came to Monrovia in March 1833. Cox was followed by several other Euro-American missionaries: Reverend S. J. Matthews, John B. Barton, Henry P. Barker, Jabez Burton, John Seys, and a single female teacher, Miss Sophronia Farrington. Afro-Americans also volunteered during these early years, notably Francis Burns, who became the first missionary bishop of the Methodist Church, and Miss Eunice Sharp, a teacher. The Methodists eventually formed a regular Annual Conference, composed of three districts, each with a presiding elder and its circuits, stations, and Sunday schools.[22] The Annual Conference consisted of twenty-one members "in full connection and on trial." Melville Cox became convinced by his experience in Liberia that Afro-Americans should be employed to conduct mission work:

Could we find men suitable, it would probably be for the interest of the mission, as well as the colony, and the interest of our Colored friends in general, to call as many of them into the field, as *auxiliaries*, as could conveniently be supported. Their constitutions, it is thought by some, are better suited to the climate than that of the white man's, and it would have a tendency to allay the many petty and fearful jealousies that exist here against *white* influence. The whole colony, with a few exceptions, seems strangely fearful of the authority of white men in any form. Time and patience, and love, however, I doubt not, will soon correct the evil.[23]

Neither time nor love and patience resolved the problem to which Cox alluded. In fact, the Methodist missionaries became the focus of a major controversy during the colonial administration of Thomas Buchanan that began in 1839. The Methodist missionaries offered economic security to settlers who became associated with their mission stations. Under the leadership of the Reverend John Seys, a Methodist newspaper, *Africa's Luminary*, was published in the colony. Methodist influence grew quickly until the government challenged its right to import goods into the colony for mission work without paying custom dues. The dispute reached the Supreme Court as the case of William N. Lewis, Collector of Customs, Port of Monrovia *vs.* Reverend

John Seys, Superintendent, Liberian Mission of the Methodist Episcopal Church.[24]

The case quickly became more than a simple legal issue. The old problem of denominational conflict threatened to polarize settlers once again. The election of new members to the Commonwealth Legislative Council in 1840 became the stage for a political test of two factions. An administration faction supported Governor Buchanan, while the Methodist faction supported the position of Reverend Seys. The resources of each faction were used to win additional adherents. Buchanan charged that Seys used money to influence voters to favor his position. "At Millsburg every voter was employed at unusually high wages on the [Methodist] Saw Mill and sugar plantation—and there *every vote* was polled for his friends."[25] An unidentified correspondent to the American Colonization Society prefaced his letter of support for the Buchanan administration by mentioning that he once worked as the colonial storekeeper but was no longer so employed:

> . . . consequently I am not influenced (like many) by Money, for I earn my living by the sweat of my brow, tho a poor one only can be earned by one person for so large a family as I have in this Country, still my situation is far more preferable than if I were placed in a condition where my "salary" must govern the dictates of my conscience.[26]

The Methodists made efforts to organize opposition to the administration in settlements away from the influence of Monrovia. Public meetings were called and anti-administration resolutions passed with speeches attacking Buchanan. One settler told of being present when Reverend Seys declared that "the citizens ought to rise up and shake off this rotten system of tyranny and oppression."[27] Whether or not this particular allegation was true, actions were taken to run candidates against Buchanan and his administration. In Edina, one of the settlements east of Monrovia, Amos Herring was one Methodist settler who was a candidate for a seat on the Legislative Council. He tried to get people to send representatives to Monrovia to defend the Methodist position against the Baptists and the government.[28] Despite the Methodist challenge, the Buchanan supporters won a majority of the council seats. The new council moved to censure the Methodist missionaries for interfering with the affairs of government by propagating subversive doctrines and maintaining a spirit of resistance, and actual stubborn resistance to authority.[29] The controversy did not finally die down until the death of Thomas Buchanan on September 2, 1841.

In 1853, the General Conference of the Methodist Episcopal Church sent out Bishop Levi Scott to report directly on the condition of their missionary activities in Liberia. The bishop was impressed with the Christian appearance of the settlers, noting that the Sabbath was observed with strictness and all the churches were crowded with orderly worshippers. With regard to the effect of the missions among the Africans, Bishop Scott was far less impressed. He reported that his inquiries in this area had produced discouraging responses, and he feared that the General Conference Board would be disappointed. The bishop added, however, that "these results were not due to any want of faithfulness on the part of the missionaries... but are the result of the peculiar condition of the native population."[30]

The Methodist missionary effort was rivaled by that of the Baptists. The Richmond, Virginia, branch of the American Baptist Missionary Union was responsible for sending Lott Carey and Collin Teague to Liberia. Although Teague settled in Sierra Leone for a time, Reverend Lott Carey established the first Baptist church in Monrovia and was active in caring for the health of many settlers. The Baptist Missionary Union sent out a Euro-American missionary, the Reverend Calvin Holton, in 1825 to work with Carey, but he died almost immediately after his arrival.[31] As a result, the activities of the Baptist mission fell totally under the control of the settlers themselves. Carey continued to reach and maintain schools in Monrovia. In 1827, he also established a mission school in Grand Cape Mount among the Vai people. In the same year, he baptized an African named John Revey and sent him to Cape Mount to run the mission school there.[32] When Carey died in 1828 from an accidental explosion, Revey was forced to leave Cape Mount and return to Monrovia.

The Providence Baptist Church that Carey had pastored since its founding was committed to the care of Collin Teague, who returned to Liberia from Sierra Leone. The church continued to grow, with its membership surpassing two hundred. A Baptist mission was established among the Bassa people run by Euro-American missionaries. Like others, they suffered high mortality and died in the land of their labors before accomplishing much. The experience of these missionaries led one survivor to observe and conclude in 1854:

That during the past twelve months, six missionaries of different denominations had died, and eight have been and are obliged to return to America; all of whom had gone to Africa within the last year. This is indeed a fearful mortality among African missionaries. . . . Educated colored men, in all probability, must and will be the only instrument employed in the conversion of Africa.[33]

The Presbyterian denomination entered the Liberian field in 1833. Their first effort was guided by the Reverend John B. Pinney. He was forced to return to America because of poor health, but he came back later that year as both missionary and temporary colonial agent. During this early period of activity, the Presbyterians planted only a few successful missions among Africans. A station was created along the coast at Settra Krow with a small school for African children. The Presbyterians also established a mission station at Cape Palmas in a place that was called Fair Hope.[34]

The American Board of Commissioners for Foreign Missions sent its first foreign missionaries to Africa in 1834, when John Leighton Wilson and his wife opened a mission at Cape Palmas, Liberia. The Cape Palmas Mission was abandoned in 1843, however, because of a high death rate among the missionaries, and the Gabon Mission was established on the banks of the Gabon River.[35]

The most successful missionary activity in Liberia during the nineteenth century was undoubtedly that organized by the Protestant Episcopal Church and directed at the Glebo people of the Cape Palmas area. The Protestant Episcopal mission began in 1836 and by 1854 included the services of six clergymen and their leader, Bishop John Payne. There were four stations, including a large one at Mount Vaughan. Both day schools and Sunday schools were operated where literacy in English was taught to Glebo children. The Glebo language was reduced to writing, and a small missionary publication was printed in the vernacular.[36] The success of the Protestant Episcopal mission in Cape Palmas soon produced conflict with the settler government authorities there. As historian Jane J. Martin made clear, the most difficult problem between the settler leadership and the missionaries was over the issue of how the Glebo and neighboring people should be treated and what would be the nature of their incorporation into the settler state.[37]

In 1854, the Disciples of Christ through the American Christian Missionary Society sent an Afro-American, Alexander Cross, to Liberia as a missionary. D. S. Barrett, a vice-president of the society, heard Cross, at the time a slave, deliver an address in Kentucky on the topic of temperance. Barrett, greatly impressed with Cross, recommended him to the Ninth Street Christian Church in Hopkinsville, Kentucky, as a potential missionary to Africa. At a meeting of the church officials on April 20, 1853, a resolution regarding Cross was adopted. They resolved to raise $530 to buy the freedom of Alexander Cross and then send him to Liberia as a missionary.[38] By October of the same year, Cross had received preparation for his work in Africa through a program of instruction supervised by the elders of the Ninth Street Christian Church. In that month, Cross was ordained in a ceremony that included "prayer, fasting, and the imposition of hands."[39] Cross left for Liberia but tragically died before he had completed one year of residence. The missionary activities of the American Christian Missionary Society in Liberia ended with his death.

The Lutheran Church did not establish its first mission in Liberia until 1860 when the Reverend Morris Officer founded the Muhlenberg Mission on the banks of the Saint Paul River. Reverend Officer stayed only one year, and not until 1874 did the arrival of David and Emily Day stir the moribund mission and lead to the expansion of Lutheran missionary work in the interior.[40]

Thus, despite the efforts of many different American Protestant denominations, the impact of mission work in Liberia was never great during the early nineteenth century.[41] The high mortality of missionaries, especially Euro-Americans, along with the limited financial means available, seriously hindered the missionary work among Africans. In 1843, for example, only 393 Africans were reported as having converted to Christianity. The number of active churchgoers, even among the settlers, was far from universal. Less than half of the total settler population in 1843 were communicants of either the Baptist, Methodist, Presbyterian, or Episcopalian churches (see Table 1).

Table 1
Christian Church Affiliations in Liberia, 1843

Denominations	Communicants			
	Americo-Liberians	Recaptured Africans	Indigenous Africans	Total
Baptists	431	63	60	554
Methodists	564	49	293	906
Presbyterians	20	4	0	24
Episcopalians	17	0	40	57
Total	1,032	116	393	1,541

The facets of Afro-American missionary activity in Liberia described in this essay were influenced in large measure by the parallel development of a settler society. Walter Lee Williams has made this very point in his general survey of the Afro-American missionary movement from 1877 to 1900: "In some ways the black church movement into Liberia was more of a denominational expansion than a true missionary movement, because the church became established by Afro-American emigrants who brought their religion with them."[42] Despite the special circumstances of this case, the experience provides an early reference point for gaining a perspective on subsequent Afro-American missionary initiatives to other parts of the African continent. Liberian colonization represented the beginning of a missionary movement that would have continental significance.

Notes

1. An excellent analysis of the influence of colonization on one influential religious leader is Stanley K. Schultz, "The Making of a Reformer: The Reverend Samuel Hopkins as an Eighteenth Century Reformer," *Proceedings of the American Philosophical Society* 115 (1971): 350-365.

2. Henry Noble Sherwood, "The Formation of the American Colonization Society," *Journal of Negro History* 2 (July 1917):212-214.

3. The most lucid account of Afro-American sentiment towards emigration and colonization is Floyd J. Miller's *The Search for a Black Nationality: Black Emigration and Colonization, 1787-1863* (Urbana: University of Illinois Press, 1975). The missionary spirit of Afro-American settlers in Liberia filled the letters that they sent back to friends and relatives in America. See Randall M. Miller, ed., *"Dear Master," Letters of a Slave Family* (Ithaca, N.Y.: Cornell University Press, 1978) and Bell I. Wiley, ed., *Slaves No More: Letters from Liberia, 1833-1869* (Lexington: University Press of Kentucky, 1980).

4. Edward W. Blyden, "The Call of Providence to the Descendants of Africa in America" in *Liberia's Offering Being Addresses, Sermons, etc.* (New York: J. A. Gray, 1862). Blyden was born in the West Indies and after coming to the United States immigrated to Liberia in 1851. His career was remarkable—including that of statesman, scholar, missionary, and propagandist. His biographer, Hollis R. Lynch, notes that for his contemporaries, Blyden represented an outstanding example of achievement at a time when much of the Western world accepted black inferiority as undisputable. See Hollis R. Lynch, *Edward Wilmot Blyden: Pan-Negro Patriot, 1832-1912* (London: Oxford University Press, 1967).

5. On March 3, 1807, Thomas Jefferson as president of the United States signed a bill that made it illegal to import Africans to the United States for the purpose of sale as slaves. For a detailed discussion of the bill and the debate over its passage, see W. E. B. Du Bois, *The Suppression of the African Slave-Trade to the United States of America, 1638-1870* (New York: Longmans, Green, & Co., 1896), pp. 94-130; and Donald L. Robinson, *Slavery in the Structure of American Politics, 1765-1820* (New York: Harcourt Brace Jovanovich, 1971), pp. 295-346. The later efforts by the American Naval Squadron to suppress the slave trade are examined in Warren S. Howard, *American Slavers and the Federal Law, 1837-1862* (Berkeley: University of California Press, 1963).

6. Philip J. Staudenraus, *The African Colonization Movement, 1816-1865* (New York: Columbia University Press, 1961), p. 50.

7. *Annals of Congress*, 15th Congress, 1st session, pp. 1771-1774.

8. Special Message of President Monroe to Congress, of December 19, 1819, in Charles H. Huberich, *Political and Legislative History of Liberia* 1 (New York: Central Book Co., 1947), p. 70.

9. Huberich, *Polticial and Legislative History* 1, pp. 77, 145.

10. Jehudi Ashmun, *Memoir of the Life and Character of the Rev. Samuel Bacon, A. M.* (Washington, D.C.: J. Gideon, 1822), pp. 241-242.

11. Daniel Coker's Diary, February 24, 1820, reprinted in Huberich, *Political and Legislative History* 1, p. 80.

12. Daniel Coker's Diary, March 2, 1820, in Huberich, *Political and Legislative History* 1, p. 81.

13. Samuel Bacon, Sherbro Island, Campelar, to Hon. Smith Thompson, Secretary of the Navy, March 21, 1820, Gunter Collection, Chicago Historical Society Library.

14. Daniel Coker, Genoy, Africa, to wife, May 26, 1820, extract printed in the *Maryland Gazette and Political Intelligencer*, January 4, 1821.

15. Diary of Daniel Coker, April 26, 1821, Manuscript Division, Library of Congress.

16. Diary of Daniel Coker, May 6, 1821.

17. *African Repository* 1 (October 1825):233-236. See also *The American Missionary Register* 6, p. 340; G. Winfred Hervey, *The Story of Baptist Missions in Foreign Lands* (St. Louis: Chancy R. Barns, 1884), p. 199; and Ralph R. Gurley, *Life of Jehudi Ashmun*, Appendix (Washington, D.C.: J. C. Dunn, 1835), p. 147.

18. Seventh Annual Report of the Baptist Board of Foreign Missions in *The Latter Day Luminary* 11, p. 399; *The American Missionary Register* 6, p. 341; *The Missionary Jubilee*, p. 215; and *African Repository* 5 (March 1829):12.

19. Diary of Daniel Coker, May 27, 1821.

20. "Treaty between King Ben of Grand Bassa, with His Princes and Head Men on One Side and Joseph R. Andrus, First Agent of the American Colonization Society on the Other," April 12, 1821, Gunter Collection.

21. For the text of the agreement, see Huberich, *Political and Legislative History of Liberia* 1, pp. 195-196.

22. David Christy, *African Colonization by the Free Colored People of the United States, An Indispensable Auxiliary to African Missions: A Lecture* (Cincinnati: T. A. & U. P. James, 1854), p. 5. See also Bennie D. Warner, *History of Methodism in Liberia: Sessions of the Liberia Annual Conference*,

1833-1972 (Monrovia: n.p., n.d.); and Wade Crawford Barclay, *History of Methodist Missions*, vol. 1: *Early American Methodism 1769-1844* (New York: Board of Missions and Church Extension of the Methodist Church, 1949), pp. 322, 336.

23. Melville Cox, Monrovia, to the American Colonization Society, May 4, 1833, reprinted in *African Repository* 9 (October 1833).

24. See *Africa's Luminary*, September 18, 1840, and October 2, 1840, for a history of the legal case from the perspective of the Methodists.

25. Thomas Buchanan, Monrovia, to Hon. Samuel Wilkeson, December 13, 1840, *Correspondence of the Colonial Agents, 1833-1842*, Archives of the Ministry of Foreign Affairs, Monrovia, Liberia.

26. Thomas Buchanan, Monrovia, to Board of Directors, American Colonization Society, April 7, 1841, Incoming Correspondence, American Colonization Society Papers, Library of Congress.

27. Francis Burns, Edina, to Thomas Buchanan, April 1, 1841, Incoming Correspondence, American Colonization Society Papers.

28. James Moore, Edina, to Samuel Wilkeson, April 2, 1841, Incoming Correspondence, American Colonization Society Papers.

29. The election results saw the administration faction win eight seats and the Methodist faction only three seats. *Commonwealth Legislative Minutes*, January 19, 1841, Archives of the Ministry of Foreign Affairs.

30. Christy, *African Colonization*, p. 7.

31. Ibid., p. 8.

32. *American Baptist Magazine* 7, p. 305.

33. Rev. W. B. Shermer, London, to the American Baptist Missionary Union, January 13, 1854, *Baptist Missionary Magazine*, March 1854.

34. Christy, *African Colonization*, p. 11 and Penelope Campbell, *Maryland in Africa: The Maryland State Colonization Society, 1831-1857* (Urbana: University of Illinois Press, 1971), p. 132.

35. William E. Strong, *The Story of the American Board* (Boston: Pilgrim Press, 1910), pp. 124-125.

36. Christy, *African Colonization*, p. 12. See also George D. Browne, "History of the Protestant Episcopal Mission in Liberia Up to 1838," *Historical Magazine of the Protestant Episcopal Church* 39 (March 1970):17-27.

37. Jane J. Martin, "The Dual Legacy: Government Authority and Mission Influence Among the Glebo of Eastern Liberia, 1834-1910" (Ph.D. dissertation, Boston University, 1968), p. 5.

38. Minutes of the Ninth Street Christian Church, April 20, 1853, Disciples of Christ Historical Society Library, Nashville, Tennessee. See also *Survey of Service* (St. Louis: Christian Board of Publication, 1928), p. 515; and Winfred Ernest Garrison and Alfred T. DeGroot, *The Disciples*

of Christ: A History (St. Louis: Christian Board of Publication, 1948), p. 476.

39. Minutes of the Ninth Street Christian Church, Lords Day in December 1853.

40. Consult Harold Vink Whetstone, "The Lutheran Mission in Liberia" (M.A. Thesis, Hartford Seminary, 1954).

41. There was an attempt to introduce Catholic missionaries to Liberia when, in 1841, Father Edward Barron, vicar-general of Philadelphia, and Father John Kelly, pastor of Saint John's Church in Albany, New York, arrived in Liberia aboard the ship *Harriet*. They were coolly received by the settlers, and a mission was never established. See Martin J. Bane, *Catholic Pioneers in West Africa* (Dublin: Clonmore & Reynolds, 1956).

42. Walter Lee Williams, "Black American Attitudes Toward Africa: The Missionary Movement, 1877-1900" (Ph.D. dissertation, University of North Carolina at Chapel Hill, 1974), p. 132. See also his *Black Americans and the Evangelization of Africa, 1877-1900* (Madison: University of Wisconsin Press, 1982).

Black Baptists, Foreign Missions, and African Colonization, 1814-1882

4

Sandy Dwayne Martin

The nineteenth century was one of missionary expansion by Euro-Americans into portions of the world inhabited by non-white peoples. This zeal for Christianizing the entire world came in the context and was greatly influenced by the religious revivals in both Europe and North America in the eighteenth and nineteenth centuries. These evangelical Christians believed they had a duty assigned by God to convert all the world to Christ. By and large, Euro-American Christian mission-minded people believed firmly that unless people were converted to Christianity, their souls would be damned to an eternity of torment in hell.[1] Besides, hearts dedicated to Christ would create for unsaved people in the present time, lives of joy, peace, and fulfillment. Christianity was seen as the one, true, perfect religion. All others were believed to be either steps upward to Christianity at best or at worst—and often—false religions.

But along with this fervent conviction concerning the uniqueness of Christianity, Euro-American supporters of foreign mission programs also believed in the unquestionable superiority of Western culture, that is, the world of the Euro-American. Whether one spoke of clothing, laws to govern society, or the habits and customs of the people, Euro-American cultures were for the most part equated with progress, "civilization," and enlightenment. Conversely, non-Western cultures were usually equated with degradation, barbarism, ignorance, and, pardon the metaphor, "darkness." Regardless of how much we reject the idea of complete cultural relativism and how firmly we assert the centrality of Christianity for the salvation of humankind, we must, nevertheless, admit its impact in the history of missions in Africa. Furthermore, this sense of cultural superiority, in some instances, might have prevented the missionaries and their supporters from grasping the truest and most comprehensive portrait of African religions.

Many American church people viewed the United States as a "chosen nation" in much the same way as ancient Israel is portrayed in the Old Testament or Hebrew Bible. The nation had been chosen by God for a special task in this world. This included spreading the blessings of Christian religion (mainly Protestantism) and Western culture throughout the earth. This duty was an important one indeed. In the minds of many, the active engagement of Christians in this mission could hasten the Second Coming of Jesus or, in the belief of others, hasten the entire world toward a golden era of peace, justice, and the universal acceptance of God's reign on earth.[2]

Black Christians and, specifically, black Baptists, cooperated in this venture to spread Christianity during the years 1814 to 1882 and thereafter. As early as 1815, two black Virginia ministers, Collin Teague and Lott Carey, with the assistance and support of a white deacon, William Crane, organized the African Baptist Missionary Society in Richmond, Virginia.[3] The goal of this convention was the Christianization of the African continent. After the Civil War, in the 1870s, independent black Baptist state conventions in Virginia, North Carolina, and South Carolina sponsored black missionaries in West Africa. In 1873, black Baptists in the Midwest founded the General Association of Western States and Territories and commissioned missionaries to Central Africa in the 1880s.[4]

These organizations generally worked in cooperation with white Baptist bodies to support personnel in Africa. The Richmond Society provided a vital core of support within the predominantly white General Missionary Convention of the Baptist Denomination in the United States of America for Foreign Missions, better known as the Triennial Convention, founded in 1814. When the

Triennial Convention divided in 1845 over the issue of slave-holding, the Richmond Society supported African missions under the aegis of the southern group, the Southern Baptist Convention (SBC). The black Baptists of Virginia also collaborated with the SBC in the 1870s to support a missionary in Nigeria. The northern foreign mission group, the American Baptist Missionary Union (ABMU), cooperated with the black state convention of South Carolina in the late 1870s and early 1880s.

Besides working with black Baptist organizations and predominantly white Baptist groups, black Baptists also utilized the American Colonization Society (ACS) to further their missionary program in Africa. This society, whose official name was the American Society for the Colonization of Free People of Color, was organized in 1816 under the leadership of the Presbyterian minister Robert S. Finley.[5] Founded to transplant Afro-Americans to Africa, it gained much of its support from Christian denominations and saw its effort in the colony of Liberia as an experiment in transmitting Christianity and "civilization," that is, Western culture, to so-called backward, heathenistic, and barbaric Africa through the agency of black colonists who had had firsthand experience with both Christianity and Western culture. The society also transported missionaries and, in some instances, core groups of people, who would comprise new churches in Liberia. Since black Baptists shared the religious and cultural assumptions of white Baptists and white Christians in general, the philosophy of the society in this regard and its financial support made it a valuable ally to the cause of foreign missions.[6]

Robert W. July in *The Origins of Modern African Thought* refers to "The Liberian Experiment." Liberia was not only an experiment for supporters of the ACS who were attempting to erect an African nation in West Africa patterned after American government and customs, but it was also an attempt by black and white Christians to establish a Christian society in so-called barbaric Africa.[7] An examination of a select number of black Baptist colonists and missionaries in Liberia shows that black Baptists on the one hand shared in the general assumption of white Christians concerning Christianity and Western culture and on the other hand had a deep sense of racial solidarity with Africans.

By examining the thoughts of Lott Carey, Hilary Teague, John Day, J. T. Richardson, and Beverly Page Yates, the religious, cultural, political, and racial views of representative black Baptist missionaries·can be demonstrated.

Lott Carey came to be a foundation for practice and theology of both white and black Baptists in Africa. Along with Collin Teague and their families, Carey journeyed to Africa in 1821 as one of the first colonists of the American Colonization Society and one of the first missionaries to Africa supported by the Triennial Convention. It is clear that Carey shared in the theological assumptions of his white Baptist counterparts. In answering the needs of the colonists, Carey, shortly after his arrival, found himself moving beyond the "spiritual" realm of mission work. For a time he practiced self-taught medicine. At one point he led a rebellion of the colonists against certain policies of the ACS agent, but the issues were eventually resolved and Carey continued in the role of a colonist. By 1828, Carey had risen to the vice-governorship and even served as acting governor in the absence of the governor. In a war between the Afro-American colonists and the indigenous Africans, Carey lost his life while preparing to defend the colony.[8]

Hilary Teague, the son of Collin Teague, was an eloquent minister, politician, and newspaper editor in Liberia and would be among those Baptists who would carry on the Carey tradition. His conception of Liberia as an outpost of Christian civilization in a barbarian wilderness survives in a hymn created by Teague to celebrate the victory of the colonists over indigenous Africans who had attacked Liberian settlements. Teague begins by praising God for his power and sovereignty. In speaking of his African enemies, Teague characterized them as a people craving the blood of the colonists, possessing limitless hatreds and malice, and having hearts devoid of love. The "barbarians" trusted in "gods of wood and stone," while in contrast the Christian and "civilized" colonists relied on the one, true God to whom alone belongs credit for victory over the Africans, Teague emphasized.[9]

Carey and, later, other Baptists, saw colonization as a significant apparatus for "redeeming and regenerating" the continent.

Just as the British people rose from savagery to the status of the most powerful people in the world, the African, too, was "swiftly rising into the light and comforts of civilization." In 1840, almost twenty years after his father's arrival in Africa, Teague was expounding a belief that would be reiterated by white missionaries a decade or so later and was also used by Europeans of the late nineteenth century as a justification for colonization. The African continent would be redeemed principally through the three agencies of Christian colonies, missionary stations, and European commerce. Colonies were especially helpful in that they stood as concrete, lasting examples for Africans to imitate. Whether colonization resulted in elimination of American slavery, Teague claimed not to know. His primary reason for supporting the colonization scheme was to redeem Africa from "barbarism."[10]

Teague, however, loathed American slavery as well as racial prejudice and discrimination. Writing from the Liberian capital of Monrovia on January 2, 1851, Teague held that the colony of Liberia was a haven for Afro-Americans seeking freedom and equality. He actually appealed for Afro-American emigration since one of the major needs of the young republic was a larger Afro-American population. The black race possessed all the capacities of any other race. But if any people were to be perfected, they must be in an atmosphere where their cravings for freedom, justice, and equality could be realized. The acquisition of classical training would not save blacks from the harshness of racial discrimination in the United States as some argued. Teague granted that there were certain shortcomings to living in Liberia, but by far it was still a much better place for blacks than the United States.[11] Noting the marginal existence of even free blacks in antebellum America, Teague wrote:

But it's so much more pleasing to be voting for one's own representatives, than to be peeping "round the corner" at those who are voting— so much more pleasant to clean one's own farm, than to clean another's boots, especially when he is conscious that it is the *ne plus ultra* of his accent.[12]

In examining the Baptist missionaries' concern for colonization and the establishment of Christian societies, one must not overlook the strong belief in the personal dimension of evangelism which characterized the theology of the missionaries. Men and women must have a personal confrontation with Jesus, be forgiven their sins, and thereafter live new lives of personal piety and holiness. John Day was one of the first black missionaries appointed for work in Liberia in 1845 and served for a time as the superintendent for Baptist missionary work in Liberia and Sierra Leone. One of his letters, dated November 17, 1853, is an example of evangelical missionary theology and method. It is imperative that the unconverted admit that he/she was a lost sinner and become "a penitent seeker after salvation." Day praised God that he had preached to the "heathen." He encouraged other missionaries to rely upon the preached words rather than trying to "prepare it by a little education; a little civilization." It was vanity to rely upon one's own judgment rather than to trust the explicit command of God. It was preaching which destroyed Satan's kingdom and built the Kingdom of Christ.[13]

The emphasis of black Baptists upon personal evangelism and personal piety, however, did not hinder them from being advocates of African colonization as a means by which to uplift black people. Three months prior to this letter by Day, he had addressed correspondence to free blacks in the United States urging them to support colonization. That letter was written at a time (the decade of the 1850s) when a resurgence of interest in colonization or emigration was taking place among black Americans. Day wondered how blacks lived in a land that placed such a number of restraints upon their activities and stifled their aspirations for progress and could still manage to escape the harmful consequences of this racial containment to the human spirit. As a result, blacks in time would be second to no other people. Day argued that this was not a fantastic dream when it was recalled that African civilizations once blossomed in grandeur when Europeans were immersed in "barbarism." "May not a reversion take place, and Africa again be the garden of the earth." Given the freedom and equality afforded blacks in Liberia, he contended that at that moment of history, Liberia was already a paradise in comparison to other places where blacks lived, places where they are "pointed out as a distinct and inferior class."[14]

In his letter, Day dealt with the major objections of the coloni-zation antagonists among black Americans. First, he discarded the notion that blacks should remain in the United States out of a feeling of obligation to their brothers and sisters in slavery—to wage an antislavery battle. Day pointed out that the presence of free blacks in the country so far had not had the effect of dis-mantling slavery, and he believed it never would. Besides, Afri-can brothers and sisters were held in a bondage much more devastating than the physical slavery in America; they were lost in the realm of barbarism—in the grips of Satan.

Second, Day addressed the concern raised by whites and blacks that the ACS was a racist organization founded upon the false principle of black inferiority. The missionary repudi-ated the racism of some proponents of colonization. Neverthe-less, he maintained that the society was the most benevolent activity being conducted on behalf of black liberation. He be-lieved that God was involved in the work and goal of the society for the good of blacks. And, regardless of the human motives—whether mainly evil or chiefly good—all things were working under the sovereignty of God's plan for the freedom and development of black people. Rather than strive against this God-approved enterprise, blacks should rise and assist the Lord in this work of colonization. "Come to the land of true liberty, where you and your children may not only be happy yourselves, but where you can assist in making Africa the praise of the whole earth."[15]

Five years later, Day was still defending the interrelation-ship between colonization and evangelism, still viewing the task of Afro-Americans as a providential one to bring Christian civilization to a "backward and lost" continent. Writing on November 13, 1858, the missionary reflected on his twenty-four years of missionary service in Africa and expressed the belief that he now stood "on the verge of Jordan." He contin-ued to view Liberia as a nation chosen by God. The economic woes of the country were interpreted to mean that God lov-ingly "rebukes and chastens" the country.[16] Day linked Afro-Americans, Liberians, and Africans as objects in a providential plan.

Ethiopia is to stretch out its hands in prayer and praise; its inhabitants are to be exalted. And American slavery, emancipation and colonization, are to perform their part in the great work. If the present colonists are recreant to their trust, God will nevertheless accomplish His purpose through them.[17]

Africa, depopulated by wars and the slave trade, now stood beckoning black Americans to return to the land of their forefathers to carry out the will of God to uplift the race.

Notwithstanding the assistance of white Baptists, North and South, the major responsibility for carrying on the work of missions rested in the hands of black Baptists in Liberia. When small amounts of aid or none at all came from Baptists in the United States, particularly during the period of the American Civil War, Liberian emigrants continued to evangelize and erect churches. In addition, just as black Baptists in the southern states served as a vanguard for African missions, so, likewise, black Baptists in Liberia, especially during the years 1868 to 1880, played a leading role in influencing white and black Baptists in the United States to renew systematic mission programs.

Most missionary efforts for the first forty or fifty years of the black Baptist presence in Liberia were directed toward the colonists rather than toward indigenous inhabitants. One factor contributing to this situation was the language and cultural differences between the two groups. In both groups, religion and culture were so closely allied that giving up one meant surrendering the other. In addition, the ACS had acquired the land by questionable means at best and by fraudulent methods most probably. The Africans understandably resented the presence of the colonists, and the superior attitude on the part of the colonists exacerbated conditions. One must also bear in mind that much of the colonists' time and energy was absorbed in adjusting to a wholly new physical environment.

At any rate, a more vigorous, concerted effort to reach the indigenous populations was inaugurated in March 1868 when representatives from ten Liberian Baptist congregations convened in Marshall, Liberia, to organize the Liberia Baptist Missionary Union. Planning to direct its attention to the evangelization of non-Christian indigenous Africans, the group designated twelve areas for missionary activities with each church responsible for the area(s) closest to it. But this organization also had significant ramifications for the African missionary movement in the United States. To gain American support, the missionary union appointed their corresponding secretary, J. T. Richardson, as an agent for the American Baptist Missionary Union in the United States.[18]

Richardson made a special appeal to black American Baptists. The Liberian Baptist leader urged young black Baptists to come to Africa as missionaries. Like many other black Baptists in the United States and Liberia, Richardson saw a link between evangelization and material progress and between the experiences of blacks in the United States and indigenous Africans on the continent. Richardson considered black Baptist participation in African missions as participation in the redemption of Africa, the fulfillment of a great promise of God for the entire black race. He wrote:

She [Africa] has long been shrouded in moral night, and her sons abroad have had to pass through a fiery ordeal, crying unto god to deliver them and their heathen brethren of his land. And it seems that Providence says their prayers are being answered, and they shall be redeemed, despite the ragings of men and devils.[19]

Besides Richardson, other black Baptists in Africa expressed concern for the evangelization of indigenous Africans. The Reverend Jacob W. Vonbrunn, an indigenous Bassa, lived with his people and conveyed the Christian message in that language. He also traveled to the United States in search of funds to erect a chapel and two or three schools for Africans.[20] Robert F. Hill of Virginia journeyed to Africa as a missionary with Thomas J. Bowen, a white Baptist, and Harvey Goodale, his assistant, in 1849. Hill chose to remain in Liberia while Bowen proceeded to Nigeria; Goodale died in Nigeria. In 1867, Hill returned to the United States. In the South, he visited old friends and conversed with potential emigrants to Liberia. In Philadelphia, Hill addressed the convention of the American Baptist Missionary Union. His delivery was well received, and his presence and appeals count

in large measure for the renewal of vigorous missionary interests in Africa among northern Baptists.[21]

Finally, Beverly Page Yates (like Hill, an emigrant from the
South) wrote in 1873 that he had served with the Southern Baptist Convention for twenty years. In a letter to Afro-American
Baptists dated May 1873, Page expressed elation at the news
that missionary interest in Africa among black Baptists was growing. Clearly, black Baptists took pride in the tradition of Carey
and Teague, the initiators of Baptist missionary work in Africa.
But Page, like others before him, made a clear connection between blackness and the evangelization of Africa. Page placed
blacks under racial as well as spiritual obligations to their African kin. Since God had so abundantly blessed Afro-Americans
with physical freedom from slavery as well as the greater liberty
of spiritual emancipation, Page found it unthinkable that Afro-
Americans would deny the blessings of redemption to, of all
people, their African kin. Whether black Baptists would come
themselves bringing their "culture and experience" or would
finance others, they must pay their obligation to Africa so that it
might be "elevated, enlightened, and saved." In cooperating
with missionary efforts to uplift Africa, religiously and culturally, black Americans would be performing a providential role,
one for which they would be held accountable on the Day of
Judgment. Thus, Page bade Afro-Americans to turn their attention to Africa:

You will not come [to Africa] as the prodigal son, wasted, weary, and
wretched; but like the Jews, hastening from the land of Egypt, laden
with precious and valuable spoils. You are one in origin with us, and
with the benighted tribes in whose behalf we plead—one in interest,
and one in worldly destiny. Come and help to make them with us one
in our most precious faith and glorious hope, that they may be one with
us throughout eternity.[22]

In conclusion, black missionary theology operated out of the
milieu of white Protestant theology and assertions of the superiority of Western culture. Black Christians joined their white brothers in lifting Protestantism as the ideal religious belief and prac-

tice. A case can be made for the presence of African survivals in the practice and worship of black religion, particularly in the invisible institution (the religion of black slaves). Nevertheless, even black Baptist and black Methodist churches, which were organized outside of white ecclesiastical structures or which broke from those structures, to a large extent carried the identical beliefs, rituals, and theology of corresponding white bodies. Blacks, too, considered Western culture superior to non-Western culture. They also prayed and expected that a period in history would arrive when Protestantism and Western "civilization" would be established throughout the world.[23] Whether one speaks of Paul Cuffee, the black merchant and member of the Society of Friends, who provided for thirty-eight Afro-Americans to return to Africa; Daniel Coker, the AME missionary to Sierra Leone; or James T. Holly, the Episcopal missionary to Haiti and exponent of black emigration, most black church people took for granted that non-Western and non-Christian peoples must come under the purview of American Christian understanding of "Christian civilization."

But blacks were not mere imitators of white Christian theology. They gleaned from scripture and their own experience in America a modification of the average white interpretation of the faith. If they accepted American ethnocentrism, they rejected both racism and slavery as inconsistent with Christian faith and the dignity and worth of their persons. But certain questions had to be faced. If, for instance, God was a God of mercy and love, and if God was a respecter of persons, both white and black, then why did God permit blacks to undergo the ordeal of a slavery that threatened familial ties, dignity, and self-respect? Black Christians generally accepted the faith of Saint Paul in Romans 8 which asserted that, from the worst of circumstances, God works to bring forth good to divine pleasure and glory. Beneath all sufferings were a purpose and a blessing. Hence, blacks, while not condoning the institution of slavery, could interpret it as a part of a divine provision for blacks to acquire Christianity and Western civilization.

Having acquired these blessings, blacks could become special instruments of God for the salvation of the African peoples who were non-Christian and without Western culture. In the eyes of many blacks, they, not whites, were the most true and most loyal adherents to the religion of Jesus. In whatever ways blacks encountered limitations, their churches provided them with one golden opportunity to express their ultimate commitment to the Christian faith. In ministerial office and lay activities, black Christians were free to express their sense of personhood and racial pride. Though deprived of all the world, they had Jesus. And, particularly in the arena of foreign missions, black Christians had instances to demonstrate solidarity with their African kin. Believing as white Christians in the efficacy of the gospel, they longed and worked for the day when Christian "civilization" would lift Africans from "degradation" and the entire race would march to a glorious future.

Notes

1. See Kenneth Scott Latourette's *A History of the Expansion of Christianity,* vol. 5: *The Great Century in the Americas, Austral-Asia, and Africa, A.D. 1800-A.D. 1914* (New York: Harper & Brothers Publishers, 1943), passim.

2. See Ernest Lee Tuveson, *Redeemer Nation: The Idea of America's Millennial Role* (Chicago: University of Chicago Press, 1968), pp. 149-150, 152-153, 154-155. Other church historians have demonstrated the influence of millennialism in American religious history, for example, Robert T. Handy, *A Christian America: Protestant Hopes and Historical Realities* (New York: Oxford University Press, 1971); and Martin E. Marty, *Righteous Empire: The Protestant Experience in America* (New York: Dial Press, 1970).

3. For accounts of these three men and the Richmond African Baptist Missionary Society, see Miles Mark Fisher, "Lott Carey, the Colonizing Missionary," *Journal of Negro History* 7 (October 1922):380-418; William A. Poe, "Lott Carey: Man of Purchased Freedom," *Church History* 39 (March 1970):49-61; and the chapter on "Lott Carey," pp. 396-444 in James B. Taylor, *Virginia Baptist Ministers* 2 (Philadelphia: J. B. Lippincott Co., 1859). The reader might also be interested in Leroy Fitts, *Lott Carey, First Black Missionary to Africa* (Valley Forge, Pa.: Judson Press, 1978).

4. William H. Moses, *The Colored Baptist Family Tree: A Compendium of Organized Negro Baptist Church History* (Nashville, Tenn.: Sunday School

Publishing Board, National Baptist Convention, U.S.A., Inc., 1925), pp. 11-12. See also Lewis Garnett Jordan, *Negro Baptist History, U.S.A., 1750-1930* (Nashville, Tenn.: Sunday School Publishing Board, National Baptist Convention, U.S.A., Inc., 1930?).

5. For a description of the American Colonization Society, the reader is directed to P. J. Staudenraus, *The African Colonization Movement, 1816-1865* (New York: Columbia University Press, 1961).

6. To examine the relationship between Western culture and Christianity in the thought of nineteenth-century black leaders, see the following: Howard Brotz, ed., *Negro Social and Political Thought 1850-1920, Representative Texts* (New York: Basic Books, Inc., 1966); Floyd J. Miller, *The Search for a Black Nationality: Black Emigration and Colonization, 1787-1863* (Urbana: University of Illinois Press, 1975); and especially Leonard I. Sweet, *Black Images of America, 1784-1870* (New York: W. W. Norton & Co., Inc., 1976).

For works on colonization, emigration, and interest in Africa by Afro-Americans, see Miller, *The Search for a Black Nationality*; Okon Edet Uya, ed., *Black Brotherhood: Afro-Americans and Africa* (Lexington, Mass.: D. C. Heath & Co., 1971); and especially for the purposes of this essay, see Louis Mehlinger's "The Attitude of the Free Negro Toward African Colonization," *Journal of Negro History* 1 (July 1916):271-301. Canadian blacks also took part in the emigration schemes of the eighteenth and nineteenth centuries, for example, James W. St. G. Walker, *The Black Loyalists, The Search for a Promised Land in Nova Scotia and Sierra Leone, 1783-1870* (New York: Africana Publishing Co., A Division of Holmes and Meier Publishers, 1976).

7. Robert W. July, *The Origins of Modern African Thought; Its Development in West Africa During the Nineteenth and Twentieth Centuries* (New York: Frederick A. Praeger, 1967), pp. 85-109.

8. See note 3.

9. *The African Repository* 12 (July 1837):231.

10. *The African Repository* 16 (October 1840):316-317.

11. *The African Repository* 27 (July 1851):199-200.

12. Ibid., p. 200.

13. *The African Repository* 30 (November 1854):341-342.

14. *The African Repository* 30 (May 1854):144-146.

15. Ibid.

16. *The African Repository* 25 (February 1859):56-57.

17. Ibid., p. 56.

18. *The African Repository* 44 (July 1868):219.

19. See Richardson letter in *The African Repository* 46 (January 1870):16-18.

20. *The African Repository* 47 (August 1871):267.

21. *The African Repository* 43 (September 1867):285 and 44 (September 1868):278-280.

22. *The African Repository* 49 (August 1873):251-253.

23. See note 6. See also Albert J. Raboteau, *Slave Religion, The "Invisible Institution" in the Antebellum South* (New York: Oxford University Press, 1978).

Ambiguous Legacy: Tuskegee's "Missionary" Impulse and Africa During the Moton Administration, 1915-1935

5

Manning Marable

Tuskegee Institute and its president, Robert R. Moton, were important elements in missionary and philanthropic activities and in the educational and economic development of Africa during 1915-1935. Booker T. Washington and his influential private secretary, Emmett J. Scott, initiated various agricultural training programs in Togo (German West Africa) and Liberia before 1915 and directly influenced British colonial policies in Africa.[1]

Under Moton's administration, Tuskegee emerged as a model for black educational systems throughout British colonial Africa. Hundreds of missionaries, political administrators, and educators studied Tuskegee Institute's programs, visited the campus, and applauded its president. Tuskegee administrators and former faculty members gave their services to colonial governments in agricultural and educational programs.

The legacy that emerged from Tuskegee's extensive involvement in African affairs, however, is ambiguous at best. The "missionary" impulse of Tuskegee under Moton reinforced white colonial rule, advocated American capitalist development within individual stages, and informally gave legitimacy to white philanthropic and paternalist domination over Africa's internal affairs.

Moton's involvement in African issues after his appointment as president of Tuskegee in 1915 began with Liberia. Several years before Washington's death, the institute's faculty and administrators began drafting proposals for the establishment of an industrial trades college in Liberia. Washington appointed a committee of four, including Emmett Scott, to study the idea. Scott and the committee urged the construction of a school "somewhere near Monrovia, up the St. Paul's River, in the Agricultural Section." The new institute "should teach agriculture as adapted to the needs of the people in Africa, the mechanical trades and academic studies, which must include hygiene and sanitation."[2]

Scott published a short essay on the impressive possibilities for economic and educational development in the country, "Is Liberia Worth Saving?"[3] His enthusiasm for the project carried into Moton's new administration. According to Scott, one of the institute's oldest friends and chief financial contributors, Olivia Phelps Stokes, was "wedded to the idea of a Tuskegee in Liberia."[4] President Moton became involved in the concept of an African Tuskegee because, in part, his chief administrative aide had already committed the college to the project. This institutional impulse to take education to Africa was one motive for missionary expansion to the continent and was found among many black American colleges and universities.

Events in Liberia coincided with the activities occurring at Tuskegee Institute. Mrs. Caroline Donovan of Baltimore, Maryland, bequeathed a substantial sum of money to the American Colonization Society "for the purpose of sending [Negro] immigrants to Liberia" and for "education in Liberia." The money was donated to the government of Liberia and was supervised by the Department of Secondary Education. Walter Walker, an Afro-American and former student at Tuskegee, was secretary of the department. Under his direction, the Caroline Donovan Normal and Industrial Institute was established in 1914. Walker was a former member of the Liberian president's cabinet, and with the support of the government he came to the United States to obtain additional financial support for the school.[5]

Walker arrived in the United States in the late spring of 1916 and immediately contacted Scott. "I know you have been extremely busy, and now that the executive work of the National Business League is upon your shoulders I realize that your time is scarcely less your own than when I was at Tuskegee," Walker explained. Nevertheless, he wrote, Tuskegee's aid was vital for the success of Donovan Institute. With suggestions and assistance in obtaining financial aid, the school "will be made a more efficient plant." The "original purpose" of the Liberian government was "to make this Institute follow the Tuskegee ideal." Hollis B. Frissell, Hampton Institute's president, had been contacted to provide support for the educational venture. Walker informed Scott that he had received assurances from the New York Colonization Society that "guaranteed" some financial aid. "I firmly believe that *one good* [Walker's emphasis] industrial school would do Liberia infinitely more good than two or three poorly equipped ones."[6] Throughout the summer and fall, Scott corresponded with Walker, made inquiries for prospective Afro-American teachers to work at the school, and informed Moton about his activities. Moton met with Walker in New York City in August 1916 to discuss the Liberian school.[7]

Moton was favorably impressed with Walker and used his influence with Olivia Phelps Stokes to provide some help for Donovan Institute. Moton assured Walker that "I will do all I can to help in the work which you are doing."[8] Walker wrote to Moton in September that he appreciated the president's efforts. "I sincerely trust," he stated, "that your interest in our work and in Liberia generally will grow in spite of the great responsibility which the work of Tuskegee imposes upon you."[9]

Simultaneously, Walker wrote to Scott and asked for assistance in removing the current principal of Donovan Institute from his position. Walker complained, "[he is] not an exact drawback, [but] he is no distinct advantage to the work." Walker suggested that Scott use his influence with Moton and Stokes to force the man's resignation. "I have just written Major Moton . . . and I trust you will do your level best to accomplish the object we are after." Walker hoped that Scott would not have "the slightest hesitation" in "making your recommendation" to the Liberian government.[10]

Although Donovan Institute became successful, it did not become the Tuskegee of Liberia. Scott informed Walker that Olivia Phelps Stokes had "the idea" that any educational effort in Liberia "should be wholly under Tuskegee Institute auspices."[11] By the mid-1920s, a group of American philanthropic interests, which included Anson Phelps Stokes, the director of the Phelps-Stokes Fund, agreed to establish the Booker T. Washington Industrial and Agricultural Institute in Liberia. A local board of trustees was created which included Liberian President C. D. B. King and members of his Cabinet. Liberian Secretary of the Interior James F. Cooper helped to coordinate the construction of the school. Moton agreed to serve on the school's American Board of Advisers.[12]

The school was dedicated in April 1929, before an audience of two thousand people. "Native chiefs resplendent in their holiday attire, Mandingo merchants in their long blue or white robes," and "European diplomats and merchants in spotless white" were in attendance. President King and Interior Secretary Cooper delivered addresses of congratulations. W. T. Francis, the American minister to Liberia, delivered the address of dedication. "We are here today," he began,

Because Booker Washington taught the world the value of systemized industrial education coupled with agricultural training, and because the chief purpose of his life was to lift the black race. Miss Olivia Phelps Stokes, who was anxious that his labor and his name be not forgotten in the land which gave his ancestors birth, provided in her will for the building of an industrial and agricultural school to bear his name in Africa.[13]

In the absence of Washington and with the sudden departure of Scott during World War I (he became the secretary-treasurer of Howard University in Washington, D.C.), Moton assumed the center stage role as a leading Afro-American decision-maker on African affairs and public policy. Hundreds of missionaries and educators in Africa, Asia, and the United States wrote to him for financial assistance, personnel from Tuskegee Institute, or advice. Moton was a representative of African interests on several occasions, for example, at the Lake Mohonk International Missionary Council Conference in 1918, the inaugural meeting of the International Missionary Council in 1921, and the Scottish Churches Missionary Conference in Glasgow in 1922. The mayor of Freetown, Sierra Leone, wrote to Moton for advice in establishing a women's industrial school. The school, named the Girls' Mechanical School and Teacher's Training Center, was started in October 1923. Principal Adelade Hayford wrote Moton in February 1924, requesting that "celebrated Tuskegee" send one of its graduates to teach at the new institute.[14]

In 1928, Leslie B. Moss, the secretary of the Foreign Missions Conference of North America, asked Moton to represent the United States at the Conference on Missions, held in Leopoldville, Belgian Congo. Moton declined the invitation.[15] A white missionary in Christchurch, New Zealand, requested his views on Christian education and racial relations.[16] Anson Phelps Stokes asked Moton to make decisions concerning the use of the Laura Spelman Rockefeller Memorial Fund and "its appropriations for African work."[17] In 1927, the Reverend Arthur C. Adams, the secretary of the Johannesburg Bantu Men's Social Center, asked Moton to help in translating *Up From Slavery* into the Sesotho language.[18] Moton, however, seemed less interested in American missionary expansion in Africa and more concerned with American educational expansion, along the lines of Tuskegee, of course.

Through his extensive correspondence, Moton became acquainted with almost every significant intellectual, religious leader, or political activist in Africa. One of Moton's closest African associates was J. E. Kwegyir Aggrey, the celebrated Gold Coast writer and educator. Both men were widely recognized as leading black educators, but Aggrey looked to Moton as a mentor and adviser. When Moton visited Salisbury, North Carolina, in 1922, Aggrey confided to him that "I should be simply delighted to do something worthwhile to assist you."[19] Aggrey wanted to meet the Afro-American leader to "talk with you and show you my plans for my country and ask your opinion, suggestion and advice about them."[20]

Both men served as advisers to the Phelps-Stokes Fund, and throughout the 1920s their friendship for each other deepened. After serving on the Phelps-Stokes Commission on Education in East Africa, Aggrey asked Moton, "as our leading [Negro] representative," to thank Thomas Jesse Jones, the educational director of the Phelps-Stokes Fund, and other commission members for their contributions on African education. Moton agreed to "address letters to other members of the Commission," adding that he "eagerly awaited the time when you can on your own native soil devote yourself without reserve to the cause which so kindles your enthusiasm."[21]

When Aggrey returned to the Gold Coast to help establish Achimoto University College in 1924, he asked Moton to forward "reports, periodicals and other publications of the Institute."[22] Aggrey clearly identified with Moton's historic political interests as well as Tuskegee's educational program. The African intellectual told Moton that the attacks against Washington and Moton by W. E. B. Du Bois were shortsighted. The "trouble with [Du Bois]," Aggrey noted, is that he should "have known that you were mastering the situation as you saw best—all the time he was criticizing."[23]

East Africa's most influential protest leader, Harry Thuku, also requested aid and support from Tuskegee. "From the books and newspapers I read...I find that your Institute has been engaged in uplifting the Negro race," he wrote. "It gives me the greatest pleasure to learn that despite the stubborn adverse evil influences the Negro in America has been successful in producing many large hearted men like Booker T. Washington and establishing Institutes like Tuskegee." Washington and Moton were "saviors," Thuku exclaimed proudly. Tuskegee was "our asylum where the hunted downtrodden and oppressed Negro may hasten to seek for help or advice." The East African Association of Kenya asked President Moton to send a number of Tuskegee pupils to begin a trade school in Nairobi. Thuku hoped that somehow a person like Moton "might be spared for founding a 'Tuskegee' in the African wilds."[24] No evidence indicates' whether or not Moton responded to Thuku's plea. Thuku's interest in Afro-American political and educational ideas, however, continued. He corresponded with Marcus Garvey in 1921 and read Garvey's *Philosophy and Opinions* while in a British prison.[25]

Afro-American and West Indian activists interested in Africa also contacted Moton. The outstanding Pan-Africanist of the period, Marcus Garvey, corresponded with Moton and thought

very highly of him until the late 1920s. Garvey's attraction to
Moton stemmed primarily from his deep affection for Booker T.
Washington and Tuskegee Institute. His initial journey to America in 1916 was "motivated by a desire to establish in Jamaica an
industrial and agricultural school along the lines of Washington's Tuskegee."[26] Garvey's organization, the Universal Negro
Improvement Association (UNIA), dedicated a "Booker T. Washington University" in New York.

A number of Tuskegee Institute alumni, including J. J. Adam,
a UNIA delegate to the League of Nations in 1922, were supporters of Garvey's black nationalist movement. Garvey had
written Moton for advice in March 1916 and visited Tuskegee
Institute in 1916 and 1923. During his 1923 visit, he donated $50
to the Tuskegee student scholarship fund and gave an address
on campus. In 1921 he invited Moton to attend the annual UNIA
convention in New York City.

Years later, after his conviction on charges of mail fraud, Garvey grew impatient and at last disillusioned with Moton. Emmett Scott, but not Moton, had dared to oppose the federal
government by objecting to Garvey's deportation. "Dr. Moton is
kept by white philanthropists," Garvey complained in 1929; "therefore, such a black man has absolutely no right talking on behalf
of the Negro race."[27]

Moton's image as a spokesman on African affairs was created,
as Garvey hinted, by his close relationship with the Phelps-Stokes
Fund and its directors. Anson Phelps Stokes was on Tuskegee
Institute's board of trustees; Moton was a trustee on the Phelps-
Stokes Fund Board. For a number of years Stokes quietly paid
Moton $500 annually as a "discretionary fund." Aggrey and
South African educator C. T. Loram also merited honoraria be-
tween $500 and $1,250 annually.

The Phelps-Stokes Fund donated $2,500 each year to the
Hampton-Tuskegee Endowment Fund, far and above the amount
this fund gave to any other black college or university. Monroe
Work, Tuskegee Institute's director of research, received $1,000
annually for the publication of the famous educational series,
the *Negro Yearbook*.[28] Stokes and Thomas Jones regularly checked
with Moton, therefore, on matters that transcended African and

Afro-American education. When Stokes forwarded an additional $300 in June 1926 for the *Negro Yearbook*'s publication, he urged Work to make several minor editorial changes that suited him.[29] Jones requested Moton's reaction when the presidency of Howard University went to Mordecai Johnson.

When the Phelps-Stokes Fund donated $500 to John Hope's Neighborhood Union of Atlanta in 1926, Moton used his influence to moderate Hope's "radical" political tendencies. "Our 'friend' [Hope] has been so vicious in some of his attacks on certain of my real friends as well as myself that I am taking pains in my own quiet way to educate him on what some of the 'enemies of the Negro race' are doing for the Negro," Moton assured Jones.[30]

Not surprisingly, these conservative, business-minded men became close comrades. As Jones departed the United States for a European tour to discuss African education in 1926, a beautiful bouquet of carnations was arranged in his stateroom as a gift. The carnations were, of course, a timely present from Robert R. Moton.[31]

African affairs in education, culture, and politics were an integral part of the Tuskegee Institute experience during Moton's administration. Twenty to thirty foreign students were in attendance at the college in any given year, most of whom were from the West Indies or Latin America. A small number of these students, however, were always from West Africa. In 1929, for example, eleven African students from South Africa, Nigeria, Sierra Leone, and Liberia were attending the institute. Students from Uganda, Kenya, the Gold Coast, and Rhodesia had been admitted in previous years.[32]

Tuskegee Institute publications attempted to acquaint Afro-American students with economic and political events involving Africa. In March 1929, the *Tuskegee Messenger* published an article on the opening of the Industrial and Commercial Bank, Ltd., of Lagos, Nigeria, and noted that the founder was a black American.[33] The journal reviewed the Gold Coast's educational system and reported achievements in African history.[34] Although W. E. B. Du Bois was the prime protagonist of the Pan-African congress movement, its August 1927 meeting in New York City was faithfully covered in the *Tuskegee Messenger*.[35]

In 1927, philanthropist George F. Peabody donated thirty-one pieces of Congolese art to Tuskegee Institute's museum, to the excitement and mixed pleasure of the staff and students. "There are fabrics of bizarre design, masks of outlandish exotic mien, fetiches and statuettes of weird proportions," the *Messenger* noted.[36] Tuskegeeans were certainly pleased to learn that South African educators had asked athletic director Cleve L. Abbott to schedule several football contests in Africa for the autumn 1929 season.[37]

Politicians and educators throughout the world made many pilgrimages to Tuskegee Institute to discover the secrets of industrial education and the Tuskegee ideal. In March 1929, E. N. Jones, a Sierra Leone educator, lectured at the institute and took notes on the school's curriculum.[38] Charles F. Andrews, a close associate of Mohandas K. Gandhi, traveled to Tuskegee from India. Andrews informed his hosts that Gandhi and other Indian leaders were interested in "establish[ing] bonds between Tuskegee Institute . . . and Sanitinikeitan," an Indian school.[39] Sir Frederick Gordon Guggisberg, governor of the Gold Coast Colony from 1919 to 1927, visited America solely "to study Tuskegee methods."[40]

An almost endless stream of foreign educators, administrators, missionaries, philanthropists, and politicians were welcomed to the campus and chauffeured by students. Each guest was met personally by one of Moton's assistants, Albon L. Holsey and G. Lake Imes, or by Moton himself. Guests of the Phelps-Stokes Fund traveling south almost always stopped for several days at the institute. L. A. Roy, the office secretary of the fund, regularly corresponded with Moton to advise him of specific dignitaries the fund was sponsoring to visit the campus. In a typical period between September and October 1926, the fund sent five Lutheran missionaries, educator C. T. Loram, and several Angolan missionaries to Tuskegee. In each instance, Moton had prepared meticulously for the visits.[41]

During any semester, a dozen African missionaries and educators might arrive at Tuskegee Institute. During the winter and early spring months of 1926-1927, a number of important figures journeyed to the campus. In December 1926, James L. Sibley, the director of the American Advisory Committee on Education in Liberia and editor of *Liberian Educational Outlook*, spoke in the Institute Chapel on Liberia.[42]

On December 26, 1926, John Langalibalele Dube of Natal, South Africa, spoke at a dinner held in his honor in Dorothy Hall. Dube reminded his audience that his college, Ohlange Institute, had been founded on the model of Tuskegee Institute, and he drew "many striking parallels between the race problem in South Africa and that in America."[43] H. H. Jones, an African missionary, lectured at the institute on March 17, 1927, on the exceptional "intelligence of African" peoples.[44] Thomas Jesse Jones visited Tuskegee in early March and lectured for several days.[45] Mrs. Anna Wicksell, the Swedish representative to the League of Nations and a member of the league's Mandate Commission, spent two weeks at Tuskegee. Speaking at the institute's chapel service on March 6, she explained: "I have come here to learn about your method of doing things. The commission wants to save Africa for the Africans and that can only be done in the same way that Dr. Washington served you." Wicksell's visit was paid for by the Phelps-Stokes Fund.[46]

Students were taught that several former Tuskegee faculty and students had assumed leading roles in African economic and educational development for decades. John Wesley Hoffman, an agricultural biologist in charge of Tuskegee's Agricultural Botany and Chemistry Department from 1894 to 1897, was one of the first black scientists to work for the British in West Africa. In 1903, Hoffman was appointed director of agriculture for what was then Lagos Colony, Nigeria. Hoffman did much of his research in the Ilogun and Ijewun districts of the Egba territory and the Ilesha and Ekiti areas of the Yoruba.

Hoffman developed a new type of cotton plant, a cross between a locally grown type and its American cousin. The new cotton was planted throughout southern Nigeria and became a major export by the 1920s. Hoffman also volunteered to serve as sanitation commissioner for the city of Abeokuta. During his work in Nigeria, from 1903 to 1908, he became a leading advocate of commercial expansion and agricultural development along Tuskegee lines. Writing to Nigeria's colonial secretary in Ibadan in December 1903, Hoffman stated that the expansion of railroads and agricultural investment would "open up to the world one of the greatest agricultural centres in all West Africa."[47]

Isaac Fisher, a former Tuskegee student, became famous as an interpreter of African culture and society during the 1920s. A protégé of Washington, Fisher had been the principal of the Branch Normal College for Negroes in Arkansas at the age of twenty-five. He subsequently became a fund-raiser for Tuskegee Institute and later a YMCA official. In 1925, Fisher received a Guggenheim Fellowship to "study race relationships."[48] Thomas Jesse Jones advised Fisher to "take a tour of Africa to study French policies, British policies, and South African policies."[49] Fisher attended the International Conference on the Christian Mission in Africa at Le Zoute, Belgium, in September 1926 and met a number of influential Africanists: the Reverend W. M. Mahabane, the president of the African National Congress; John Langalibalele Dube; Anson Phelps Stokes; C. T. Loram, then South African commissioner for Native Affairs; and J. H. Dillard, president of the Slater and Jeanes Funds.[50]

Fisher's writings on his travels throughout Africa captured the imagination of many Afro-Americans. C. L. Fisher, the minister of Birmingham's Sixteenth Street Baptist Church (Alabama), wrote his brother that Fisher's letters had caused much excitement among his congregation. "We were all very favorably surprised to learn of the important, and I presume lucrative positions held by our people [in the Gold Coast]. Such information," he observed, "has not reached us through missionaries."[51]

In May 1926, Charles Winter Wood, the executive secretary of the Hampton-Tuskegee Endowment Fund, informed Fisher that his exploits were being watched proudly at Tuskegee. "I have read your interesting letter over and over again," Wood wrote, "and have showed it to many of my friends who have enjoyed it immensely." Wood continued:

You would be surprised to know how many of our boys and girls here at Tuskegee whom you do not know, but who are following your career with most remarkable interest, first, because you are a Tuskegee man, second, because you are an extraordinary man, and third, because you are a man of our race. These boys and girls look up to you as an ideal, and you are an inspiration to the Negro youth here because of your remarkable personality and your scholarly attainments.[52]

The only official expedition sponsored by Tuskegee to Africa during the 1920s was to the Gold Coast and Liberia. Moton asked R. R. Taylor, vice-president of the institute, to visit West Africa for six months in 1929. Taylor's primary duty was to attend the dedication exercises of the Booker T. Washington Institute in Liberia and to advise officials there "as to the layout of the [new] buildings and grounds." Taylor was Tuskegee Institute's principal architect, and his skills were used to draft plans for the new school.

During his visit, Taylor also completed a study on "the possible economic needs of the country," reported the *Liberian Educational Outlook*, "with the view of recommending courses at the school which will be in keeping" with "agricultural and industrial training."[53] Taylor discussed his plans with President King and Interior Secretary Cooper. D. A. Ross, the manager of the Firestone Company in Liberia, invited Taylor to survey his company's massive rubber plantation on the Du River. Taylor agreed.

The Liberian government had granted the Firestone Company one million acres of forest land, and industrial development was occurring at a rapid pace. Taylor was awed by the Firestone effort, and he came away a firm proponent of American capitalist development in Liberia and all of Africa. Before leaving Monrovia, Taylor cabled Moton immediately on the Firestone Company's effort:

I am amazed at the magnitude of the development. It seems almost a miracle that such a large undertaking could be organized and achieve such results in so short a time; especially interesting is the favorable attitude of the native employees who were interviewed, as time permitted, without reservations. This development will in my opinion, mean the greatest benefit to the country.[54]

Taylor's correspondence suggested that the Booker T. Washington Institute could be a successful training ground for potential Firestone employees. If only the Liberians could appreciate and learn from the Tuskegee doctrine of self-help, capitalist initiative, and accommodation, he believed, the country could inevitably progress. Returning to Tuskegee, Taylor summed up what he thought was the key to Liberia's problem: "one of the greatest difficulties is the [Liberian] attitude toward work."[55]

Moton's personal involvement in Liberian internal affairs increased during the Great Depression. The Liberian government was unable to pay its foreign debts, and the legislature renounced most of its obligations in early 1933. The possibility that a European government might occupy Monrovia became a reality. In February 1933, Moton and Jones discussed Liberia's difficulties with William Phillips, President-elect Franklin D. Roosevelt's new under-secretary of state. Moton wrote to Major General Blanton Winship, Herbert Hoover's appointed negotiator with the Liberians. Moton stated that it was "futile" for the League of Nations to solve Liberia's economic woes. "I am more than ever convinced," he told Winship, "that the United States has a more vital interest in Liberia than any European country. On the long view I believe that such relationship is the best guarantee of Liberian sovereignty."[56]

Moton was an active member of the Advisory Committee on Education in Liberia, an organization consisting of the leaders from the American Colonization Society, the Phelps-Stokes Fund, and several American missionary groups.[57] Tuskegee's president attempted to transform the rather negative image of Liberia in the American press. When Henry L. West, the president of the American Colonization Society, mailed five hundred copies of *The Liberian Crisis* to Moton, he informed West that he would "distribute" them "advantageously" to influential people aware of African problems.[58]

Moton provided support for the Liberian Research Society of Los Angeles, a black organization that "attempt[ed] to foster a program which will spread favorable opinions about Liberia in the Negro group in America."[59] Officials of the Liberian government continued to rely on Tuskegee for advice. In March 1934, Walter Walker, then serving in the Liberian Consulate in New York, asked G. Lake Imes to review Liberia's request to the League of Nations for medical supplies and consultants.[60]

When Moton resigned the presidency of Tuskegee Institute in 1935, a significant phase of Tuskegee history ended. Frederick Patterson, the new president of the institute, did not have the same political and educational perspectives as the college's first two presidents. African political and educational issues were reported less frequently in the Tuskegee Institute publications, although student and faculty involvement in colonial Africa continued. With the Great Depression and World War II, the age of white philanthropy and paternalist politics was being transformed. Moton's and Tuskegee's contribution to Africa had been determined largely by the conservative political realities of the 1920s. As African nations moved swiftly toward independence, Tuskegee's "missionary" impulse and accommodationist political philosophy lost much of its relevancy and appeal.

Notes

1. See Louis R. Harlan, "Booker T. Washington and the White Man's Burden," *American Historical Review* 71 (January 1967):441-467; and W. Manning Marbale, "The Pan-Africanism of Booker T. Washington: A Reappraisal," *Claflin College Review* 2 (May 1978):1-14.

2. Memorandum, E. J. Scott, John Whittaker, A. F. Owens, and J. B. Ramsey to Booker T. Washington, no date, Moton Papers, Tuskegee Institute Archives, Tuskegee Institute, Alabama (10).

3. Scott to I. B. W. Barnett, May 17, 1916, Moton Papers (10).

4. Scott to Walter Walker, October 25, 1916, Moton Papers (10).

5. W. Walker to Robert R. Moton, September 2, 1916; and E. Scott to W. Walker, October 3, 1916, Moton Papers (10).

6 .W. Walker to E. Scott, July 28, 1916, Moton Papers (10).

7. Ibid. See also E. Scott to W. Walker, June 20, 1916; R. Moton to W. Walker, September 15, 1916; W. Walker to E. Scott, October 21, 1916; and W. Walker to E. Scott, June 6, 1916, Moton Papers (10).

8. R. Moton to W. Walker, September 15, 1916, Moton Papers (10).

9. W. Walker to R. Moton, September 2, 1916, Moton Papers (10).

10. W. Walker to E. Scott, September 2, 1916, Moton Papers (10).

11. E. Scott to W. Walker, October 25, 1916, Moton Papers (10).

12. "Dr. Taylor's Visit," *Liberian Educational Outlook* 2 (May 1929):4.

13. "Hold Dedication Exercises for 'Tuskegee in Africa,' " *Tuskegee Messenger* 5 (May 1929):3. Copies in Tuskegee Institute Archives.

14. A. Hayford to R. Moton, February 4, 1924, Moton Papers (148).

15. L. B. Moss to R. Moton, March 29, 1928, Moton Papers (143).

16. E. T. Early to R. Moton, March 13, 1924, Moton Papers (148).

17. A. P. Stokes to R. Moton, November 10, 1926, Moton Papers (125).

18. "Africans Seek Translation of 'Up From Slavery,' " *Tuskegee Messenger* 3 (February 1927):3.

19. J. E. Kwegyir Aggrey to R. Moton, September 21, 1922; and J.E.K. Aggrey to R. Moton, September 22, 1922, Moton Papers (78).

20. J. E. K. Aggrey to R. Moton, May 7, 1922, Moton Papers (78).

21. J. E. K. Aggrey to R. Moton, September 4, 1924; and R. Moton to J.E.K. Aggrey, October 16, 1924, Moton Papers (78).

22. J. E. K. Aggrey to R. Moton, October 10, 1924, Moton Papers (78).

23. Ibid. Aggrey wrote to Du Bois in 1913, but no contact appears to have been maintained between the two men. Aggrey to W. E. B. Du Bois, July 1, 1913, in *The Correspondence of W. E. B. Du Bois* 1, ed. Herbert Aptheker (Amherst, Mass.: University of Massachusetts Press, 1973), pp. 182-185.

24. Harry Thuku to R. Moton, September 8, 1921, Moton Papers (7).

25. Tony Martin, *Race First: The Ideological and Organizational Struggles of Marcus Garvey and the Universal Negro Improvement Association* (Westport, Conn.: Greenwood Press, 1976), p. 116.

26. Ibid., p. 36.

27. Ibid., pp. 36, 45, 281-282, 284, 290, 324.

28. Phelps-Stokes Fund Budget, November 9, 1926, copy in A. P. Stokes to R. Moton, November 10, 1926, Moton Papers (125).

29. A. P. Stokes to Monroe N. Work, June 10, 1926, Moton Papers (125).

30. Thomas Jesse Jones to R. Moton, July 6, 1926; T. J. Jones to R. Moton, July 20, 1926; and R. Moton to T. J. Jones, July 24, 1926, Moton Papers (125).

31. R. Moton to T. J. Jones, August 4, 1926, Moton Papers (125).

32. *Tuskegee Institute Bulletin* 22 (May 1928):141; *Tuskegee Institute Bulletin* 23 (March 1929):136; and *Tuskegee Institute Bulletin* 26 (May 1933):177. Copies in Tuskegee Institute Archives.

33. "Native Africans Open New Bank in Nigeria," *Tuskegee Messenger* 5 (March 1929):5.

34. "West Africa Needs Schools," *Tuskegee Messenger* 3 (June 1927):3 and "Africans Tanned Leather," *Tuskegee Messenger* 3 (October 1927):7.

35. "Fourth Pan-African Congress," *Tuskegee Messenger* 3 (June 1927):3.

36. "Institute Museum Gets African Art Specimens," *Tuskegee Messenger* 3 (April 1927):5.

37. "Decline South African Offer," *Tuskegee Messenger* 5 (March 1927):7.

38. "Education in Africa," *Tuskegee Messenger* 5 (February 1929):7.

39. "Tagore, Gandhi Send Messages to Tuskegee," *Tuskegee Messenger* 5 (March 1929):1.

40. "British Colonial Governor to Study Tuskegee Methods," *Tuskegee Messenger* 3 (October 1927):1.

41. L. A. Roy to R. Moton, October 28, 1926; R. Moton to L. A. Roy, September 13, 1926; L. A. Roy to R. Moton, October 6, 1926; and R. Moton to Clark Foreman, October 30, 1926, Moton Papers (125).

42. "Liberian Scenes Shown," *Tuskegee Messenger* 3 (January 1927):5.

43. "Education Redemption of Africa Says Native," *Tuskegee Messenger* 3 (January 1927):5.

44. "Finds Africans Intelligent," *Tuskegee Messenger* 3 (April 1927):2.

45. "Dr. Thomas Jesse Jones Speaks on Near East," *Tuskegee Messenger* 3 (March 1927):7.

46. "Swedish Educator Observes Tuskegee," *Tuskegee Messenger* 3 (April 1927):3.

47. J. W. Hoffman to Colonial Secretary, Ibadan, December 26, 1903, J. W. Hoffman Papers, Tuskegee Institute Archives (1).

48. Resident Trustee on Committee for the Branch Normal College, University of Arkansas, to Booker T. Washington, August 14, 1905, Isaac Fisher Papers, Tuskegee Institute Archives (1).

49. Thomas Jesse Jones to I. Fisher, August 19, 1925, Fisher Papers (1).

50. "Who's Who, International Conference on the Christian Mission in Africa," Le Zoute, Belgium (London: International Missionary Council, 1926), copy in Fisher Papers (1).

51. C. L. Fisher to I. Fisher, December 6, 1926, Fisher Papers (1).

52. C. W. Wood to I. Fisher, May 31, 1926, Fisher Papers (1).

53. "Dr. Taylor's Visit," *Liberian Educational Outlook* 2 (May 1929):4.

54. Ibid., and "Firestone Developments Amaze Mr. R. R. Taylor," *Tuskegee Messenger* 5 (May 1929):3.

55. R. R. Taylor, "The Outlook in Liberia," *Tuskegee Messenger* 5 (October 1929):8. Despite the critical differences in educational policy that separated Du Bois from the Tuskegee tradition of Moton, their approaches to the problem of African economic development were quite similar. In 1924, Du Bois visited Liberia and accompanied the American minister, Solomon P. Hood, and a Firestone executive into the forest "with a view to deciding whether it would be worthwhile for the Firestone

Company to invest in Liberia." In October 1925, Du Bois wrote to Harvey Firestone, suggesting that his company hire Liberians and black Americans to work with "white American rubber experts" in the country. "You can inaugurate one of the greatest and far reaching reforms in the relations between white industrial countries like America and black, partly developed countries like Liberia," Du Bois declared. W. E. B. Du Bois to Harvey Firestone, October 26, 1925, in *The Correspondence of W. E. B. Du Bois* 1, ed. Aptheker, pp. 320-323.

56. Moton to Major General Blanton Winship, March 3, 1933, Moton Papers (189).

57. T. J. Jones to Henry L. Stimson, February 24, 1933, Moton Papers (189).

58. R. Moton to H. L. West, May 20, 1933, Moton Papers (189).

59. Alfred R. Green to R. Moton, October 21, 1933, Moton Papers (189).

60. W. Walker to G. Lake Imes, March 10, 1934; and W. Walker to G. Lake Imes, March 19, 1934, Moton Papers (189).

Black American Missionary Influence on the Origins of University Education in West Africa

6

Thomas C. Howard

Among the least recognized but most lasting consequences of the black American missionary presence in Africa is the inspiration it provided to generations of young Africans to seek higher education in the United States, very often at predominantly black, church-related institutions. Less chronicled still is the considerable impact on African higher education of American educational models introduced by Africans returning from their North American sojourn. This essay addresses several aspects of the Afro-American impact on African education by focusing on the widespread influence in African education of Nnamdi Azikiwe, one of the most prominent political figures of the late colonial and early nationalist period.

Educated at missionary schools during his early years, Azikiwe was encouraged while still in his youth to travel to the United States by James Aggrey, a Fante from the Gold Coast, who had spent over twenty years in North Carolina teaching at a college operated by the African Methodist Episcopal Zion (AMEZ) Church, one of the largest American Protestant denominations.[1] During the 1920s, Aggrey, who first traveled to America under the sponsorship of an AMEZ missionary, Bishop John Bryan Small, became the most widely recognized African of his generation, inspiring thousands of other Africans by his example to seek education in America. Of the many touched by Aggrey, however, Azikiwe became one of the most distinguished. In addition to his well-known career as a nationalist spokesman and statesman (he ended his public career as the first president of independent Nigeria), Azikiwe emerges under examination as a highly successful academic entrepreneur who almost single-handedly instigated and presided over the most dramatic experiment in higher education hitherto attempted in West Africa, the founding of the "American" University of Nigeria at Nsukka.

It was a bold experiment which went far beyond the aspirations of those early black American missionaries who used every possible opportunity to foster educational development at all levels in Africa and who urged the creation of at least one major West African university. It should be added, however, that even though the experiment swept far beyond the most fanciful ambitions of the early missionary advocates, it also failed to realize its full promise. The plans of missionaries, like the grandiose schemes of African nationalist spokesmen, tended to be excessively optimistic and therefore a major cause of subsequent disappointment. Had the promises and anticipations of the late colonial and early independence years in Africa been less millennial, the hangover today would be less painful.

In probably no other sphere had this been more the case than in higher education, for it was on the returns from massive investment in the higher learning of African universities that modern African society was to be constructed—and constructed in short order. The singular magic of formal education still lingers more enticingly in Africa than in America, although as all the shibboleths about "nation-building," "modernization," and "university development" so common to the 1950s and 1960s recede, disillusionment is growing.[2]

All the universities of tropical Africa are the heritage of alien cultures, a fact that is at the root of most of the continuing dilemmas with which those concerned with higher education in Africa must contend. This is true notwithstanding the many suggestions, arguments, and schemes for the creation of more genuinely indigenous African universities, universities that more effectively "reconcile innovation with the African tradition."[3] Historically, such aspirations have clashed with what has appeared to many to be the incompatible imperative that African universities adhere to an international criterion, a kind of academic gold standard that would assure acceptance of African degrees abroad and the participation of African-trained scholars in international conferences. This latter argument has clearly been the more widely influential. Its success has guaranteed that, among other things, African universities largely remain conservative institutions in situations that demand radical departures and function as conduits for conveying to Africa the academic culture of the West.[4]

In the former British sectors of West Africa, disputes regarding the "Africanization" and ideology of university education have in effect been subordinated to the struggle over which alien tradition ought to serve as the dominant model. The officially sanctioned model during the colonial era was that of the British civic university. The competitive, but nonetheless foreign, transplant proposed has been American, first in the Tuskegee tradition and later, in its logical extension, the land-grant university.[5]

Proposals for the creation of a West African university date at least from 1862. It was not until 1920, however, that these ideas coalesced in the widely debated public demand by the National Congress of British West Africa for an institution of higher education that would combine the resources of the Gold Coast, Nigeria, Sierra Leone, and the Gambia.[6] It was also in 1920 that the famous Phelps-Stokes Commission on Education toured West Africa. Although the crucial influence of its critique of West African primary and secondary education, published two years later, is well known, its implications for African higher education remain largely unexamined. The recommendations of the commission suggested that even the idea of a university in tropical Africa was so premature as to be ludicrous. In the case of the one West African institution where university degrees had for forty-four years been obtainable, Fourah Bay College in Sierra Leone, it was urged that the curriculum be altered to stress industrial education of the Tuskegee style rather than the traditional academic and classical subjects.[7] The Phelps-Stokes Commission was not the first intrusion of American educational theory in West Africa, though it was for many years the most powerful inducement for collaboration between specialists in Afro-American education and those missionaries and Colonial Office officials concerned with African education. The commission was also significant because one of its members inspired a future generation of young Africans to seek university education in the United States.

James E. K. Aggrey was the only African member of the Phelps-Stokes Commission, a position for which he had been selected largely because of his outspoken advocacy of the Tuskegee philosophy of education and his reputation as an "interpreter" of one race to the other. Aggrey became the most widely acknowledged black proponent of racial accommodation after the death of Booker T. Washington in 1915. By 1920, his remarkable life had already been divided by twenty-three years in his native Gold Coast and twenty-two in the United States where he earned an undergraduate degree and then remained on the faculty of a black liberal arts college in North Carolina.[8] Through Thomas Jesse Jones, for thirty-eight years the educational director of the Phelps-Stokes Fund, Aggrey found himself back in Africa in 1920 at the start of the first of two remarkable African tours that would make Aggrey the most widely traveled and visible African of his generation.[9]

As mentioned earlier, among the thousands of Africans who encountered Aggrey was Nnamdi Azikiwe, at the time a student in the Wesleyan Boys School in Lagos. The experience for the sixteen-year-old Azikiwe was electrifying and lasting. As he described it eight years afterward: "Dr. Aggrey's appeal moved me and since then [1920] I have doggedly plodded along and plugged my way to America."[10] More than this, Azikiwe added in this same letter that he had decided "to be among those who will take up the mantle left by the immortal Aggrey."[11] Elsewhere he expressed it even more forcefully: "I became a new man and my ideas of life changed so much that I lived in day-dreams, hoping against hope for the time when it would be possible for me to be like Aggrey."[12] It was a commitment to which Azikiwe remained completely faithful throughout his career. A full grasp of the implications of this commitment is fundamental to our understanding of Azikiwe's role as a proponent of American educational thought and strategy in Africa, first proposed by black American missionaries stationed in Africa.

During the 1920s, Aggrey became the most famous legatee, in the tradition of Africanus Horton, William Blyden, and J. E. Casely Hayford, of the moderate, liberal, mainly Christian nationalist heritage of nineteenth-century West African intellectual life. Simply put, this was a tradition that sought gradual evolutionary reform within the framework of the British empire, and the articulate elite of Lagos and other West African centers from which this philosophy emanated might be characterized as "Africans of a Victorian persuasion."[13] The tradition included tacit acceptance of the style of philanthropic imperialism and missionary Christianity contained in such phrases as "civilizing mission" and the "white man's burden." For many of this persuasion the purpose of education was to place themselves, as individuals, in a better position to help their people through the medium of Western civilization. The society they sought to emulate in externals was that of Victorian England, though much of their intellectual life was Pan-African, based on increasingly close and complex ties with the British West Indies and the United States.

In the Lagos frequented by Azikiwe during the years of his early intellectual development—and his meeting with Aggrey—there was a widespread image abroad of the United States as a country where even the most obscure, even a black man, could rise to a position of importance and even of worldwide distinction. Prominent among those who imparted this image were missionaries of the black American churches who seemed to be proof of the results possible. These individuals were successful professionals who had profited from American education and who now sought to use their talents for the benefit of their ancestral home. The message seemed clear that through patience, hard work, and the proper education almost anything could be accomplished.[14]

Patience, hard work, and education are the signal words, for they best summarize the evolutionary philosophy and the Social Darwinism which, together with pseudoscientific theories of race, dominated so much of Western thought at the turn of the century. Yet, those who were the victims of such racial slander often attempted to use the same evolutionary concepts to their own advantage. Thus, Booker T. Washington advised that members of his race cast down their bucket where they were, to be patient, and slowly to demonstrate that they could evolve into the equal of their betters.[15] Aggrey preached that with time, with patience, with cooperation, and through the proper education, Africans, too, could fly.[16]

Aggrey's philosophy of racial evolution was clothed in the garb of Christian sacrifice—sacrifice for Africa. Only the best, Aggrey would say, was good enough for Africa, but the best could only come with time and through the crucible of Western education. Supported as it was by lofty rhetoric, it was for many an appealing doctrine, though it served to deflect American intellectuals and statesmen from potentially more constructive avenues of thought. This very doctrine inspired Azikiwe, as he prepared in 1925 to leave for the United States, to seek the educational kingdom that would elevate him to a position of power and influence, enabling him to coax his people into following his example. First he would demonstrate that he could evolve as an individual, and then he would show others how they could follow.[17]

Azikiwe spent two years in the United States as part of the thin but steadily widening stream of what has been felicitously phrased the "second middle passage" of Africans seeking independently in America the higher education denied them at home.[18] A profile of these travelers from Africa reveals a dedicated group of young men, virtually all supported by their own labors or that of relatives. In the main they congregated at traditionally black institutions in both the North and South or, less frequently, at large urban universities throughout the country. Although some enrolled in medicine and other professional courses, the majority tended to register in the social sciences, especially in sociology, anthropology, and political science.[19]

Azikiwe, who was one of probably twenty Nigerians who left for the United States between 1920 and 1937, fits the pattern very well.[20] Between 1925 and 1927, he was enrolled in the general arts curriculum at Storer College at Harper's Ferry, West

Virginia, all the while working at a variety of odd jobs, including traveling salesman and strike-breaker in Pennsylvania.[21] Transferring to Howard University in 1928 with the aid of funds from the Phelps-Stokes Fund, Azikiwe studied political science and education, attaining high averages in both subjects.[22] In January 1929, he wrote to Anson Phelps Stokes, chairman of the fund, expressing his gratitude for intervention on his behalf. "My ambition," he wrote, "is to study the administrative phases of education, especially as it affects the African educational problem . . . this is but trailing the path immortalized by my fellow African— the lamented Aggrey."[23]

Azikiwe spent only a short time at Howard. Reacting unfavorably to the urban setting of the university, Azikiwe transferred to Lincoln University in Pennsylvania in the autumn of 1929. He wrote to Jones that he preferred it to Howard because the fellowship was warmer and the rural location was one "where nature challenges one's intelligence and fires his imagination to be more creative."[24] Lincoln had enrolled students from Africa, mostly from Liberia and South Africa, since the day of its opening in 1856 and had provided numerous volunteers for the African mission field. But it was Azikiwe who was to make the name of this small, relatively obscure Afro-American college virtually synonymous with American higher education for a succeeding generation of West African youth.[25] The most famous of his successors at Lincoln was Kwame Nkrumah who, having failed entrance examinations for the University of London, followed Azikiwe's advice in 1935 to apply at Lincoln.[26] Nkrumah was, of course, also to return to Africa with his own conception of higher education based in part on his American experiences. Much that he attempted in Ghana to transform the university system provides a useful comparison for Azikiwe's activities in Nigeria.

Azikiwe remained at Lincoln, first as a student and then as an instructor in political science for five years. In 1930, he completed requirements for the A.B. degree, and between 1931 and 1933, he continued graduate studies at the Columbia University Summer School (as had Aggrey) and at the University of Pennsylvania. In 1932, he was awarded an M.A. degree in philosophy and religion by Lincoln and in 1933 an M.S. in anthropology by Pennsylvania.[27] Clearly, Azikiwe was gathering much first-hand knowledge of the American university system, knowledge that he hoped soon to put to use.

In 1933, Azikiwe applied for a variety of teaching positions both in missionary and government schools in West Africa, including Achimota College, the famous government school near Accra where Aggrey had returned as assistant vice-principal in 1924. Convinced that the rejections he received from virtually all those approached reflected racial discrimination, Azikiwe determined to return to Africa where he would start a school that would serve as "a nucleus for a University."[28] His plans included two alternatives, the first of which was to establish a university at Monrovia in Liberia that would welcome students from all parts of Africa. If, however, insufficient funds were collected from philanthropic Americans for this venture, he would return to Nigeria and establish a University of Nigeria, depending on his patriotic countrymen to develop the scheme. Azikiwe then proceeded to make elaborate plans for the university of his dreams, plans that were thoroughly American in concept and detail. There would be thirteen faculties, including education, commerce, journalism, agriculture, and technology, and degrees in most fields through the Ph.D.[29]

To raise capital, Azikiwe looked to the example of Wilberforce University in Ohio which had conducted a successful fund-raising campaign by listing contributors on a "Roll of Honor." Azikiwe calculated that if a million Nigerians subscribed £1 each as a permanent endowment, this could gather interest at 5 percent, providing an annual income of £50,000.[30] In the meanwhile, to obtain initial working funds, to fulfill this "desire to revolutionize African intellectual life," Azikiwe made a direct appeal to American and African friends. The letter he prepared for circulation read in part:

For eight years (1925-33) I have laboured and struggled in the United States to secure an education for service to those who are not privileged as I have been. My tutelage is invaluable and I feel that no greater service could I render to African youth than to share with them the joys of my new life in the West. Towards the realization of my aims and dreams, it is proposed to establish an institution in West Africa for the intellectual and manual education of Africans, male and female.[31]

Many replies to this appeal came in, but accompanying them were contributions of less than £40, all of which Azikiwe refunded. His "pet scheme for the founding of a University of Nigeria" having been thwarted, Azikiwe turned his attention "towards earning a livelihood elsewhere in Africa."[32]

This was not, however, entirely the case, for Azikiwe did not abandon his interest in learning more about American strategies of black education for ultimate application in Africa. In May 1933, he requested additional funds from the Phelps-Stokes Fund to "realize a lifetime dream" of studying at first hand the educational philosophy of Hampton Institute in Virginia. As he expressed it to Jones: "Hampton is such a famous site. I have read so much of that shrine of Negro education. . . . I would like to stay there and see how the school which prepared Washington and Moton carries on the old tradition of Armstrong."[33] Jones's marginal notation, "this is important," on Azikiwe's appeal anticipated an award of the requested funds, and Azikiwe spent several weeks at Hampton in the summer of 1933.[34]

The next year Azikiwe made further attempts, with the aid of Jones, to locate suitable employment in education somewhere in Africa.[35] When these yielded nothing positive, Azikiwe was further embittered and attributed the rejections not only to racial prejudice but also to official British suspicion of mission-educated Africans and Africans educated in America. Such people, Azikiwe was convinced, were assumed to be disloyal and anti-British.[36] It was not the last time that this issue would arise in Azikiwe's career, and on this occasion it provided the background for a critical juncture in his life. Azikiwe determined that if no future was immediately open to him in education, he would turn to journalism as a means of helping to popularize his developing conception of a new, or as he soon would characterize it, "renascent" Africa. Education was vital, he still believed, but for the time being, "the press is a much wider and more potent avenue for this particular mission."[37]

He had not abandoned his plans for a university, but he saw

that it would have to wait. He appealed again to Jones for advice, expressing his belief that "true African education" is possible if only the African peoples realize their own capacities. This he knew was consonant with Jones's philosophy of education and "that of our Aggrey."[38] So again the name of Aggrey was sounded to legitimize Azikiwe's ambitions to establish a future educational center in Africa. Furthermore, advice was sought from Jones regarding other American foundations and organizations that might be approached for later financial backing for such a center.[39] In the meanwhile, however, a university would have to wait the achievement of other goals in Africa, namely, the attainment of "spiritual balance, social regeneration and economic determinism."[40]

The terminology represented here is indicative of the eclectic ideology which for Azikiwe was still in the initial stages of formulation. His years in the United States provided him with just enough half-digested knowledge of the thought of figures as diverse as John Dewey, Karl Marx, and Marcus Garvey to enable him to embellish the Christian and evolutionary views that remained at the core of his thinking. In 1934, Azikiwe was embarking on a new course which would perpetuate in West Africa the intellectual traditions of the past half century, tempered by the catch words and slogans of the various theorists and philosophers he encountered intellectually or directly while in America.[41] The most thoroughly embraced influences on Azikiwe in America were those of pragmatism, individual philanthropy, liberal democracy, and that nebulous quality which Americans still enjoyed referring to as "rugged individualism."[42]

For three turbulent years, Azikiwe worked "in the land of Kwegyir Aggrey," as the editor of the *African Morning Post* in Accra. He returned to Nigeria in the summer of 1937 to edit his own newspaper, the *West African Pilot*, the first of a succession of publishing ventures organized by the limited liability company which Azikiwe incorporated.[43]The reporting and editorializing of Azikiwe's newspapers, particularly the *Pilot*, contributed appreciably to the growth of West African nationalism, and Azikiwe himself was increasingly viewed as the most visible and annoying gadfly of colonial officialdom. More than any other

African figure during these years, Azikiwe contributed to and symbolized the politicization of African thinking, though basically it was still the old Darwinian law of natural selection, both for the self and for the race, now couched in the language of the "new Africa." Azikiwe's book, *Renascent Africa* (1937), reflected most dramatically both the continuation of his nineteenth-century evolutionary grounding and his American education. It was his single most significant testament and because of its influence perhaps the most important African political manifesto of the years between the wars. Ultimately, between 1946 and 1950, it even contributed to the inspiration for a radical philosophical movement, that of Zikism, a movement that Azikiwe himself disowned when it clashed too severely with his accommodationist policies.[44]

Azikiwe never forsook his ambition for the educational future of Nigeria, and he used every opportunity to promote his views. The opportunity arose in large measure because Azikiwe's return to Africa coincided with the first, though still highly tentative, steps taken to formulate an official colonial policy of university development. When Azikiwe reached West Africa in 1934, Fourah Bay College, through its affiliations with Durham University, was still the only institution in tropical Africa that awarded fully recognized undergraduate degrees.[45] In 1935, Achimota College had also begun offering degree courses in engineering using the University of London syllabus, though on a scale that was to remain extremely limited.[46] Achimota was widely regarded as the most logical core around which a future West African university would develop, although in reality neither its successive headmasters nor most of those in decision-making roles saw it as a potential university except perhaps in the most distant future.[47] Closer to Azikiwe was another colonial experiment in higher education, the Higher College at Yaba in Nigeria which was formally opened in 1934. The origins of Yaba lie in the reluctance of the Colonial Office to respond to missionary and African demands for higher education. From the start, however, its object was only to "give a training of a university or professional character."[48]

These demands led ultimately to the appointment of a succession of British advisory commissions to investigate the question of higher education in British Africa. This investigation got under way with the 1933 study of James Currie, a former director of education in the Sudan and a member of the Colonial Office Advisory Committee on Education. Currie called for immediate plans to begin university development; the Colonial Office, which received the report favorably, requested responses from the various African colonial governments. The lukewarm response from virtually all the governors was indicative of the indifference, and even hostility, of most local colonial officials.[49] The only encouraging response came from Uganda, leading to the creation of a commission to investigate the feasibility of transforming Makerere School into an institution of higher education.[50] The hope was to raise Makerere to full university status within ten years.

In 1938, another commission was appointed to report on the status and future of Fourah Bay College in view of its troubled financial situation. The report concluded in part that Fourah Bay might supply the theological and arts faculties of a "united West African college or university," but only when such an institution might be founded "at some distant date."[51] Similarly, the next year at the West African Governors' Conference in Lagos, a similar project for a West African university was considered, but only as a very long-range concept.

During World War II, plans for future university development continued with more concrete results. The most important initial development was the report of a sub-committee of the Colonial Office Advisory Committee which pressed for a comprehensive scheme of higher education for the colonies. The enthusiasm of the subcommittee chairman, H. J. Channon, led to the establishment of two commissions in 1943; one, under the chairmanship of Cyril Asquith, was to focus on the general issue of higher education in all of the colonies, and the other, chaired by Walter Elliot, was to concentrate on the question in West Africa. Both commissions published their recommendations in 1945, therein finally committing Britain to a policy of colonial university development commencing at once.[52] The importance of these documents cannot be stressed too much, for many came to view their recommendations as decrees to be followed with little or no deviation. The underlying assumption of the reports was a belief that the pattern and purpose of university education in Great Britain, particularly those of the British civic university, were equally appropriate for Africa. These colonial universities were to begin in embryo as "university colleges," later to be elevated to full university status after a satisfactory probationary period. The examinations of the University of London would be administered and the external degrees of that university awarded until such time that independent status could be assured. These "Asquith colleges" were to be entirely residential, to adhere to the international standards of British universities, and, as had traditionally been the British pattern, to educate a small elite who would "have the standards of public service and capacity for leadership which the progress of self-government demands."[53]

The Elliot Commission spent most of the first four months of 1944 in West Africa, visiting sixty-nine towns and cities in the Gold Coast, Nigeria, Sierra Leone, and, briefly, the Gambia.[54] In addition to the many planned meetings with colonial officials, missionaries, and representatives of the African populations, the commission at every turn encountered reporters from the African press. In Nigeria particularly, the commission found itself constantly questioned by representatives of Azikiwe's newspapers, with Azikiwe himself foremost among the critics.[55] By the time the commission visited West Africa, journalism there had long been an important source of information for the literate urban masses. Azikiwe, who had been fascinated by the unifying power of the American black press during his years as a student, had been since his return among the most effective in applying its strategies to the African situation.

In addition to interviews with its members and exhaustive coverage of its activities, the commission also served as the excuse for a succession of widely reported speeches by Azikiwe on education. Typical was the address delivered before the Onitsha Improvement Union in March 1944, timed to coincide with the visit of Arthur Creech Jones and other commission representatives. As reported in his own press, Azikiwe emphasized in his remarks the importance of various American assessments (including those of the Phelps-Stokes Fund) of African preparedness for equal education and responsibility with Europeans. Using a

recent American study of the applicability of the principles of
the Atlantic Charter to Africa, Azikiwe called for educational
self-determination for Africans—peoples who clearly in the past
had "demonstrated social capacity and educability."[56]

The American study cited, *The Atlantic Charter and Africa from
an American Standpoint*, was one of the most influential responses
to the controversies generated by the signing of the Atlantic
Charter in 1941 and the application of the Roosevelt-Churchill
"Eight Points" to Africa. The drafters of this study, the Committee on Africa, the War, and Peace Aims, had first met in the
autumn of 1941 at the initiative of the Phelps-Stokes Fund. Both
Anson Phelps Stokes and Thomas Jesse Jones were on the committee, as were several African students then studying in the
United States. Kwame Nkrumah, then at Lincoln University,
was one. Although the report did stress the ultimate goal of
self-government by the African colonies and the need to prepare
for it, it also reiterated most of the old paternalistic views on the
applicability to Africa of low-level agricultural and industrial
education as developed in the American South.[57] Azikiwe does
not appear to have opposed this old message, particularly its
stress on the need somehow to adapt American concepts of "education for life" to the African environment. The year prior to the
visit of the Elliot Commission in West Africa, Azikiwe had reinforced these attitudes during a visit to London as secretary of the
West African Press Delegation to the United Kingdom. In a memorandum prepared largely by him entitled "The Atlantic Charter
and British West Africa," the first listed demands for postwar
reconstruction in British West Africa were reforms in education.
As the memorandum worded it, education should be "designed
to fit the citizen to his environment; to enable him to fulfill his
obligations and responsibilities as a citizen; to develop him intellectually and socially; to train him as a useful member of society;
to train him for a trade or profession."[58] Such a demand, in the
context of the rest of the document, was at once a perpetuation of
the old message of differentiated black education and the harbin-
ger of a new era of American impact on Africa.

The end of the war in 1945 signaled the beginning of a period
of massive expansion of higher education in the United States

and, to a lesser extent, in Great Britain, which, before its momentum slowed in the late 1960s, witnessed a fundamental reordering of attitudes toward the approaches to university education. For British Africa this was to have at least two important consequences. First, British colonial universities in Africa were to be provided with the funds to develop, but along the lines of an older, traditional, elitist, mainly Oxbridge pattern, even as newer concepts were making inroads in Great Britain itself. Second, African nationalist politicians who had received their higher education in America, of whom Azikiwe continued to be the most prominent, pressed for the application of what they conceived to be the greater adaptability of American universities to the needs of Africa. To facilitate this there was also the availability of American funds, in part a product of Cold War strategy, but also the result of the increasingly fashionable support in the United States of international projects and area studies by the federal government and American-based philanthropic foundations. The result was an often uneasy marriage between British educational traditionalism, particularly on matters related to academic standards and curricula, and what was frequently described as American "flexibility."[59]

From the outset, strong emotions surrounded the recommendations of the British educational commissions which were acted upon between 1945 and 1948. With final agreement on the status of Fourah Bay College still unresolved, two new university colleges, that of the Gold Coast and that for Nigeria at Ibadan, were formally opened in the autumn of 1948.[60] University College Ibadan, incorporating the old Yaba Higher College, enrolled 104 students during its first session and began a period of gradual development which by 1960 only allowed an enrollment of 1,250.[61] The pace was intentionally gradual, and the pattern was almost exclusively English, mainly that of Cambridge, from high table and the passing of after-dinner port to the constitution and curriculum and, above all, the social function. Despite movement away from the outlook in England itself, those who planned and structured Ibadan conceived it as the training ground for a small social and intellectual elite who would gradually inherit the instruments of power from the departing colonial hierarchy.

From the beginning Ibadan was tutorial and entirely residential, with halls of residence modeled insofar as reality would permit on the colleges of Cambridge as they were recalled by the planners from their own student days. As so often occurred in the imperial experience, the metropolitan pattern was replicated in the colony with a time lag. Ibadan was in many ways an Edwardian, even a Victorian, institution that suited not only its British sponsors but also those Anglicized and Anglophile intelligentsia who would inhabit its halls and send their sons for education. These latter, British-educated, Nigerians firmly believed that education was indivisible and that the classical training characteristically received by the upper echelons of the colonial establishment was just as correct for those Africans who would eventually succeed to the mandarinate. At last, many believed, Nigeria would have a university of international standards that would award degrees with the same currency as the University of London until the British sponsors deemed Ibadan worthy of awarding its own degrees. Such a development did not in fact come until 1962; ironically, Ibadan was therefore the youngest of the five Nigerian universities then in existence.[62]

But not all subscribed to the colonial university plan, and it continued to generate opposition. The arguments and press attacks against the university were wide-ranging, including alleged racist policies governing staff appointments and salary differentials, the exclusion of qualified students, architectural extravagance, and the limited London-based curriculum.[63] Implicit in many of these charges was the view that while the Cambridge pattern and London curriculum were inappropriate for Africa there were other imports, mainly American, that were not. There is more than slight irony in the fact that while Ibadan was being denounced for its thralldom to England, preliminary plans were already under way to create a competitor institution that would be no less effectively bound to another foreign nation, the United States.

Among the heated questions surrounding the new university college, the most dominant were the nature of the curriculum and the problem of standards. As early as 1944, the Nigerian Union of Teachers submitted to the Elliot Commission a memorandum proposing a department of education at the new institution. Neither this nor subsequent proposals for departments of engineering economics, or other "practical" additions to the curriculum were received favorably, and neither new faculty nor departments were added during the first six years of the college.[64] During these years, the very few admitted to Ibadan and the numerous failures among the students added to the number and impatience of critics.[65]

Azikiwe was among those annoyed by the curriculum which he believed to be too rarified and too bound by what he considered an unrealistic reliance on "standards." By the early 1950s, he was able to count on great numbers of secondary school graduates who saw no chance for admission to Ibadan. As Nigeria moved more steadily toward independence, university admission also became a political question with far-reaching implications which Azikiwe was too astute to ignore. He began to extend new feelers to the United States for funds and advice. As early as 1947, during the first of a succession of American pilgrimages in search of moral and material support for his political ambitions and educational projects, Azikiwe made numerous public appeals. In one of his New York speeches, after excoriating British colonial policy as deceptive and autocratic, Azikiwe called for "the establishment of a university in West Africa, organized and administered by the American and African peoples."[66] He continued:

Surely, if we can have "Yale in China," "American University in Turkey" and "American University in Beirut" I see no reason why we should not have "Lincoln University [or] Howard University in Africa." I trust that all those who are interested in this project of adjusting human relations will bear in mind this idea of establishing a university in West Africa in order to make the bridgehead in Africa more secure and more intrinsic in its value to the cause of understanding, goodwill and fellowship with the United States.[67]

Clearly, Azikiwe had not forgotten his plan of 1934 and was approaching that stage of his career where he was in a position to act on it. This was increasingly advantageous for him politically, for the question of university development in Nigeria was governed more and more by political maneuver and bargaining. Nigeria was in the initial stages of the process which by the 1960s would lead to virtually complete politicization of university issues. Higher education became the focus of regional and national infighting and bargaining at the same time that it increasingly fell into a pattern of complex negotiations with American and British universities and a variety of foreign and international agencies.

The main political developments can be sketched quickly. Since 1944, Azikiwe had taken the lead in forming the National Council of Nigeria and the Cameroons (NCNC), a movement intended to be national in its appeal but which in reality became an Ibo political instrument. Neither the NCNC nor other mainly ethnically based rival groups advocated the creation of a unitary state. In general, the NCNC pushed for a large number of regions, while the Yoruba and northern parties—the Action Group and Northern Peoples' Congress (NPC)—agitated for a few large regions.[68] The constitution of 1951 provided for a new central government constituted mainly of indirectly elected members, but it allowed important ministerial experience for Africans at many levels. In 1954, final concessions from the British allowed the creation of a fully federal system with an elective central legislative chamber which determined the appointment of a number of federal ministers. Parallel arrangements were made for the regional assemblies.[69] The realization that independence was in the wind caused an intensification of intrapolitical struggles between 1954 and 1960. In 1957, with the creation of the new position of federal prime minister, the predominately Yoruba western and the largely Ibo eastern regions attained self-government in internal affairs (the politically less experienced northern region followed in 1959) and agreed in conference in 1958 on a final independence constitution. In the 1959 federal elections, the NPC and NCNC combined tactically to form a government with a northerner as prime minister and Azikiwe as president of the Senate and, sometime later, governor-general. When Nigeria became a republic in 1963, Azikiwe became its first president.[70]

In 1955, the year after he became premier of the eastern region, Azikiwe traveled to Washington and New York again to seek assistance in materializing his plans to establish an American-style university in the east. He had already determined to call it the University of Nigeria, therein preempting the concept of a national university for his own region. By 1955, he had developed an antipathy to the pattern developing in Ibadan. Two years before, he had confronted the second principal, J. T. Saunders, on the latter's home ground at Cambridge with his aspirations for curriculum changes at Ibadan that would reflect both greater Africanization and the vocational stress of American universities.[71] When changes of this sort did not appear to be forthcoming at Ibadan, Azikiwe proceeded with his own plans.

When American foundations and federal agencies responded with initial reluctance to Azikiwe's overtures in 1955, he returned to Nigeria where at his urging the eastern legislature passed a law establishing a University of Nigeria with funding provided mainly by the Palm Oil Marketing Board.[72] The financial arm-twisting at home to achieve his ambition was Azikiwe's first major foray into what has been called the "economics of euphoria," the exuberance that pushed ahead university formation because it was believed to be the necessary percursor of all future economic development.[73]

In seconding the motion in the eastern House of Assembly which passed the "Law to Establish a University in the Eastern Region of Nigeria," Azikiwe once more associated himself with the memory of Aggrey and cited at some length the report of the Phelps-Stokes Commission of 1920 which he hailed as still timely for Nigeria. "I believe," said Azikiwe, "that, side by side with higher vocational education, opportunities should be created to enable the trained individuals to play a useful role in the development of the country." He added:

It is my fondest wish that when the University of Nigeria ultimately becomes a reality, our young men and women will find opportunities for gaining experience in life's battle, so that lack of money will not deter them from obtaining higher vocational education in any of the facilities or institutes of the university. I hope that the training in self-help and the experience in self-reliance will make them confident of themselves and enable them to puncture the myth of the proverbial lack of initiative and drive on the part of the Nigerian worker.[74]

It was the Azikiwe of 1934 and of 1920 speaking still.

Further attempts to obtain American financial backing were more successful, and Michigan State University, with federal backing from the Agency for International Development (AID), contracted to guide the creation of the new university. Azikiwe selected Michigan State as one of the best known exemplars of the land-grant concept, a concept that Azikiwe believed more effectively combined the virtues of vocational education with more traditional studies. For Azikiwe, the land-grant idea contained enough of the older "practical education for life and service" virtues of the Tuskegee philosophy to be acceptable. In his mind, the land-grant university also symbolized the "American way" of education by the 1950s, an approach as far removed from the British pattern as he could imagine. Equally aware of this and apprehensive about it were British colonial and academic spokesmen. The Colonial Office, reflecting this concern, obtained agreement from the Inter-University Council to become involved and insofar as possible to deflect potentially excessive American influence.[75]

In 1958, after the presentation of a joint report by British and American academics, two proclamations of the eastern region outlined the rationale and plans for the new university.[76] These documents, which sketch the philosophy of the new university, also reflect Azikiwe's views, which were fundamentally unchanged since his youthful proposals for a university in 1933. The new university was clearly going to be created in Azikiwe's image. Even the site was selected at least in part because it was near the village of Nsukka, the location of the eastern premier's summer home. Although it was hoped that the institution would be a "full adaptation to the needs of the indigenous culture," it is clear that the important stress was on the "desire to draw fully upon the educational philosophies, methods, and experience of other cultures."[77] Those clearly in mind were American. These documents are optimistic both in their analysis of the anticipated educational contributions to Nigeria and the implicit faith in the continuing availability of outside funding. (Shell Oil is cited specifically as a potential source of funds.) American higher education and American industry had arrived.

With Michigan State acting as the key agency for securing outside financial aid and staffing, plans proceeded for the new university to open officially with 220 students during the celebrations of independence week early in October 1960.[78] Despite the astonishing speed with which the American advisers acted, conditions during the first weeks were disorganized and, from the point of view of skeptical or disapproving British observers, primitive: students even had to unpack their own linen, an unheard of inconvenience at Ibadan.[79] Such a reaction was typical of most British and British-educated observers throughout the formative years of Nsukka. Many wished to redirect the new university along British lines, and although the arguments were most often couched in terms of Nigerianization, the basic questions turned on the issue of which of the two alien patterns would prevail. Even with the best intentions such conflicts could not but hinder, and hinder in costly fashion, the progress of higher education in Nigeria.

If the British had moved with gentlemanly ease at Ibadan, the Americans proceeded with frantic speed at Nsukka. Between the opening of the university in 1960 and the military coup of January 1966 which expelled him from office, Azikiwe, combining as he did so many key offices in the region, nation, and university, presided over and frequently personally directed the development of what he clearly viewed as "his" university. It would be the greatest personal monument he would leave his people. Rarely, in fact, has a university during its formative years reflected so deeply the personal imprint of one man, and whatever historic parallels might be cited would undoubtedly have to be drawn from the American experience. Hampton Institute reflected General Samuel Armstrong and Tuskegee, Booker T. Washington. Michigan State also appeared to Azikiwe as proof of what one man's vision had been able to accomplish.[80] Shielded insofar as Azikiwe could arrange from outside public attack, the

University of Nigeria moved toward institutionalizing the land-grant ideal of mass higher education, elevating "practical" vocational fields to university status in the interest of social reconstruction and economic development.[81] Journalism, home economics, and education joined agriculture, a general studies program, and an American-style extension system in rapid order. In haste, the rudiments of an American "multi-university," awarding its own degrees, was implanted on Nigerian soil. Even under the best of circumstances, such a development would tend to lead to difficulties. The widespread identification of Nsukka as "the American university" was, paradoxically, both its greatest asset and its most serious liability. It was an asset because of the official and financial support it received, and a liability because of the widespread suspicion that American education was not of sufficiently high quality to compete with Ibadan or other British or British-model institutions.[82]

American-educated Africans had always been patronized by those of their fellows holding British degrees, and this frequently grew into open distrust or hostility. Africans who had received their education in America had long been feared by the colonial governments and by those Africans beholden to them as enemies of the status quo. These feelings were quick to be carried over into the new university where American functionalism was often viewed as quixotic and substandard. Indeed, the issue of standards encompassed most of the other objections raised by opponents of the American system. This issue became increasingly the battleground between the supporters and the enemies of the American "experiment."

A fairly typical assessment of American higher education appeared in a book by two British-educated members of the Ibadan faculty published in 1960, the same year that the university at Nsukka opened its doors. Education in the United States was perceived as the "product of a misguided conception of democracy which may be...summarized as 'identical education for all at the pace of the slowest.' "[83] They continued with the opinion that the "appalling backwardness" of American schools creates a "vast hunger for further education," comparable to that to be found in West Africa, which in turn leads to a "vast proliferation of so-called universities which have no academic standards and precious few of any other sort."[84] In response to such charges, the proponents of American university education could only express their view that standards were not universal and developed naturally in response to the needs of a given time and place.[85] The issue was never satisfactorily settled at Nsukka, though in the main the British preoccupation with standards eventually created enough pressure to force modification of the entrance requirements, the curriculum, and the examination procedures more to reflect British practice. A British honors degree system was also blended with the American credit system.

Yet, the University of Nigeria at Nsukka remained for years—certainly until the tragedies of the civil war between 1967 and 1970—as the most dramatic effort to create a noncolonial university in the former British sphere of West Africa. It also occupies a unique place in the history of African higher education because it was conceived and largely founded by one man, Nnamdi Azikiwe, not only as a personal tribute to himself, but also as the academic center for his "new Africa." The truth, however, is that the new Africa was really the old Africa—the future was still in the hands of outsiders who had shouldered the "white man's burden." This time, however, the outsiders were American rather than European, for Azikiwe was in the tradition of Aggrey. And even more than in Aggrey's case, Azikiwe had absorbed through his American experiences an image of the United States, with its material abundance, its promise of prosperity and happiness as the ideal state. Africa could likewise move ultimately to this stage of human evolution through proper education of the American vocational variety. In 1940, Azikiwe had looked forward to his own retirement years which he hoped would be spent

in an idyllic atmosphere, in an environment of pastoral grandeur, in a campus, where the shades and spirits of by-gone eras, the bubbling youths of Renascent Africa, shall gather round a cloistered hearth with me, firing the imagination of African youth, and building the foundation and superstructure of a new Africa.[86]

The reality turned out to be far different. Despite the rhetoric about the ideal of a radical departure for African higher educa-

tion and the creation of a truly African university adapted to the
needs of the African people, the clash between rival alien traditions took center stage and in the process became increasingly
politicized. The Americans who came to supervise the building
of the new educational Jerusalem were quickly drawn into the
intricacies of African political struggles which they never fully
understood. They promised a great deal; in retrospect, they clearly
promised far too much. In the full glow of the most phenomenal
educational expansion in their own history, they held before the
eyes of Africa the spectacular image of university expansion.
American missionary education on the primary and secondary
levels had been one thing, but this was university education. With
such know-how and such generous financing, the African evolutionary process could be accelerated and Africa might actually be
dragged into the modern world even before full recovery from the
shock of colonialism. The prospect fascinated Azikiwe and many
others, and it was a near fatal fascination. While the Africans
argued over which foreign model to copy, they institutionalized a
system of higher education inappropriate to their needs.

   This dilemma may be viewed as a somewhat curious and distorted legacy of those early black American missionaries who
urged and contributed to the development of African education.
Of course, this contribution took many different forms, and the
example focused upon here illustrates only one. The attempt
has been made to trace the genealogy of an idea from the first
black AMEZ missionary who in 1898 sponsored James Aggrey to
Nnamdi Azikiwe who had in turn been inspired by Aggrey to
travel for his education to America in 1925. Through this lineage
the first African university drawn fully from American educational models came to be founded in 1960. In the process, many
new ingredients were clearly added to the mix, though the even-
tual influence of black American churches and educational institutions on African university education is undeniable.

Notes

   1. The African Methodist Episcopal Zion Church is the outgrowth
of a black congregation established in New York in 1796. Incorporated

in 1801 with its present name, the denomination expanded throughout the Northeast until the 1860s when it moved into the southern states as well. The basic account of these years is David H. Bradley, *A History of the African Methodist Episcopal Zion Church* (Nashville, Tenn.: Pantheon Press, 1970). Also of importance is Alexander Walters, *My Life and Work* (Chicago: Fleming H.Revell Co., 1917). Walters was a bishop of the AMEZ Church, one of the founders of the NAACP, and an organizer of the first Pan-African Conference in London in 1900. For an account of the early work of the AMEZ in the Gold Coast, see Cameron C. Alleyne, *The Gold Coast at a Glance* (New York: Hunt Publishing Co., 1931). Alleyne was one of the first resident AMEZ bishops in West Africa.

2. See, for example, Mark Blaug, *Education and the Employment Problem in Developing Countries* (Geneva: ILO, 1973); and Theodor Hanf, et al., "Education: An Obstacle to Development? Some Remarks About the Political Functions of Education in Asia and Africa," *Comparative Education Review* 19 (February 1975):68-87.

3. J.F.A. Ajayi, "African Universities and the African Tradition," *East Africa Journal* 8 (November 1971):5. See also J. Ko-Zerbo, "Africanization of Higher Education Curriculum," in *Creating the African University*, ed. T. M. Yesufu (Ibadan: Oxford University Press, 1973), pp. 20-26.

4. See Arthur T. Porter, "University Development in Africa," *African Affairs* 71 (January 1972):73-83. Recently, some have come to view the African university in the even more sinister role of educational analogue of the multinational corporation, an institution that serves foreign rather than African interests. See, for example, Ali A. Mazrui, "The African University as a Multinational Corporation: Problems of Penetration and Dependency," *Harvard Educational Review* 45 (May 1975):191-210.

5. The principal source for the development of official British universities remains Eric Ashby's magisterial *Universities, British, Indian, African* (London: Weidenfeld & Nicolson, 1966); for an excellent study of the Tuskegee industrial influence in colonial Africa, see Kenneth J. King, *Pan-Africanism and Education* (Oxford: Clarendon Press, 1971).

6. See "Education with Particular Reference to a West African University," *Gold Coast Independent*, May 26, 1923, p. 370. Here the 1923 Resolutions of the National Congress of British West Africa are listed and discussed; on education they reaffirm and expand on the resolutions of the 1920 session. The first recorded appeal for a West African university was made in 1862, and again in 1868 by James Africanus Beal Horton, the famous Sierra Leonean physician. On Horton see

Christopher Fyfe, *Africanus Horton* (New York: Oxford University Press, 1972).

7. Fourah Bay College, established as an Anglican missionary institution in 1827, had offered a program leading to a Durham University degree since 1876. In response to the Phelps-Stokes recommendations, action was set in motion by the Colonial Office during the mid-1920s to alter the Fourah Bay curriculum as far as possible along basic industrial and agricultural lines. For a detailed discussion of these plans, see Great Britain, Public Record Office CO 879/121/1100, "Minutes of the Advisory Committee on Native Education in Tropical Africa, September 14, 1927." For the full report of the Phelps-Stokes Commission, see T. J. Jones, *Education in Africa* (New York: Phelps-Stokes Fund, 1922).

8. Aggrey studied and then taught at Livingstone College in Salisbury, North Carolina, a small liberal arts college operated by the African Methodist Episcopal Zion Church. It had been a black missionary of this church who inspired Aggrey to leave the Gold Coast in 1898. The major source on Aggrey remains Edwin W. Smith, *Aggrey of Africa: A Study in Black and White* (London: Student Christian Movement Press, 1929). Also see Thomas C. Howard, "West Africa and the American South: Notes on James E. K. Aggrey and the Idea of a University for West Africa," *Journal of African Studies* 2 (Winter 1975-76):445-465.

9. In the course of the two Phelps-Stokes Tours (1920-1921 and 1923-1924), Aggrey traveled and spoke in virtually every sub-Saharan African territory. To the multitudes who observed him he was the embodiment of what education appeared able to accomplish for Africans. For the itinerary of the two tours, see Jones, *Education in Africa*; and T. J. Jones, *Education in East Africa*, (New York: Phelps-Stokes Fund, 1925). For a more candid appraisal by Jones of Aggrey's role on these journeys, see his *Private Journal*, Box 263, Edinburgh House (Headquarters of the British Conference of Missionary Societies of Great Britain and Northern Ireland), London.

10. Azikiwe to T. J. Jones, June 16, 1928, Azikiwe Correspondence Files, Phelps-Stokes Fund Archives (hereafter PSFA), New York.

11. Ibid.

12. V. C. Iketuonye, *Zik of New Africa* (London: P. R. Macmillan, 1961), p. 38.

13. The phrase is that of Michael J.C. Echeruo in "Nnamdi Azikiwe and Nineteenth-Century Nigerian Thought," *Journal of Modern African Studies* 12 (1974):249. For a general account of the intellectual history of West Africa, see Robert W. July, *The Origins of Modern African Thought* (London: Faber & Faber, 1968). Also of value are the selections in J. A.

Langley, *Ideologies of Liberation in Black Africa, 1856-1970* London: R. Collins, 1979).

14. Soon after meeting Aggrey in 1920, Azikiwe was awarded as a school prize a biography of James A. Garfield, W. M. Thayer's *From Log Cabin to the White House* (New York: Scribner's, 1881). A classic rags-to-riches tale, it more than ever confirmed Azikiwe's belief in the virtue of American institutions. See Azikiwe's autobiography, *My Odyssey* (New York: Praeger, 1970), pp. 40-42.

15. Booker T. Washington's role in American racial history has been widely analyzed, though the best feeling for the climate of his times can be obtained from a reading of his own *Up From Slavery*, first published in 1901. For Washington's own involvement in Africa, see Louis B. Harlan, "Booker T. Washington and the White Man's Burden," *American Historical Review* 7 (January 1966):441-467.

16. The reference is to one of Aggrey's famous metaphors, that of the eagles trained to behave like chickens until they were encouraged to fly into the sun.

17. For a contemporary account illustrating the implications of this philosophy of missionary dedication among African students of this era, see "Negro Students in Africa, America and Europe," Special issue of the *Student World* (April 1923). A copy is located in the files of the Missionary Research Library, New York.

18. Richard D. Ralston, "A Second Middle Passage: African Student Sojourns in the United States During the Colonial Period and Their Influence upon the Changing Character of African Leadership" (Ph.D. dissertation, University of California at Los Angeles, 1972).

19. Imanuel Geiss, *The Pan-African Movement* (New York: Africana Publishing Co., 1974), p. 375.

20. The number of Nigerians seeking higher education in the United States during this period was proportionally far less than those going to Great Britain, and this remained the case until at least the 1960s. As late as 1963-1964, of the estimated 14,200-17,200 Nigerians studying abroad, between 11,000 and 12,000 were in the United Kingdom, approximately ten times greater than the number estimated to have been in the United States. See Ladislav Cerych, *The Integration of External Assistance with Educational Planning in Nigeria* (Paris: IIEP, 1967), p. 40.

21. Many details of Azikiwe's academic record and activities in the United States are available in the archives of the Phelps-Stokes Fund. See especially the autobiographical statement in his letter to Jones, May 11, 1934 (Student file, B-4) which provides useful additions to and checks the episodes revealed in his autobiography.

22. Azikiwe to Jones, May 21 and June 16, 1928, Azikiwe Correspondence Files, PSFA. In 1928, Azikiwe received $200 from the Phelps-Stokes Fund for his studies at Howard, the first of a number of such grants he was to be given throughout his stay in America. Through the direct intervention of Anson Phelps Stokes, chairman of the fund, with university officials, Howard provided Azikiwe with a scholarship. See correspondence between Anson Phelps Stokes, D. W. Woodard, and Emmett J. Scott, Dean of Liberal Arts and Secretary-Treasurer of the University, December 1928, Azikiwe Correspondence Files, PSFA. At Howard, Azikiwe obtained part-time work as private secretary to Alain L. Locke of the Philosophy Department.

23. Azikiwe to Anson Phelps Stokes, January 12, 1929, Azikiwe Correspondence Files, PSFA.

24. Azikiwe to Jones, September 17, 1929, Azikiwe Correspondence Files, PSFA. It is perhaps not projecting too much to see already the roots of Azikiwe's later preference for an isolated, rural university in Nigeria.

25. For the history of Lincoln, with stress on its African ties, see Horace Mann Bond, "Forming African Youth: A Philosophy of Education" in *Africa Seen by American Negroes* (Paris: Présence Africaine, 1958), pp. 247-261. Also of interest is "Africa Sends Fifteen to Lincoln—Proteges of Azikiwe," *Lincoln University Bulletin* 44 (February 1939):6, for a discussion of Azikiwe's impact on African applications to Lincoln in the years soon after his return to Nigeria. For an account of the serious difficulties over the question of the appointment of black faculty at Lincoln just prior to Azikiwe's arrival there, see Raymond Wolters, *The New Negro on Campus: Black College Rebellions of the 1920s* (Princeton, N.J.: Princeton University Press, 1975), pp. 276-293.

26. Geiss, *Pan-African Movement*, p. 369. Azikiwe's influence in gaining admission at Lincoln for Nkrumah is emphasized in his autobiography, *My Odyssey*, p. 275. Nkrumah makes no mention of it in his own later reminiscences. See Kwame Nkrumah, *The Autobiography of Kwame Nkrumah* (London: Thomas Nelson & Sons, 1959).

27. Azikiwe to Jones, May 11, 1931; March 29, 1932; and February 20, 1933, Azikiwe Correspondence Files, PSFA. After initial efforts to work on the Ph.D. at Columbia on "colonial relations with backward peoples" under Parker T. Moon, the historian of imperial diplomacy, Azikiwe began doctoral studies at the University of Pennsylvania. It is of note that Kwame Nkrumah also obtained Master's degrees from Lincoln and Pennsylvania in subjects similar to those studied by Azikiwe.

28. Azikiwe, *My Odyssey*, p. 167.

29. Ibid., p. 168.

30. Ibid. Azikiwe seem's unaware, or at least says nothing, about the serious disputes over financial management that raged at Wilberforce, a small liberal arts college operated by the African Methodist Episcopal Church, throughout the 1920s. In 1927, a state investigation finally resulted in the appointment of a state-supported board of control to approve all university expenditures. See Wolters, *New Negro on Campus*, pp. 293-313.

31. Azikiwe, *My Odyssey*, p. 169.

32. Ibid., p. 170.

33. Azikiwe to Jones, May 4, 1933, Azikiwe Correspondence Files, PSFA. The references are to General S. C. Armstrong, founder and long-time president of Hampton, and to R. R. Moton, Washington's successor at Tuskegee.

34. This is not to suggest that Azikiwe was an unqualified proponent of Hampton-Tuskegee methods, but that he thought aspects of the American industrial and agricultural educational traditions were worthy of emulation in Africa.

35. See, for instance, the correspondence between Jones, Hanns Vischer (Secretary of the Colonial Office Advisory Committee on African Education) and E.R.J. Hussey (Director of Education for Nigeria) in Azikiwe Correspondence Files, PSFA.

36. Azikiwe, *My Odyssey*, p. 181.

37. Nnamdi Azikiwe, *Renascent Africa* (London: Frank Cass, 1968), p. 17. The book was originally published in 1937.

38. Azikiwe to Jones, February 28, 1934, Azikiwe Correspondence Files, PSFA.

39. Ibid.

40. Azikiwe, *Renascent Africa*, p. 18.

41. Next to Aggrey, the most lasting influence of a black thinker on Azikiwe was, surprisingly, that of Marcus Garvey. Mainly, it was Garvey's style that appealed—his flaming oratory which called for racial pride and the redemption of Africa through a new black nationalism. Although in style, and seemingly in philosophy, Garvey was the antithesis of Aggrey, Azikiwe was able to reconcile the two and to see perhaps correctly that the aims of his two heroes were not all that dissimilar. The literature on Garvey has grown immensely during the past few years, though the basic biography remains E. D. Cronon, *Black Moses, The Story of the Universal Negro Improvement Association* (Madison: University of Wisconsin Press, 1955). Also see the useful selections in John Henrik Clarke, ed., *Marcus Garvey and the Vision of Africa* (New

York: Random House, 1974) and Tony Martin, *Race First: The Ideological and Organizational Struggles of Marcus Garvey and the Universal Negro Improvement Association* (Westport, Conn.: Greenwood Press, 1976).

42. See, for example, Azikiwe's "solemn vow" for the New Year, 1934, in *My Odyssey*, p. 174. Also see pp. 121-122.

43. Zik's Press, Ltd. was incorporated in August 1937 and continued to expand its holdings and its influence, primarily as the vehicle for expression of Azikiwe's plans for the "new Africa."

44. The term "Zikism" seems to have been used first by A. A. Nwafor Orizu, a young eastern Nigerian, in his book *Without Bitterness: Western Nations in Post-War Africa* (New York: Creative Age Press, 1944). For more on Zikism and its fate in Nigeria, see Richard L. Sklar, *Nigerian Political Parties: Power in an Emergent African Nation* (Princeton, N.J.: Princeton University Press, 1963), pp. 72-83.

45. See note 7. For details of Fourah Bay, consult Omotayo Ogunsulire, "The History of Fourah Bay College and Its Influence in West Africa from the Foundation of the Elliot Commission, 1943" (Diploma in Education thesis, University of Durham, 1956).

46. During the period 1935-1942, only eight students passed the final B.Sc. examination of London University in this subject. See Great Britain, Colonial Office, *Report of the Commission on Higher Education in West Africa*, Cmd. 6655 (London: HMSO, 1945), p. 167.

47. Interview with Bishop Robert W. Stopford, 1973. Bishop Stopford, retired bishop of London, was principal of Achimota during the visit of the Elliot Commission. He expressed the opinion that most of the leadership at the college did not wish expansion into a university because it would destroy the "soul" of Achimota, that is, its role as an exclusive boarding school of the English public school type.

48. "Higher Education in Nigeria," *Overseas Education* 6 (October 1934): 17-19. A valuable source on Yaba is F. E. Ogunlade, "Yaba Higher College and the Formation of an Intellectual Elite" (M.A. thesis, University of Ibadan, 1970). For Azikiwe, Yaba had more than symbolic meaning, for the origins of his party, the National Council of Nigeria and the Cameroons, may be found there. Most of the young men who gathered at Azikiwe's house at Yaba in 1942 were connected with the college.

49. Opposition of the colonial officials on-the-spot, as opposed to most of those in London, to the further development of education was founded mainly on the fear of African competition for their jobs. For a discussion of this phenomenon, see Ade Fajana, "Colonial Control and Education: The Development of Higher Eduction in Nigeria, 1900-1950," *Journal of the Historical Society of Nigeria* 6 (December 1972):323-340.

50. On Makerere, see Great Britain, Colonial Office, *Higher Eduction in East Africa: Report on the Commission Appointed by the Secretary of State for the Colonies* (London: HMSO, 1937). For a semi-official history of Makerere, see Margaret MacPherson, *They Built for the Future* (Cambridge: Cambridge University Press, 1964). Also see Arthur Mayhew, *Education in the Colonial Empire* London: Longmans, 1938), p. 170ff.

51. Great Britain, Colonial Office, *Fourah Bay College: Report of the Commission Appointed in 1938 by the Secretary of State for the Colonies to Report on Fourah Bay College, Freetown* (London: HMSO, 1939), p. 26.

52. See note 46 for reference to the Elliot Commission. Also refer to Great Britain, Colonial Office, *Report of the Commission on Higher Education in the Colonies*, Cmd. 6647 (London: HMSO, 1945).

53. *Report of the Commission on Higher Education in the Colonies*, p. 104.

54. See "Elliot Commission, Itinerary" in A. Creech Jones Papers, MSS British Empire 332, Box 12, File 2, Rhodes House, Oxford. Arthur Creech Jones, a member of the Elliot Commission, became secretary of state for the colonies in the Attlee government founded in 1945.

55. Interview with Dr. Margaret Read, 1973. Dr. Read, who was a member of the commission, recalls that Azikiwe's newspapers had a highly "radical" reputation among the members of the commission and that their reporters asked many difficult questions.

56. *West African Pilot*, March 11, 1944, p. 2. The study cited by Azikiwe was *The Atlantic Charter and Africa from an American Standpoint* (New York:Committee on Africa, the War and Peace Aims, 1942).

57. *Atlantic Charter and Africa*, p. 92ff.

58. West African Press Delegation to Great Britain, "The Atlantic Charter and British West Africa: Memorandum on Post-War Reconstruction of the Colonies and Protectorates of British West Africa," August 1934. A typescript manuscript of this memorandum is located in the library of the Institute of Commonwealth Studies, University of London.

59. The time had long passed since the Phelps-Stokes Fund was the only American nonmissionary agency directly involved in Africa. As early as the 1930s, the Carnegie Corporation through its British Dominions and Colonies Program, and its later equivalents, had become increasingly concerned with education. See, for instance, "Education and Research in British Dependent Territories—the Role of the United States," *Universities Quarterly* 12 (August 1958):399-406. Later added to the spectrum were such offices as the Federal Agency for International Development and the Overseas Liaison Committee of the American Council on Education.

60. A new Inter-University Council for Higher Education in the Colonies was created to coordinate the policies of the new university colleges, and the University of London undertook to guarantee standards through the use of its examinations.

61. For the standard official history of Ibadan, see J. F. Ade Ajayi and Tekena N. Tamuno, eds., *The University of Ibadan, 1948-73: A History of the First Twenty-five Years* (Ibadan: Ibadan University Press, 1973). In addition, there are accounts by the first two principals, the more useful of which is Kenneth Mellanby, *The Birth of Nigeria's University* (London: Methuen & Co., Ltd., 1958). Ibadan has also been subjected to a scathing sociological analysis in Pierre L.vanden Berghe, *Power and Privilege at an African University* (London: Routledge & Kegan Paul, 1973).

62. A. Babs Fafunwa, *History of Nigerian Higher Education* (Lagos: Macmillan & Co. of Nigeria, Let., 1971), p. 191.

63. Mellanby, *Birth of Nigeria's University*, pp. 248, 252.

64. Fafunwa, *History of Nigerian Higher Education*, p. 116.

65. Robert Koehl, "Educational Culture and Nigerian Universities," *Comparative Education Review* 15 (October 1971):368.

66. Typescript press release of speech delivered by Azikiwe before the African Academy of Arts and Research, New York, June 27, 1947. Copy located in Azikiwe Correspondence Files, PSFA.

67. Ibid.

68. For the early history of the NCNC, see Sklar, *Nigerian Political Parties*, pp. 57-64.

69. The transition from unitary foundations to federalism is discussed in Sklar, *Nigerian Political Parties*, p. 133ff.

70. Ibid., p. 509.

71. Davidson Nichol, "Politics, Nationalism and Universities in Africa," *African Affairs* 62 (January 1963):25.

72. Eric Ashby, *Universities*, p. 277; *The University Looks Abroad: Approaches to World Affairs at Six American Universities* (New York: Walker & Co., 1965), p. 61.

73. C. W. DeKiewiet, *The Emergent University: An Interpretation* (Washington, D.C.: American Council on Education, 1971), p. 7.

74. *Zik: A Selection from the Speeches of Nnamdi Azikiwe* (Cambridge: Cambridge University Press, 1961), p. 285.

75. Ashby, *Universities*, p. 277.

76. Nigeria, Eastern Region, *University of Nigeria, Eastern Region Official Document No. 2 of 1958* (Enugu: Government Printer, 1958); and Nigeria, Eastern Region, *University of Nigeria, Eastern Region Official Document No. 4 of 1958* (Enugu: Government Printer, 1958).

77. Nigeria, Eastern Region, *University of Nigeria ...Document No. 4*, p. 2.

78. T. M. Yesufu, ed., *Creating the African University: Emerging Issues in the 1970's* (Ibadan: Oxford University Press, 1973), p. 186. There is some dispute regarding the number of students who enrolled the first year at Ibadan. Ashby (*Universities*, p. 278) cites the figure as 256.

79. Ashby, *Universities*, p. 278.

80. John Hannah had been president of Michigan State since 1941 and had been highly successful in guiding his university through many hazardous political battles. Even the existence of a parallel rivalry to the Nsukka-Ibadan relationship—that between Michigan State and more "traditional" University of Michigan—could hardly have escaped Azikiwe. Hannah became directly involved with the Nsukka project and developed a close personal relationship with Azikiwe.

81. For studies of the land-grant philosophy in general, see James L. Morrill, *The Ongoing State University* (Minneapolis: University of Minnesota Press, 1960); and Mary J. Bowman, "The Land Grant Colleges and Universities in Human Resource Development," *Journal of Economic History* 12 (December 1962):547-554. For the application (by a participant) to Nigeria, see John W. Hanson, *Education Nsukka* (East Lansing: Michigan State University Press, 1968).

82. Throughout the first six years of its existence, Nsukka was drawn steadily into the vortex of NCNC politics, and the gradual erosion of Azikiwe's authority was reflected in the university.

83. Adegoke Olubummo and John Ferguson, *The Emergent University with Special Reference to Nigeria* (London: Longman, 1960), p. 13.

84. Ibid.,p. 14.

85. Hanson, *Education Nsukka*, p. 80.

86. Cited by Echeruo, "Nnamdi Azikiwe and Nigerian Thought," p. 263.

THE MISSIONARY: METHODS, INTERESTS, AND ACTIVITIES

THE MISSIONARY: INTRODUCTION

Walter L. Williams

This section, on representative Afro-American missionary activities in Africa, provides case studies of the impact which black Americans had on Africa. The articles in this section demonstrate the varied nature of Afro-American involvement: three articles focus on missions sponsored by white churches in areas of Africa that had not seen much previous Western involvement, while another article discusses a black church located in an area where many Africans were already Westernized and Christian. The black missionaries' common activities and problems tell us much about their motives and the results of their involvement in Africa.

The Afro-Americans who volunteered as missionaries had much of the same motivations as missionaries in general. They tended to be individuals who had a strong sense of social duty to helping others, and this sense of duty was focused on mission work because of their intense religious upbringing. Many of the missionaries received their interest from the example of other mission advocates, who spoke at their churches or schools. Moreover, many came from relatively well-to-do families and did not have a strong need to build their success in monetary terms. They could become concerned for others, precisely because they were financially secure from their own backgrounds and did not have to worry about financial matters. On the other hand, they were extremely concerned about their social status, and they had a strong need for social approval. By going into mission work they could.

hold an occupation that was highly respected within the black community. Their emphasis on "sacrificing" themselves to go to Africa was not merely for fund-raising purposes; it also was a call for social approval which was so important to them.

For Afro-Americans of the late nineteenth and early twentieth centuries, mission work was also valued because it was one of only a few occupations that was respected by whites as well. Especially for those blacks within white churches who envied refined upper class whites, mission work proved a means of gaining white approval while at the same time offering a rare chance to exercise leadership. For those blacks who rejected such white approval, independent black missions provided a means of escape from white society and a competition with white churches on an equal level. In either case, they could hold an elite status and an independence of action available to few black Americans.

For the Afro-American missionaries, more was at stake than religion and social status. All of them, whether they were sponsored by white or black churches, felt a strong sense of duty to their African homeland. The fact that the black churches, especially the African Methodist Episcopal Church (AME) and the National Baptist Convention (NBC), sent their missionaries to black-populated nations reflects their race pride. They believed that Africa was in degradation and "barbarism" because it did not have Christianity and "civilization." As refined and educated individuals themselves, the black missionaries believed fervently in the Victorian ideal of Western culture. Anyone who was different was considered to be "heathen savage." By bringing Christianity and Westernization to Africa, the black missionaries thought they had the key to redeeming the continent. If they could convert and educate the indigenous people, they were sure that Africa would begin a rise into "civilization" and world respect. This new rise, they felt, would improve the status of black people all over the world, including those in the United States.

Black missionaries were not as ethnocentric as white missionaries, but they did condemn indigenous African cultures as inferior. However, once African persons were Westernized, the Afro-Americans dropped their negativism and accepted them as equal brethren in Christ. It was in their attitudes toward Westernized

Africans that the black Christians differed most significantly from their white counterparts. While white missionaries continued to hold ideas of racial inferiority toward Africans, black missionaries did not. The close feeling between the two black groups was the major reason why independent African Christian churches were so attracted to affiliation with Afro-American denominations. This connection did much to contribute to the rise of Pan-African sentiments in the twentieth century.

In terms of their daily duties, the black missionaries concentrated on religious conversion, but even more so on "civilizing" Africans by teaching them a Western life-style. Education, focusing on American ways of doing things, was greatly emphasized. The women missionaries felt an additional sense of duty to African females, and this incipient feminism provided them with stronger emotional ties than they seemed to receive from the male missionaries. They concentrated their efforts on the training of girls into traditional Western women's work. By all their educational efforts, the black missionaries hoped to plant the seeds of "civilization" in their converts.

The mission efforts toward conversion did not have as dramatic an impact as many of the Christians hoped. Beyond some superficial changes in dress and behavior, the Africans mainly continued their previous cultural world-view and customs. Most of those individuals who did change were ransomed slaves or social outcasts, and often the changes did not go as deep as the missionaries wanted to believe. Among the previously acculturated blacks in South Africa, the Afro-Americans did not have as much control over them as they might have liked. The Africans had already declared their religious independence from white churches before affiliating with black Americans, and they often were considerably more militant than black evangelists from the United States.

The Afro-American missionaries were rather conservative in their challenges to the European colonial system. Sometimes, as in the case of Presbyterian William Sheppard in the Congo, they challenged imperialist authority, but even in Sheppard's case he was careful to limit his attack to the exposure of atrocities rather than to question the right of European takeover. More often, the Afro-Americans believed that imperialism was a temporary stage that was necessary to unify Africans and "civilize" them. Their missions' positions, within the white-controlled colonial system, were too weak to do otherwise. It was often the Africans themselves who were more militant.

Nevertheless, the very presence of Afro-American missionaries provided an unsettling influence on imperialism. By operating in positions of authority, the blacks provided tangible evidence that with education Africans could also rise to higher levels than their white mentors had suggested. Such a feeling contributed to nationalism among Westernized Africans and increased their Pan-African sentiments.

William Henry Sheppard, Afro-American Missionary in the Congo, 1890-1910

7

Walter L. Williams

Black Americans of the late nineteenth century expressed much more interest in Africa than historians have recognized. A major focus of this interest was the idea of emigrating "back to Africa," by black people who were dissatisfied with their second-class status in the United States.[1] Yet, the black churches also exerted a primary role in awakening an interest in Africa among black Americans, which extended beyond the emigration question. Even though the importance of black religion has been recognized, few scholars have adequately investigated the influence of the African mission movement in forming Afro-American attitudes toward the homeland and thereby contributing to the rise of Pan-African identity.

Since the 1820s, various white American churches had sponsored black clergymen as their missionaries in Africa, primarily because of the belief that Afro-Americans could survive in the tropical climate better than whites. However, by the last two decades of the century, Afro-American missionaries came to be increasingly sponsored by the independent black denominations. After having consolidated their institutional and financial backing in their expansion among the freedmen of the South follow-

This chapter is adapted from Walter L. Williams, *Black Americans and the Evangelization of Africa, 1877-1900* (Madison: The University of Wisconsin Press; © 1982 by The Board of Regents of the University of Wisconsin System). Reprinted by permission.

ing the Civil War, these independent sects began to look to Africa as their next logical area for expansion.[2]

Within this context, it is remarkable that one of the most influential Afro-American missionaries of this era was sponsored by the white Southern Presbyterian Church. While other white churches were dismissing or segregating their black missionaries, the Presbyterians were becoming involved in Central Africa primarily through the efforts of a black man: William Henry Sheppard.

The Southern Presbyterians, separated from their northern brethren since the Civil War, clearly treated their black constituents as second-class members. Yet, they saw no inconsistency between their policies of racial discrimination and their desire to spread the gospel in Africa. Like the other white churches, they were attracted to the use of Afro-Americans as missionaries in Africa because of the health factor, but they also saw the mission movement as a means of exerting their influence over rising black leaders. Therefore, they had established Stillman College, in Tuscaloosa, Alabama, specifically to train black missionaries. The faculty and students of this college, in turn, became a major force for the establishment of an African Presbyterian mission.[3]

The most prominent early graduate of Stillman College was William Henry Sheppard. Although his parents had only been freed a short time before his birth in 1865, Sheppard grew up in a moderately well-to-do family of Waynesboro, Virginia. His father was a barber and his mother managed a Ladies' Health Bath, so both had unusually close ties to southern whites. This relationship produced a bond of affection toward whites that characterized Sheppard's entire career.[4]

His parents were devoted Presbyterians, and they imparted a strong sense of religious and social duty to their son. At age sixteen Sheppard entered Virginia's Hampton Institute, where the white president of the school, Samuel Armstrong, became his ideal. While at Hampton, Sheppard's experiences teaching Sunday school caused him to be directed to the ministry. After graduation, he entered the theological seminary of Stillman College and was soon ordained as a minister in the Southern Presbyterian Church.[5]

Exactly when he became interested in Africa is uncertain, but it may have been due to a speech given at Hampton in 1882 by the distinguished West African nationalist Edward W. Blyden. At that time, while Sheppard was a student there, a Hampton alumnus was serving as a missionary in Sierra Leone. This missionary, Ackrell E. White, wrote reports to his school encouraging his fellow blacks to "redeem Africa" and to follow Blyden's advice to "look to Africa as his country and his home."[6]

As a young preacher, William Sheppard did not adapt well to his first congregations in Montgomery, Alabama, or Atlanta, Georgia. By 1887, he was petitioning the Presbyterian Executive Committee of Foreign Missions to send him as a missionary to Africa.[7] But the Presbyterian leaders refused to send a black man as leader of one of their missions, so they delayed Sheppard's requests until a white missionary could be found to lead the proposed mission. The Southern Presbyterians had been most active in China missions, and it was difficult to attract a southern white to devote his life to Africa, but finally in 1890 such a man volunteered. Samuel Norvell Lapsley was from a prominent Alabama family of former slaveowners, and he absorbed the evangelical spirit from his missionary grandparents. He evidently became interested in the Congo through Senator John T. Morgan, his father's law partner. Lapsley had done some missionary work among American blacks, and he felt comfortable with the idea of working with Sheppard. Therefore, the two men, white and black, were soon appointed Presbyterian missionaries to the Congo.[8]

Sheppard and Lapsley arrived in the Congo in 1890, but it was a year before they established their mission. The Mission Board directed them to choose a site in the interior, well removed from other missions, in a densely populated area. The missionaries' choice, at Luebo in the Kasai Valley of the southern Congo, met all these conditions. Since Luebo was nine hundred miles in the interior, and in 1890 there were less than a thousand Westerners in the whole Congo, Sheppard and Lapsley were almost isolated from outside contact. But a Belgian trading company had recently established a station at Luebo, and its principal advantage was that it was located at the meeting ground of five major ethnic groups.[9]

Upon leaving America, Sheppard expressed some sadness "to leave home, friends and native land and seek a home among strangers."[10] This attachment to America was soon overcome, for Sheppard wrote back to the Presbyterian missionary journal soon after arriving in the Congo that "I am certainly happy in the country of my forefathers."[11] Besides a feeling of identity with the Africans, his first impressions of the Africans were favorable. After meeting a local indigenous king, Sheppard referred to him as "his most gracious majesty." Sheppard was also impressed by the attentiveness and "intelligent interest" displayed by the Congolese Christian converts.[12]

Sheppard did make unfavorable statements about Africans, using the common missionary observations on "spiritual darkness" and "moral gloom." But he soon realized significant differences among Africans and, unlike many missionaries, refused to stereotype them: "How different the people are at different towns; here they have nothing too good for us, and just a little distance away at another town, we can get nothing they have."[13] Even when criticizing the Africans, as he did for their heavy use of alcohol, Sheppard identified himself with them (even if he was sometimes paternalistic) and called them "my people." After a year in the Congo, Sheppard could report: "We have on the whole been treated very kindly by all the [African] people. We have received many nice and useful presents from different kings. . . . I always wanted to live in Africa, I felt that I would be happy, and so I am."[14]

Evidently, he was well like by the Africans, because Lapsley wrote that Sheppard was a "great favorite" and that the Congolese referred to him as " 'Shoppit Monine,' the great Sheppard."[15] In numerous photographs of the Presbyterian Congo Mission, Sheppard is shown in close contact with the Africans and usually in the midst of great activity.[16]

Lapsley and Sheppard worked well as a team. Sheppard, with his gift for learning the African languages, his skill as a hunter, and his physical strength, was the primary contact with the Africans and directed the practical needs of the mission. Lapsley, on the other hand, managed the finances and dealt with the white colonial officials. Together they toured the Kasai, introducing themselves, preaching, teaching, providing medical aid, and ransoming slaves. Within three years the mission had ransomed about seventy African slaves, mostly children who had been captured in intertribal wars, and these became the first mission converts. Other Africans came to the mission to obtain refuge from local wars or to get medical care.[17]

The biggest problem of the two missionaries was health. Sheppard ultimately suffered twenty-two bouts of the African fever, but his strength helped him survive. The weaker Lapsley, however, could not adapt to the tropical climate and finally succumbed in March 1892. Sheppard keenly felt the death of his friend, since he was now entirely alone among the Africans.[18] Thus, whether or not they liked it, the white Southern Presbyterians were left in 1892 with a black man heading their missionary effort in Africa.

Alone, Sheppard continued the mission work. The Bakete, the first group with which the missionaries had had contact, were friendly and helpful, but they were satisfied with their own religion and saw no reason to switch to an alien one. Therefore, Sheppard decided to concentrate on the Bakuba, even though no foreigner had ever visited their kingdom. Bakubaland was a highly organized state with a law forbidding any of their people to direct outsiders into their territory. By this means they had resisted European penetration. The Bakuba were most noted for their art and their oral traditions.[19]

Even though Sheppard learned the language and was treated considerately by the border town chief, he could not gain directions for entering the capital. By an ingenious plan, Sheppard persuaded the chief to allow his guide to go to the next town to purchase eggs. The guide would mark the trail and secretly guide Sheppard on to the next town. By repeating this process, Sheppard was able to move from town to town toward the Bakuba capital. In the effort to exhaust local supplies of eggs, Sheppard performed wonders at egg-eating, downing thirty at one meal. His ability to get so far into the forbidden land and his fluency in the language, as well as his reputation for eating eggs, caused the Bakuba king to have Sheppard brought into the capital. Sheppard so impressed the king that he was welcomed as the reincarnation of an ancestor.[20]

In his attitudes toward the Bakuba and the Bakete, Sheppard was sometimes derogatory. He mentioned the Africans as having "weak and warped minds" and being "enveloped in the blackness of an awful midnight."[21] While staying with the Bakuba, Sheppard preached against and actively resisted the custom of killing a slave to accompany a recently deceased master.[22] He also protested against the practice of trial by poison, but was dumbfounded to learn that even the accused person had such faith in the method that he was anxious to take the poison in order to prove his innocence. This practice provoked one of Sheppard's few righteous outbursts:

Seeing these awful customs practiced by these people for ages makes you indignant and depressed and also fills you with pity. Only by preaching God's word, having faith, patience and love will we eradicate the deep-rooted evil. Everything to them is run by chance, and there are evil spirits and witches everywhere.[23]

Sheppard's general lack of identity with the Africans and his periodic censure of specific customs did not change his whole attitude toward them. Even his condemnations were directed toward saving African lives rather than merely being ethnocentric. In fact, Sheppard's autobiography, which was based on the diary he kept during his first five years in the Congo, had much objective ethnographic description.[24] He recognized differences among different African societies, without stereotypes, and did not allow an isolated incident to turn him against a group. For example, even though he once had his money stolen and had to deal firmly with a town to have it returned, he could still remark that, "all the natives we have met in the Kasai are, on the whole, honest."[25]

More often, Sheppard lavished compliments on the Congolese. He noted that nothing was wasted by the people, that they were "economical" and "industrious."[26] Sheppard gave evidence of an understanding of cultural relativism by showing respect for African customs. For example, soon after arriving in the Congo he once carelessly threw a palm nut against a house. Unknown to Sheppard, such an act was a curse upon the home. When the village panicked, Sheppard recalled: "Immediately I went over to the excited crowd and explained my ignorance of the fact and promised to make reparation." Rather than dismiss the belief as a silly custom, Sheppard respected the life-style of the Africans and thus gained their confidence. On another occasion, Sheppard "consented at once" to stop hunting near farmlands because of the Bakuba belief that his rifle fire would cause their corn to die.[27]

Furthermore, Sheppard had the strength of character to acknowledge his mistakes and to learn from the Africans. To aid a village during a famine he shot a hippotamus for them, but in disregard of their pleading he swam into the lake to tie a rope around the carcass. Suddenly a crocodile appeared and Sheppard barely escaped to shore. To the villagers: "I begged their pardon and was ashamed of my bravery....Many times in Central Africa foreigners get into serious difficulties from which they cannot extricate themselves by disregarding the advice of natives."[28]

Even though he objected to some of their customs, Sheppard admired the Bakuba most. He complimented their dancing, dress, and personal appearance. He was amazed at their moral family life, with strict prohibitions on polygamy, adultery, and drunkenness. Their industriousness impressed him, as did their custom of reserving every third day as a day of rest.[29] His admiration for the Bakuba was summarized by his statement that, during his 1892 visit:

I grew very fond of the Bakuba and it was reciprocated. They were the finest looking race I had seen in Africa, dignified, graceful, courageous, honest, with an open, smiling countenance and really hospitable. Their knowledge of weaving, embroidering, woodcarving and smelting was the highest in equatorial Africa.[30]

But even though the Bakuba liked Sheppard, they were psychologically satisfied with their own religion and were not interested in conversion. After four months in Bakubaland Sheppard returned to Luebo, where the mission grew primarily by the addition of freed slaves and social outcasts. With the loneliness beginning to affect him, he decided to visit the United States.

After he left for the United States in 1893, three white couples were persuaded to come to the Presbyterian Congo Mission, but two soon died and three more left because of illness, so that by 1896 only one white missionary was left. The church had difficulty getting white missionaries for the Congo and keeping those who did go. Because of the expense and the relative lack of converts, the Presbyterian leaders considered ending their Congo Mission.[31]

Probably because he realized that his mission might be abolished, Sheppard decided to use his 1893 visit to America as a recruiting drive for more black missionaries. Presented with more volunteers, while their white missionaries were dying or leaving, the Southern Presbyterians would thus be unable to refuse more offers, even if they were from blacks. Sheppard's fame on arriving in America was increased by his having been made a fellow in the Royal Geographical Society, an English tribute to his explorations into Bakubaland.[32]

Almost as if he were fighting for his life, Sheppard traveled through the South speaking about his Congo Mission. Evidently, he was successful in arousing interest because the *Missionary Review of the World* reported that he "has been speaking to crowded houses, capturing all by his eloquence, fund of humor, and his histrionic qualities."[33] Likewise, a Presbyterian pamphlet stated: "Dr. Sheppard told the story of his experience in numerous churches and before church assemblies so vividly and so appealingly that the whole Church took the Congo Mission to its heart."[34]

Undoubtedly Sheppard's biggest effect was upon southern blacks. The Presbyterian mission journal reported that the most notable aspect of Sheppard's visit was "the interest awakened in it amongst our colored friends." The journal quoted a white Virginia church official:

The people of his own race listened with deepest interest to his accounts of Africa, and the sad condition of her millions of people. A strong desire was kindled in their hearts to do something to aid in the great work of their redemption. They formed a society, which they called "The Congo Missionary Society." . . . They are Baptists, but knowing no Baptist missionary society on the Congo or in all Africa, they preferred for their first aid to be given to Mr. Sheppard in his work.[35]

It is significant that, while there were a substantial number of American Baptist missionaries in the Congo, the blacks preferred to contribute to a black missionary of a different denomination whom they had met.

Sheppard had written to the *Indianapolis Freeman*, one of the largest black newspapers in the nation, about "my central African home," saying that "we have found the natives kind and obliging with a few exceptions."[36] Even Sheppard's parents, who were proud of their son for "carrying light into the dark places of the earth," publicized his reports from Africa.[37] But Sheppard's biggest impact on black American attitudes toward Africa was a result of his speeches in black churches and schools. In November 1893, he gave a speech to the student body of Hampton Institute which was printed in the *Southern Workman*. Much of the speech was humorous, with Sheppard telling about having to eat so many eggs in traveling into Bakubaland, and remarking that only a dog fight was eventful enough to interrupt one of his church services. He spoke of the Zappo-Zaps, a cannibal people: "You can trust them as far as you can see them—and the farther off you can see them the better you can trust them."[38]

On the Bakuba, Sheppard described his amazement on entering Ifuka, King Lukenga's capital city: "for I had seen nothing like it in Africa....[The Bakubas] make one feel that he has again entered a land of civilization." He complimented their industriousness, cleanliness, and morality, and he described the Bakuba religion without condemnation. Sheppard was quick to point out that they "are not idolators" and had a vague belief in a Supreme Being and in a spiritual afterlife. After complimenting the Africans, however, Sheppard also criticized them for their belief in witchcraft and trial by poison. In addition, he said, the Bakuba "enslave their prisoners captured in war; the slaves are kindly treated in life, but are often killed when their master dies." Sheppard could understand the African reasoning that the slave was killed in order that his soul could accompany his dead master, but he still could not accept this custom. Nevertheless, Sheppard ended his speech with a talk on Bakuba superiority: "Perhaps they got their civilization from the Egyptians—or the Egyptians theirs from the Bakuba!"[39] In all, Sheppard presented the Africans in a favorably objective light, and while not slighting their faults he displayed much less moralizing than was customary for nineteenth-century missionaries in Africa.

The most direct evidence of Sheppard's influence on black Americans, besides their offers of monetary contributions, was represented by those blacks who volunteered to return with him to the Congo as missionaries. The first to join Sheppard was Lucy Gantt, a graduate of Talladega College, an American Missionary Association school for blacks in Alabama. On a visit to her hometown, Gantt met William Sheppard, then a student at Stillman, and they corresponded while Sheppard was in Africa. Upon Sheppard's return she volunteered as a missionary, and they were married on February 21, 1894.[40] Sheppard also attracted Henry P. Hawkins, a newly ordained minister from Stillman Seminary, and two more Talladega graduates, Lillian Thomas and Maria Fearing.[41]

This group of four new missionaries accompanied Sheppard to Luebo in May 1894.[42] A year later they were joined by another black missionary, Joseph E. Phipps from Chicago's Dwight L. Moody Bible Institute. Although he resided in Virginia, Phipps had been born and raised in Saint Kitts, West Indies, and he claimed that his grandfather was Congolese. Thus, his feeling of duty to the land of his ancestors was even more specific than the usual black identity with Africa. The Presbyterian mission committee reported: "He impressed the Committee as a man of humble, earnest, and simple piety, and one who will probably be fitted to reach his own people more readily and effectually than even one of our Southern born and educated colored people."[43] Such statements demonstrate that the white church officials believed the black missionaries felt an identity with the Africans.

Sheppard and the black missionaries led the mission until 1897, when the Presbyterian leaders prevailed upon two white missionaries to join the Luebo Mission. William M. Morrison, already a notable missionary in Asia, took over the leadership at Luebo. Morrison seemed unprejudiced toward his black co-workers, and he aided race relations by his approach to missionary work. He advised his mission to treat the Africans "as kindly and courteously as white people." As he explained: "We are their servants and not their masters. Under their black skins they have feelings and sensibilities similar to ours, which ought to be respected. If we laugh at their customs, appearance, or fetishes, we destroy their confidence in us and repel them."[44] Such an attitude could not fail to impress the black missionaries.

Another reason for the good race relations was the respect shown to the blacks. During an era when few southern whites acknowledged any titles of respect to black people, the Presbyterian officials consistently referred to their black missionaries as "Reverend," "Mr.," "Mrs.," or "Miss." The black personnel received pay equal to that of white missionaries, and they had an influential voice in mission affairs.[45]

Probably the major reason for good relations in the integrated mission had to do with the attitude of the black missionaries. Sheppard gracefully transferred his leadership role to Morrison, and he worked hard to cultivate good feelings with the whites. He wrote to a white Presbyterian:

I am proud of our Southern Church, which is doing so much for the evangelization of the negro in America and Africa. I owe all that I am, or ever expect to be, to that Church. When you turn your back upon us, to whom shall we go? No, stand by us, and we will prove your trust![46]

Sheppard and his colleagues might be open to charges of "Uncle Tom-ism," but as missionaries entirely dependent on white church support they had little choice but accommodation. Since the Americans of both races recognized they had more in common with each other than with either the Belgians or the Congolese, the status of the black missionaries was probably far better than it would have been among whites in the United States.[47]

The mission work at Luebo continued to make gains. Sheppard reported that: "We are happy and feel at home; [we] seldom speak of returning to America." In 1896, he stated that he felt more satisfied with his work in Africa than he would have anywhere else, and he hoped to be able to stay many more years in the Congo.[48] By 1898, Sheppard had established a new branch mission on the Bakuba frontier, and two years later the two mission stations had a total of three hundred and fifty converts.[49]

Even though Lucy Sheppard's first two children died in infancy, she continued to serve as a teacher and nurse at the mission. However, with the birth of a third child, and after almost succumbing to disease herself, Mrs. Sheppard decided in 1898 to take the child back to America to be cared for by relatives.[50]

Some of the black missionaries had trouble relating to Africans, and there is little evidence that the Congolese thought of the Afro-Americans as anything other than black-skinned white men.[51] Henry Hawkins, the Stillman graduate who had followed Sheppard to the Congo in 1894, reported five years later that his most difficult task was to make the Africans feel Christian guilt. That is, after converts had agreed to accept the new religion, they could not understand why their declarations of belief had not immediately "made them the children of God, despite all we could say along the line of total depravity of the heart."[52] This statement not only reveals African psychological self-assurance, but also the missionary's need to produce feelings of inadequacy in his converts.

The Presbyterian missionaries' biggest problems were not with the Africans but with their Belgian rulers. Leopold II, king of Belgium, had had expansionist dreams since the 1860s, and in 1879, he commissioned the explorer Henry Stanley to set up a commercial empire on the Congo. However, as Leopold's "Congo Free State" was encircled by European occupation in the late nineteenth-century "scramble" for Africa, the Belgian monarch became more and more suspicious of foreigners in the Congo. In addition, non-Belgian Protestant missionaries were doubly suspect to the Catholic Leopold.[53]

From the missionary viewpoint, Leopold's form of indirect rule through concessionaire companies was tragic. The relentless pressure for greater profits caused many abuses of the Congolese people by the company officials. The unsettled condition of society in the late 1890s naturally disrupted missionary progress, so the clergymen had ample reason to complain. For example, the 1899 report of the Luebo Mission, written by Hawkins, complained about the effect of government actions in the Kasai area:

A goodly number of our people, or rather the people around us here, had been taken away by the State [for forced labor], and those who were permitted to remain were mightily perturbed in spirit lest a similar fate would be theirs.... [Consequently] the interest of the people about things spiritual was being converted into base indifference.[54]

The Protestant American missionaries, with neither national nor religious loyalties to Leopold, openly criticized the Free State government. Foremost among these critics were the principal men of Luebo, Sheppard and Morrison. In 1898, a government officer imposed a heavy food tax upon the Kasai peoples, to force them to work for Europeans in order to have cash to pay the tax. Thus, by this arrangement, the company got cheap labor and the government ended up with most of the cash. In addition, the government used feared cannibalistic Zappo-Zap soldiers to collect the tax. Because he could speak the languages and was "much beloved by all the tribes," Sheppard was chosen to make an investigatory tour of the Kasai. Not only did he find that a more exploitative system could hardly be devised, but he also discovered that the Zappo-Zaps were using their tax-collecting forays as a cover for slave raids and cannibalism.[55]

On the basis of Sheppard's findings, the Presbyterian mission called for a state inquiry. When the inquiry did not punish the officials responsible, and with no improvement in the situation, Sheppard and Morrison made the exposé public.[56] This story caused the Presbyterian Mission Board to appeal to the U.S. Department of State, to protest directly to King Leopold. The exposé became internationally famous and had great effect on American and British mission organizations.[57]

Sheppard's thoroughness and persistence in exposing the Congo atrocities was a mark of his deep concern for Africans. The *Southern Workman*, in publicizing his exploits, explained Sheppard's success as a product of his "tact, heroism, and friendly relations with the natives."[58] The black missionary, fully supported by Morrison, continued his campaign so relentlessly that the concessionaire Kasai Company took him to court in 1909 for libel. Sheppard's "crime" consisted of writing an article in the mission newspaper which traced the decline of Bakuba society. Before the coming of the Europeans, he wrote, the Bakuba farmed their own lands and were prosperous. However, with the entry of the Kasai Company the people were forced to work for the whites making rubber. The cash wages they received, after taxes, were too meager to buy the goods they needed but no longer had time to produce for themselves. Thus, the introduction of a cash economy, on Belgian terms, had produced a dramatic decline in their standard of living. In the trial, which was publicized internationally, Sheppard's defense not only showed his love for the Africans but his own identity with his Kasai home as well. After proving the truth of his statements Sheppard was found not guilty.[59]

Although Sheppard was acquitted in his trial, strained relations with the government continued. As the whites established more intensive control over the Congo, Sheppard as a black man had less freedom to operate. While he cultivated good relations with the white missionaries, one suspects that Sheppard preferred exercising his own authority independent of close supervision. His happiest letters were written between 1894 and 1897, when he headed a predominantly black mission. The establishment of his own branch mission soon after the coming of Morrison suggests Sheppard's independence more than it does racial conflict. In many ways, Morrison and Sheppard were similar personalities, and they got along well together. But the realization of loss of his independent black world in the Kasai, plus the psychic strain of the trial, caused Sheppard to retire in 1910. He returned to America with a trunkful of photographs and artifacts made by his beloved Bakuba.[60]

William Henry Sheppard was not a successful missionary in terms of the number of converts he won into the Presbyterian Church. Perhaps he respected Africans too much to interfere grossly in their whole way of life. Certainly, he condemned aspects of their culture, but never to the extent that was typical of most nineteenth-century missionaries. Sheppard rejected the view that soul-saving excluded earthly considerations, and he worked hard to aid those Congolese whom he met. Whether giving medical aid, ransoming slaves, or protesting colonial exploitation, Sheppard tried to improve African standards of living. While he did not express a Pan-African ideology, the black missionary did feel a closeness to the Kasai peoples that was felt by few white Americans. William Sheppard, because of his influence on black Americans and his efforts in behalf of Africans, deserves to be ranked among the most important of early Afro-American missionaries.

Notes

1. This interest in African emigration is beginning to receive deserved interest by scholars. The best study of emigrationist thought in the era is Edwin Redkey, *Black Exodus: Black Nationalist and Back-to-Africa Movements, 1890-1910* (New Haven, Conn.: Yale University Press, 1969). The opposition to emigration in one professional group is emphasized in Walter L. Williams, "Black Journalism's Opinions About Africa During the Late Nineteenth Century," *Phylon* 34 (September 1973): 224-235. For a more general overview of the subject, see Walter L. Williams, "Black American Attitudes Toward Africa, 1877-1900," *Pan-African Journal* 4 (Spring 1971): 173-194.

2. Walter L.Williams, *Black Americans and the Evangelization of Africa, 1877-1900* (Madison: University of Wisconsin Press, 1982); and Walter L. Williams, "Ethnic Relations of African Students in the United States, with Black Americans, 1870-1900," *Journal of Negro History* 65 (Summer 1980): 228-249.

3. Stanley Shaloff, *Reform in Leopold's Congo* (Richmond, Va.: John Knox Press, 1970), pp. 13-18. This book is the best study of the American Presbyterian Congo Mission.

4. William H. Sheppard, *Pioneers in Congo* (Louisville, Ky.: Pentecostal Publishing Co., 1917), p. 11. This autobiography is the single most valuable source of Sheppard's life. See also *Southern Workman* 29 (April 1900): 218.

5. *Missionary Review of the World* 8 (1895): 327; and Shaloff, *Reform*, pp. 18-20.

6. *Southern Workman* 12 (January 1883): 9; Kenneth J. King, *Pan-Africanism and Education* (London: Oxford University Press, 1971), p. 8; and Hollis Lynch, *Edward Wilmot Blyden: Pan-Negro Patriot* (London: Oxford University Press, 1967).

7. *Missionary Review of the World* 8 (1895): 327; and Shaloff, *Reform*, pp. 18-20.

8. Ruth Slade, *English-Speaking Missions in the Congo Independent State, 1878-1908* (Brussels: Académie Royale, 1959), p. 104; and Shaloff, *Reform*, pp. 17-18.

9. The five ethnic groups near Luebo were the Bakete, Bakuba, Bena Lulua, Baluba, and Zappo-Zap. Slade, *English-Speaking Missions*, pp. 104-106; Shaloff, *Reform*, pp. 23, 26; and Charles P. Groves, *The Planting of Christianity in Africa* 3 (London: Lutterworth Press, 1948-1958), p. 120.

10. Sheppard, *Pioneers*, p. 16.

11. W. H. Sheppard letter, May 17, 1890, printed in *The Missionary* (September 1890): 352-355.

12. Ibid. and Sheppard, *Pioneers*, pp. 29-30.

13. W. H. Sheppard journal, December 1890-February 1891, printed in *The Missionary* (July 1891): 254-259.

14. Ibid.; and Unpublished W. H. Sheppard letter, January 5, 1892, Sheppard Papers, Manuscript Number 55644, Presbyterian Historical Foundation, Montreat, North Carolina.

15. Samuel Lapsley letter, printed in *The Missionary* (April 1892): 151.

16. Photograph Collection, Sheppard Papers. Although the other missionaries are shown solemn and unmoving, Sheppard is usually smiling and striking a masterful pose. Many photographs show him with his rifle and wild game, indicating the he enjoyed hunting. Others show the Africans giving him a rifle salute; Sheppard holding a spear with a group of Bakuba hunters; Sheppard in a river captain's uniform; leading a brass band; or playing a banjo for the Africans. He habitually dressed in an entirely white suit, complete with pith helmet.

17. Shaloff, *Reform*, pp. 26-30; Slade, *English-Speaking Missions*, pp. 104-107, 197; *Annual Report of the Executive Committee of Foreign Missions of the Presbyterian Church in the United States* (1894), p. xxxvii.

18. Shaloff, *Reform*, pp. 30-31.

19. Ibid., pp. 26-27. The only good ethnohistory in English is Jan Vansina, *The Children of Woot: A History of the Kuba Peoples* (Madison: University of Wisconsin Press, 1978). But there is considerable literature in French. According to Jan Vansina, *Les Tribus Ba-Kuba et Les Peuplades Apparentées* (Tervuren, Belgium: Annales du Musée Royal du Congo Belge, 1954), pp. 8-9, the Bakuba king was sacred and powerful. Each group within the Bakuba nation paid tribute to the king, but retained autonomy over its own internal affairs. In the nineteenth century, the Bakuba had to repel invasions by neighboring peoples, but they preserved their kingdom. Even though a European trading post was established at Luebo in 1885, and the Presbyterian missionaries came six years later, the Bakuba were not greatly affected by the Euro-

peans until after 1904. See also Vansina's *De la Tradition Orale* (Tervuren, Belgium: Annales du Musée Royal du Congo Belge, 1961); and E. Torday, *Notes Ethnographiques sur les Peuples Communement Appelés Bakuba* (Bruxelles: Annales du Musée Royal du Congo Belge, 1910).

20. Shaloff, *Reform*, pp. 31-35; *Missionary Review of the World* 8 (1895): 329-330; and Sheppard, *Pioneers*, pp. 93-104.

21. Sheppard, *Pioneers*, pp. 87, 154.

22. Ibid., p. 135; and Sheppard letter, printed in *The Missionary* (June 1896): 48-49.

23. Sheppard, *Pioneers*, pp. 135, 137, 149.

24. Ibid., for example, pp. 59-61.

25. Ibid., pp. 96-97, 101, 123.

26. Ibid., pp. 76-77.

27. Ibid., pp. 93-94, 134.

28. Ibid., pp. 37-38.

29. Ibid., pp. 127-129, 140; *Missionary Review of the World* 8 (1895): 330.

30. Sheppard, *Pioneers*, pp. p. 143.

31. Shaloff, *Reform*, pp. 36-39.

32. *Missionary Review of the World* 8 (1895): 331; and *Southern Workman* 29 (April 1900): 221.

33. *Missionary Review of the World* 8 (1895): 327.

34. *Memorial of Dr. William H. Sheppard* (Louisville, Ky.: Presbyterian Colored Mission, n.d.), p. 2, copy in Sheppard Papers.

35. *The Missionary* (August 1894): 319.

36. William Sheppard letter, *Freeman*, February 27, 1892, p. 7. Sheppard went on to say that he often read the newspaper to the Africans, and he recommended the paper as evidence of "the vast and solid strides of the Negro in material, industrial and spiritual wealth."

37. *Southern Workman* 29 (April 1900): 218-219.

38. Ibid., 22 (December 1893): 182.

39. Ibid., pp. 184-187.

40. Groves, *Planting of Christianity* 3, p. 120n; Julia Lake Kellersberger, "Lucy Gantt Sheppard, Shepherdess of His Sheep on Two Continents" (Atlanta, Ga.: Committee of Women's Work, Presbyterian Church in the U.S., n.d.), pp. 5-10; Lucien V. Rule, "A Daughter of the Morning," Unpublished typescript of interviews with Lucy Gantt Sheppard in 1940, Sheppard Papers.

41. *The Missionary* (July 1894): 272-273; *Annual Reports* (1894): xxxvi, (1895): 28-29; and Shaloff, *Reform*, p. 39.

42. Kellersberger, "Lucy Gantt Sheppard," p. 11.

43. *The Missionary* (November 1895): 491; see also *Annual Report* (1896):

12-13. Other black American missionaries who later served at the Presbyterian Luebo Mission, and their dates in Africa, were: Lillian Thomas DeYampert (1894-1915), L.A. DeYampert (1902-1915), Althea Brown Edmiston (1902-1937), A. L. Edmiston (1903-1941), and Annie Katherine Taylor Rochester (1906-1914). Ironically, while the Presbyterian mission was integrated during the age of segregation, it was all-white from 1941 to 1958; see Shaloff, *Reform*, p. 39.

44. Shaloff, *Reform*, pp. 40, 182.

45. Ibid, p. 49.

46. W. H. Sheppard letter, December 9, 1896, in Rosa Gibbons, "Historical Research on Rev. William H. Sheppard, D. D., F.R.C.S.," Unpublished typescript in Sheppard Papers, p. 52.

47. Shaloff, *Reform*, pp. 47-49.

48. Sheppard letter, November 30, 1896, in Gibbons, Sheppard Papers, p. 54; *Annual Report* (1897): 14.

49. *Missionary Review of the World* 11 (1898): 798; and *Southern Workman* 29 (April 1900): 221.

50. Kellersberger, "Lucy Gantt Sheppard," pp. 20-21. After Mrs. Sheppard rejoined her husband in the Congo, she bore a son named William Lapsley Sheppard in honor of Sheppard's first white co-worker. However, the Congolese named him "Maxamalinge," and that became the name by which the son was called even after he returned to America. Photograph collection, Sheppard Papers.

51. This African tendency to define people culturally rather than racially is much more logical than American racial classifications. Shaloff, *Reform*, p. 48. While Shaloff is doubtless correct in seeing the black missionaries as culture-bound like their white counterparts, there is little evidence to support his speculation that the Afro-Americans were more intolerant of the Africans than were the white clergymen. In Sheppard's case, at least, there is much evidence to suggest the contrary.

52. Henry P. Hawkins letter, *Annual Report* (1900):25.

53. Slade, *English-Speaking Missions*, pp. 162-163.

54. Henry Hawkins letter, *Annual Report* (1900): 21. See also Slade, *English-Speaking Missions*, pp. 240-242.

55. *Southern Workman* 29 (April 1900): 220-221; *Missionary Review of the World* 13 (1900): 340-344; Sheppard, *Pioneers*; Slade, *English-Speaking Missions*, pp. 244, 254; and Groves, *Planting of Christianity* 3, p. 268.

56. William Sheppard and William Morrison letter, *The Missionary* (February 1900).

57. Slade, *English-Speaking Missions*, pp. 254, 306.

58. *Southern Workman* 29 (April 1900): 221.

59. Slade, *English-Speaking Missions*, pp. 359, 367-372; and Sheppard, *Pioneers*.

60. Sheppard Collection, Historical Foundation of the Presbyterian and Reformed Churches, Montreat, North Carolina. Also in his collection is a silver trophy presented to Sheppard by the white missionaries at Luebo, in tribute to his twenty years of mission work and as evidence of continued close relations in the integrated Congo Mission. On his return to the United States, Sheppard preached in Louisville, Kentucky, until his death in 1927. Pamphlet, *Sheppard*, p. 10, Sheppard Papers. I wish to express gratitude to the Historical Foundation in Montreat, North Carolina, for allowing me full access to the Sheppard Papers, without which this study would have been incomplete.

Their "Special Mission": Afro-American Women As Missionaries to the Congo, 1894-1937

8

Sylvia M. Jacobs

Over the years, many black Americans have returned to Africa in various capacities—as emigrants, sailors, diplomats, missionaries, and/or travelers, among others. Before 1940, however, the majority of Afro-Americans who went to Africa and returned to the United States went as missionaries. In this role, they were able to fulfill their "special duty" to their homeland, to help in the development and Christianization of the continent.

Although the majority of black missionaries who went to Africa were males, females also met this call. Generally, the women who went accompanied their husbands and were active partners in missionary duties. Because men were the actual appointees to these positions, they frequently were given all the credit for the accomplishments and improvements. In many instances, the missionary wives made a significant impact on Africans in particular locales, especially on women and children. In other cases, women went alone as missionaries to Africa, because of their personal desires to help in the growth of the continent, and they were instrumental in bringing about positive results.[1] A number of black missionaries sponsored by white-dominated American churches began working in Africa during the nineteenth century, and women many times made up the core of workers for African missions. They were ordinarily interested and involved in the status of females of the continent.[2]

Beginning in 1890, the Southern Presbyterian Church sent black missionaries to the Congo, thus initiating what was to become one of the largest Presbyterian missions in this country. In that year, an Afro-American, William Sheppard, along with Samuel Lapsley, opened the American Presbyterian Congo Mission. Between 1890, when the first black missionary was stationed in the Congo, and 1941, when the last missionary of this period left, a total of nine Afro-Americans were missionaries there. After 1958, additional black Americans were appointed to work in the Congo. Among the earlier missionaries, five were women. These black American women who represented the Southern Presbyterian Church to the American Presbyterian Congo Mission served from 1894 to 1937. They were: Maria Fearing (1894-1915), Lillian Thomas DeYampert (1894-1915), Lucy Gantt Sheppard (1894-1910), Althea Brown Edmiston (1902-1937), and Annie Katherine Taylor Rochester (1906-1914).[3]

Maria Fearing was born in 1838 in Gainsville, Alabama, to Mary and Jesse Fearing, both bondservants. As a child, she was brought up in the Presbyterian Church and her mistress told her many stories about the children of Africa, which prompted her to predict: "I will go to Africa some day if I can." When slavery was abolished, Fearing, then twenty-seven years of age, had already learned how to care for children, in addition to housekeeping, cooking, sewing, mending, washing, ironing, and other such domestic chores. She did not begin her formal education until the age of thirty-three, but she eventually completed the ninth grade at Talladega College (Talladega, Alabama), taught at a rural school in Anniston, Alabama, and later returned to Talladega as assistant matron in the boarding department.[4]

In 1893-1894, William Sheppard was on furlough from the Presbyterian Congo Mission and traveled throughout the United States addressing religious and educational audiences. He spoke at Talledega in 1894 and made an appeal for volunteers to work in Africa. Fearing, who had vowed as a young girl that she would go to Africa, offered her services to the Congo Mission. Already fifty-six years of age, with less than a high school education, she nevertheless applied to the Executive Committee of Foreign Missions for an appointment as a missionary. The Executive Committee would not subsidize her because of her advanced age. Undeterred, for she saw this as her "special mission," she sold the house she had bought while teaching in Anniston to Judge J. W. Lapsley, father of the other pioneer in the Congo. With the money from the sale of her house, her life's savings, and $100 pledged by the women of the Congregational Church in Talladega, she again appealed to the Executive Committee for appointment in the Congo, promising to pay for all of her expenses. With this financial backing, she was given permission to accompany the party going to the Congo with Sheppard. On May 26, 1894, Fearing, along with Sheppard and three other Afro-Americans, sailed from New York bound for the Congo Free State.[5]

Upon her arrival at the mission station, at Luebo, Fearing immediately began religious teaching among the Baluba-Lulua and learning their language, which had not as yet been reduced to written form. During the week, she traveled to nearby villages, teaching religious lessons to small groups. Eventually, she won the friendship of the local people, particularly the children, who followed her home to hear stories of America. Soon Fearing became known by the children as "mamu wa Mputu," the "foreign mother."

Fearing believed that her major duty in Africa was to improve the lives of the women and children. She thought that the best way to do this was to take a few girls under her care, keeping them separate from the local population. She decided it could be done by raising orphaned and kidnapped girls, who would have no reason for returning to the villages. News spread and Fearing eventually had enough girls to begin her home. During her stay in Africa, the "Fearing family" grew to almost one hundred, as she managed the Pantops Home for Girls at Luebo until her departure from the Congo in 1915.[6]

Four months after Fearing sailed from New York, the Executive Committee for Foreign Missions informed her that they would allot her enough money to buy food. Less than a year later, she was employed at a "reasonable cost" for the mission work she was doing and, after two years in the Congo, appointed as a regularly stationed missionary. In addition to her salary, from time to time she received small gifts of money from friends to be used for the Congo Mission. Aside from a little amount put away for emergencies, Fearing spent the remainder for the maintenance of the home for girls.[7]

From the beginning, Fearing trained the girls of the home in how to care for themselves. They were organized into groups and learned domestic science and sewing. The work around the Pantops Home was arranged so that all could help. Various age groups performed different jobs. There were daily tasks of sweeping the rooms and the yard, of husking and shelling corn, scraping manioc, and pounding grain. Others did the cooking. Fearing also taught the girls to make beds, set tables, and wash dishes. Assignments changed periodically to allow each girl the opportunity to learn all the things she would do in her future home. Along with these chores, Fearing taught the girls prayers and verses. She instructed them on how to conduct themselves and, as much as possible, since she had never married, about courtship and marriage. In addition, the girls were required to attend day school and all the religious services of the mission.[8]

Fearing along with the other workers at Luebo built small dwellings to accommodate six to eight girls. The younger girls were placed in houses under the supervision of an elder girl; and a senior girl was also chosen as monitor for the older girls. The houses were built close together and formed a private enclosure. Fearing was able to secure corn, peas, manioc, peanuts, bananas, plantains, pumpkins, sweet potatoes, greens, and palm oil for the home from the people of the surrounding areas. Two or three times a week, the girls were given goat's meat or fish. The girls of the home were generally better fed than the village children.[9]

For the girls of the Pantops Home, Fearing was their only mother. Although in total numbers she reached only a few of the Congolese children, her impact was surely considerable over twenty-one years. Most of the girls she trained married, became mothers, and eventually did some kind of civic work in the communities in which they lived. Fearing referred to them as "our little home missionaries," and in 1904, she asked the Presbyterian Church to join in prayer that the girls would grow up to be Christian women, "and that line, upon line, taught to them each day, much good may be done through them among their people in years to come."[10] William Sheppard made an appeal from a more practical perspective by insisting that the church "think of the Pantops home with more than a hundred girls in training for Christian work."[11]

In a letter to the secretary of the Executive Committee of Foreign Missions, early in the twentieth century, Fearing reported on the status of the home: "The Girls' Home has a larger number in it than it has ever had, and more are begging to be permitted to come. They are being taught all kinds of useful work, and best of all most of them have become Christians and are trying very hard to live better lives." A letter written by one of the girls of the Pantops Home, published in the *Missionary Survey*, explained that there were many girls under Mother Fearing's care and that she was always helping them and showing them the Christian way.[12]

The finances of the Pantops Home for Girls were eventually subsidized by the home church. Although Fearing had initially supplied almost all of the necessary funds for the school, the Presbyterian Church finally realized the benefits of such an endeavor and assumed all of the financial burden.

In addition to her activities with the home, Fearing taught a class in the mission Sunday school and day school. Although she had mastered the Baluba-Lulua languages as spoken in the Upper Kasai and Congo River Basin, they had not been written down, and the lessons and religious readings were translated each day.[13]

Fearing, likewise, continued her work in the surrounding villages and was active in the church campaign of "civilizing and Christianizing" Africa and Africans. In one of her many trips, she observed: "Going around the natives and visiting them in their different villages and seeing them in their homes is very interesting indeed; their lives are so unlike ours. One may gain quite a good deal of knowledge of their customs and the everyday life."[14] She later went on to caution: "I am thankful to say that there is quite an improvement in many of the natives, yet there is room for more." Months afterward, during a trip to the

Basonga region, she insisted that "there are at this place a great many people who know nothing about the true God, and there are none to teach them about the Lord Jesus who came to save them."[15] This was obviously a call for more missionaries and a justification for continuing missionary work.

Fearing went to the United States for a furlough in 1906 but returned to the Congo a short time later. While in America, she spoke to religious groups, telling them of her work in the Christianizing of Africa. Because of signs of weariness, she took a second leave of absence in 1915, unaware that she would never return. Another Afro-American missionary couple, and Fearing's closest friends, the DeYamperts, were also taking a furlough at this time. After a year of rest, she informed the Executive Committee of Foreign Missions that she was ready to return to Africa. However, because of her advanced age, and unforeseen circumstances involving the DeYamperts who were to accompany her, she did not go back to Africa. Denied the opportunity to continue her work on the continent, Fearing accepted an invitation to live with the DeYamperts. She became active in the First Presbyterian Church in Selma, Alabama. Unsurprisingly, the work she had begun at the Pantops Home for Girls continued in her absence. Maria Fearing eventually returned to the place of her birth, Gainesville, Alabama, where she died on May 23, 1937.[16]

Lillian May Thomas was a student at Talladega College during the time Maria Fearing was assistant matron in the boarding department. Thomas was appointed by the Executive Committee of Foreign Missions as a missionary to the Congo Mission in 1894 and traveled to Africa in the same party with Fearing. Thomas was born on September 14, 1872, in Mobile, Alabama, to James and Lydia Randolph Thomas. At the age of twelve, she joined the Congregational Church. After finishing studies at Emerson Institute in Mobile, she entered Talladega College. During her senior year, in 1894, William Sheppard visited the campus and issued a call for missionaries to Africa. According to her husband, Lucius A. DeYampert, she had long desired to be a missionary and responded at once. She sailed for the Congo, in the party with Fearing, on May 26, 1894. During their stay in Africa, Thomas and Fearing became close friends and for fourteen years lived in the same house. On June 18, 1908, Thomas married DeYampert at Luebo.[17]

Thomas, too, worked among the women of Luebo. She was engaged in the Pantops Home for Girls, ultimately becoming superintendent. Like Fearing, she taught the Baluba and Lulua girls how to clean and dress themselves and how to wash, iron, cook, and sew. In the early days when printing was introduced into the Congo, she helped to teach the Congolese how to set type. Thomas was instrumental in starting the Luebo day school which eventually educated thousands.[18]

Thomas was as dedicated to building and developing schools in the Congo as Fearing was to establishing a home for girls, and she wrote many articles in the *Kassai Herald*, a journal devoted to the work of the American Presbyterian Congo Mission, concerning the need for education. In one article, Thomas described the condition of schools in the Congo: "We began school at Luebo in December 1894 with just a few children who were on the station at that time. We had no books, charts, black-boards or anything to teach with." She went on to explain that by 1900, there were thirty-seven pupils in the school. At the beginning of 1901, the number had increased to eighty, and two years later, in 1903, it reached almost two hundred and fifty. However, Thomas complained that there were more students than the present three teachers could instruct, and she asked: "Will not some one come and help in this good work?" She believed that schools were "the greatest and most important task before us" and explained that "there is a great awakening in the educational work, as well as in the spiritual."[19]

In 1909, Mrs. DeYampert in a letter to *The Missionary*, a monthly magazine published by the Executive Committee of Foreign Missions of the Presbyterian Church in the United States, extolled the Presbyterian Church and missionary work in Africa: "These people are now in the sunshine of the wonderful blessings of God. The good Master put it in your hearts, your good and generous hearts, to send the gospel to them." She apparently believed that religion and education would bring Africa out of "darkness."[20]

In 1915, the DeYamperts joined Fearing in a furlough to the United States. However, when the Executive Committee of Foreign Missions gave them permission to return to the Congo, a medical examination revealed that Mrs. DeYampert had high blood pressure, which made it unadvisable for her to go back to Africa. The DeYamperts returned to Selma, Alabama. This physical problem finally caused a heart attack which on May 29, 1930, resulted in Mrs. DeYampert's death.[21]

The third woman to join the party of five bound for the Congo Mission in 1894 was Lucy Gantt Sheppard, who was at that time William Sheppard's new bride. Lucy Gantt was born on February 21, 1867, in Tuscaloosa, Alabama, to Eliza Gantt, an orphaned ex-slave who had been deserted by her husband. At the age of eleven, she entered Talladega College where she studied for nine years. Ironically, Gantt, the youngest student in the school, was placed under the personal supervision of the oldest pupil of the school, Maria Fearing. At the age of thirteen, Gantt joined the college Congregational Church. With tutoring and encouragement by the wife of the college president, Gantt developed a trained singing voice, became a member of the college choir, and later traveled throughout the United States for one year with the Loudin Jubilee Singers. (The Fisk University Jubilee Singers, which had disbanded in 1878, was reorganized by Frederick J. Loudin in 1882 as the Loudin Jubilee Singers.) In June 1886, she was graduated from Talladega College. For two summers she taught in a one-room school in Grayton, Alabama. She then taught in the Birmingham City Schools for over seven years. It was on a visit to her old home in Tuscaloosa that she met her future husband, then a theology student at Stillman Institute. On February 21, 1894, she married William Sheppard in Jacksonville, Florida, where her mother had moved because of failing health. The newlyweds spent several weeks touring the country, with Sheppard calling for missionaries for the Congo Mission. It was then that two other Talladega students, Maria Fearing and Lillian Thomas, and a Stillman graduate, Henry P. Hawkins, volunteered for missionary work and sailed with the Sheppards from New York on May 26, 1894.[22]

Mrs. Sheppard's activities in the Congo paralleled those of the other two women who went in 1894: she taught school, held evangelistic services in surrounding villages, and instructed the women and girls on Western cooking, sewing, washing, and ironing. However, as a trained teacher, her major task when she arrived at Luebo was to work in the school. According to Mrs. Sheppard, the educational methods employed were of the crudest form, and even compared to the school she taught at in rural Alabama, they were. There were no textbooks, pencils, or desks, and most of the students were rescued slave children who had been sold by their parents. It was not until 1900, when money was given for a small printing press, that first and second grade readers, biblical parables, and song sheets were reproduced. But during the entire sixteen years of her missionary work in the Congo, neither a dictionary nor a grammar book was printed to aid in the study of the Baluba-Lulua languages.[23]

Mrs. Sheppard volunteered her home at Luebo as a place to train girls of the Pantops Home. She boasted that "the making of a Christian home was part of my missionary task and I was glad that my house could be used as a demonstration and practice center." All of the women missionaries took a part in the training of the young men and women at the mission. In relating her experiences, Mrs. Sheppard mentioned that "Congo girls took their turns, by twos, working in my home learning new methods of more abundant living. . . . Boys were trained in my kitchen to cook, for I had ever in mind the future homemaking of young men and women." Mrs. Sheppard also worked as a practical nurse in the medical clinic that was open at Luebo six days a week.[24]

Mrs. Sheppard's early years in the Congo were not easy ones. Her first child was born prematurely and lived only a few weeks. Her second child lived barely eight months. When her third daughter was born, the other missionaries agreed that she should return to the United States for a well-deserved rest. Mrs. Sheppard remained in the United States for over a year, leaving her daughter in the care of her sister-in-law. In 1900, she had a fourth child, William Lapsley Sheppard.[25]

When Mrs. Sheppard returned to the Congo in 1899, her husband had been reassigned to the new Ibanche station in Bakuba territory. Again she had to learn a new language. In 1900, she began the first school at Ibanche. When it opened, there were fifteen students with Mrs. Sheppard as the only teacher. One year later, she bragged that there were "seventy enrolled, sixty-five in regular attendance and two native teachers."[26] While at Ibanche, Mrs. Sheppard worked in the Marie Carey Home. She did the same basic things that she had done at the Pantops Home at Luebo, training young women for adult life.[27]

It was at Ibanche, in 1902, that Mrs. Sheppard formed the first women's society of the Congo Mission. According to her own account, the society began:

When I saw the first native woman in her strip of cloth, her hair daubed with paint, her body smeared with grease and her mind filled with sin and superstition, I could not help but wonder if she could be changed. . . . Some weeks ago, I invited a few to meet with me at my home for a prayer service. Fifty have been coming and we have emerged into a missionary society whose aim is to care for the sick, look up indifferent members, and help others in need. We are learning to pray and sing together.

The women met once a week, every sixth day.[28] She pointed out that the gatherings were simple, and "the one great object in these meetings is to get these women, interest them, and by God's help keep them." Mrs. Sheppard expressed a recurrent theme among women missionaries when she announced that "there is a great work here among the women, alas sadly neglected for want of workers."[29]

The Sheppards returned to the United States on another furlough in 1906. While there, most of their time was spent traveling and securing new recruits for missionary work. In September 1909, William Sheppard was tried at Leopoldville in the Congo because of an article he wrote in the *Kassai Herald*. He was found not guilty of malicious slander against the Kasai Company, but in March 1910, the Sheppards left the Congo Mission permanently. When they returned to the United States, they lived in Virginia for a year and finally moved to Louisville, Kentucky. Sheppard became pastor of Grace Presbyterian Church, and his wife taught in the Sunday school, trained the church choir, organized a junior choir, and lectured about their work at the Presbyterian Congo Mission. After her husband's death in 1927, she continued work in the church and the community. Lucy Gantt Sheppard died in 1955.[30]

It was eight years after the first three black women went to the Congo Mission in 1894 that the fourth woman joined them. Althea Maria Brown was the fifth child of ten and the second daughter of Robert and Molly Suggs Brown. She was born eight days before Christmas in 1874, in Russelville, DeKalb County, Alabama. When she was one and a half years old, her parents sold their home and moved near Rolling Fork, Mississippi. As a young child, Brown secured her education at home. Her father taught her the alphabet and a neighbor taught her to read.[31]

In the fall of 1892, Brown, then eighteen years old, left her home in Mississippi and, because of her previous education at home, entered the seventh grade at Fisk University in Nashville, Tennessee. Three months after her arrival at Fisk, she joined the Congregational Church. Brown had always dreamed of being a teacher, and at the conclusion of each school year she taught at a district summer school. She also occasionally substituted in the city schools of Nashville. In 1901, she was graduated from Fisk with the highest honor and was the only woman to speak on the commencement program. Her graduating address was "What Missions Have Done for the World." After graduation, she studied for one year at the Chicago Training School for City and Foreign Missions.[32]

Althea Brown had an absorbing interest in Africa and a lifelong desire to aid in the Christian "redemption" of the continent. She decided she wanted to serve in the Congo Free State and applied to the Executive Committee of Foreign Missions of the Presbyterian Church for appointment. She received her commission on May 14, 1901, and sailed for Africa on August 20, 1902.[33]

Brown arrived at Luebo in November 1902 but remained there only seven weeks. During her stay, she began studying the Baluba-Lulua languages under William M. Morrison, who was reducing them to writing and preparing a grammar and dictionary. He inspired her to do the same thing with the Bakuba language. During her temporary stay at Luebo, Brown lived with Maria Fearing at the Pantops Home for Girls. She was permanently stationed at Ibanche, forty miles north of Luebo. The station was only three years old when Brown arrived. William and Lucy Sheppard had been at Ibanche since its inception.[34]

Ibanche was intended not as a permanent station but only as a stepping-stone to the Bakuba kingdom; it nonetheless remained for sixteen years until it was abandoned in 1915. Brown's duties at Ibanche included preparing a grammar and dictionary in the Bakuba language, teaching in the day school and Sunday school, and working among the women and children. She became the head of the day school, supervisor of the Marie Carey Home for Girls, and leader in the missionary assignments in the surrounding villages.[35]

In 1904, Alonzo Edmiston came to the Ibanche station. Althea Brown and Edmiston were married on July 8, 1905. Henry P. Hawkins was the best man and Lillian Thomas bridesmaid. Their first child, Sherman Lucius, was born on May 26, 1906, but because of the child's poor health, Mrs. Edmiston took him out of Africa in 1908. Her husband joined them a year later, but the two did not return to the Congo until 1911 because of lack of church funds. However, through lectures and exhibits on Africa, they were able to pay for their passage back to the Congo. Another child, named Alonzo Leaucourt, was born to the couple on May 27, 1913. Mrs. Edmiston took another furlough in 1914 because this child, too, became ill, and she remained in the United States until August 1917. Both sons were left in the care of relatives. Because of delays in New York City, Cape Town, South Africa, and Saint Paul de Loanda, Angola, she did not reach Luebo until January 1918.[36]

From 1918 until 1920, the Edmistons were located at Bulape, a new station sixteen miles from the Bakuba capital. For one year they were resident missionaries at Mushenge, a substation of Bulape. While there, they organized day schools and catechism classes. The Sunday services were often attended by as many as two thousand people. After a year, it was decided that only the Bulape station should be maintained in Bakuba territory, and the Edmistons were withdrawn from Mushenge.[37]

The Edmistons took another furlough in April 1920. While in the United States, Mrs. Edmiston delivered the commencement address at Fisk University. On May 29, 1921, twenty years after her valedictory speech, she again emphasized the importance of missions. Mrs. Edmiston disclosed:

After the Civil War the Christian world turned towards the Negro race in America for the evangelization of Africa.... Many felt that the Freedman had not only a great work to do here in America, but also a large share in carrying Christianity to the millions of less fortunate ones in Africa.... I am convinced that it is the purpose of God that many of us should, like Moses, return to our people in Africa and lead them forth from the land of bondage into the promised land of life more abundant on this earth and life eternal in the world to come.... In my mind the highest post of honor that one can fill is the place where there is the greatest need, and where one can render the largest service.

The Edmistons returned to the Congo in December 1921. In December 1922, they were transferred to the Mutoto station, one hundred and sixty miles east of Luebo.[38]

While at Mutoto, Mrs. Edmiston was in charge of the girls' home, principal of the day school system, in which more than five hundred students were enrolled, and assisted in the Bible school. In addition to her educational work, she on occasion assumed the duties of a nurse.[39]

Mrs. Edmiston's work in the villages was principally among the women. She believed that the women were "urgently in need of help and instruction in the Christian ideals of womanhood." As early as 1904, she made a plea for more missionaries to work among African women. She described their situation:

Nothing is more touching to us foreign women as we enter the "Dark Continent" than the condition in which we find our heathen sister.... We see the heathen woman in her totally depraved and degraded state. With blank, inexpressive face, greased, matted hair, her only garment the size of two hands, she may be seen paddling a canoe, or bartering her garden products. Life has no meaning to her. She simply seeks an existence.

In her appeal, she sadly noted that "Because of our [missionaries'] limited number and strength, we are able to reach out a helping hand to a comparatively few. There are scores within our reach whom we do not touch, yet *no work is so far-reaching in its influence as that done among the women and children"* [emphasis added]. Like other women missionaries, Mrs. Edmiston's call was for the uplift of the women of Africa.[40]

At Ibanche, caring for the girls at the Marie Carey Home, at Bulape and Mushenge, working among the women, and at Mutoto, overseeing the Home for Girls, Mrs. Edmiston found satisfaction in seeing these females become educated leaders among their own people. One of her colleagues at Mutoto wrote of Mrs. Edmiston's work among the women and children: "Who can measure the results of a life given to teaching boys and girls?"[41]

Comparable to her activities for the uplift of Congolese womanhood was Mrs. Edmiston's outstanding contribution to the Bakuba work. She began translating the Bakuba language immediately upon her arrival at Ibanche in 1902, a task that took her eleven years to complete. Yet, her grammar and dictionary were not published until 1932. When her book was finished, there was no money to have the printing done. The matter periodically came up before the annual mission meeting, but the feeling was that the expense of publication could not be justified. Finally, permission was granted for publication on the condition that Mrs. Edmiston raise the funds herself, from sources outside the regular mission budget. She began to raise the funds— Fisk University contributed $400, Mrs. Edmiston's parents, $100, the women of the First Presbyterian Church of Selma, Alabama, $100, and the Foreign Mission Committee the bulk of the remainder necessary for printing the book. The 619-page *Grammar and Dictionary of the Bushonga or Bukuba Language As Spoken By the Bushonga or Bukuba Tribe Who Dwell in the Upper Kasai District, Belgian Congo, Central Africa* was finally printed at a cost of $2,000 in 1932.[42] Besides the grammar and dictionary, Mrs. Edmiston also translated school books, hymns, parables, proverbs, lullabies, folk stories, fairy tales, and conundrums.[43]

In December 1924, trypanosomes (sleeping sickness) was found in Mrs. Edmiston's blood, and two months later her husband also became a victim of the disease. On March 30, 1925, the

Edmistons left Mutoto, taking treatments in Brussels, New York, and Nashville. They returned to the Congo cured in 1927. They took furloughs again in 1929 and 1935. Between 1927 and 1937, the Edmistons continued their work at Mutoto station and during this period, translated and printed the entire Bible into the Baluba-Lulua languages.[44]

In her last missionary address, delivered before the Missionary Conference of Negro Women, in Indianapolis, Indiana, in 1935, Mrs. Edmiston revealed her deep love for mission work:

I have suffered many adversities. I have had days of cloud and of sunshine, and have been called upon to make sacrifices that have caused my heart to bleed. But, in spite of it all, I have found inexpressible joy and happiness in the Master's service in this far-off land, and I have never had cause to regret the decision made when a girl in school. God has verified all His promises to me and I have never wanted for any of the necessary comforts of life. And, he has permitted me, along with my colleagues, to see the abundant fruits of our labor.

Mrs. Edmiston was able to realize her dream. She acknowledged: "My one desire is to spend and be spent in the service of God and my race."[45]

Althea Brown Edmiston died on June 9, 1937, of malaria and sleeping sickness. She was buried on Mutoto station in the Congo. The Women's Auxiliary of the Presbyterian Church in the United States, which Mrs. Edmiston had represented in Africa for almost thirty-five years, donated $49,651.82 to set up the Althea Brown Edmiston Memorial Fund, to continue maintenance of the homes for girls where Mrs. Edmiston had worked for so long.[46]

One other Afro-American woman represented the Southern Presbyterian Church in the Congo Mission: Annie Katherine Taylor, who was a missionary in the Congo from 1906 to 1914. Taylor was born in Tuscaloosa, Alabama, and was educated at Scotia College, (now Barber Scotia) in Concord, North Carolina. Little is known of her parents or her early life. In 1906, she sailed to Africa. She was first stationed in Luebo and worked in the Pantops Home for Girls with Maria Fearing and Lillian Thomas. Later, she was transferred to Ibanche where she became superintendent of the Marie Carey Home and taught in the day school. In her eight years of service, she proved herself to be a devoted missionary. One of her colleagues recalled that she possessed the four virtues necessary for a successful missionary: efficiency, consecration, temperament, and industry.[47]

Taylor's particular interest while at Ibanche was in the Marie Carey Home. There, she taught the girls sewing, laundering, sweeping, cooking, and general housework. She spoke of her work with the girls with enthusiasm:

We are so thankful to have them while they are young and hope we may not fail in trying to train them up in the way that they should go, trusting that when they are older and go from us to their own homes and people, they may be christian mothers of christian families and so help hundreds of villagers to whom we cannot go.

She indicated that the missionaries tried to get the girls during their formative years, believing that then their work would be lasting.[48]

On May 4, 1911, Taylor married Reverend A. A. Rochester, a Jamaican missionary in the Congo (1906-1939), representing the Southern Presbyterian Church of the United States. In November of that year, they took their first furlough visiting her family in Alabama and his in Jamaica. They arrived back in the Congo in June 1912.[49] After their return to the Congo, the Rochesters were sent to the new station at Mutoto. While there, Mrs. Rochester was a teacher, the girls' home superintendent, a house-to-house visitor, a gardener, and a nurse.

In February 1914, Mrs. Rochester complained of severe abdominal pains, which were diagnosed as appendicitis. She prepared to go to Great Britain for an operation, but was later advised against it because she seemed to have recovered. In April, she had another attack and died on May 14, 1914. She was the first missionary buried at Mutoto. Mrs. Rochester was known among the Bakuba as Bulape, and in 1915, the Bulape station was established and named in order "to perpetuate the memory of Mrs. A. A. Rochester, a colored missionary of high ability, who died at Mutoto on May 14, 1914, after eight years of efficient and consecrated service."[50] Charles L. Crane, a distinguished missionary in the Congo, praised Annie Katherine Taylor Rochester:

In her death in 1914 our Mission sustained a loss at a time when there were few like her to carry on the work among the women and girls. Many native women of today at Ibanche and Mutoto remember her as one of their best friends and teachers, and those of us who knew her personally still think of her as one of God's choice spirits.[51]

In 1941, Alonzo Edmiston left the Congo. He was the last Afro-American missionary appointed to the Congo during this period. The Southern Presbyterian Congo Mission was all-white after that date, until the late 1950s.

Afro-American missionaries made a valuable contribution to the establishment and extension of missionary work in the Congo,[52] and women played a substantial role in this process. All five of the black women who were assigned to the Presbyterian Congo Mission before 1937 by the Southern Presbyterian Church were interested in the Christian "redemption" of Africa. Interestingly, all five were born in Alabama and attended southern black colleges. Exposure in these schools during the missionary era to the idea of the "manifest destiny" of black Americans to "save Africa" for Christianity may help to explain their interest in mission work. This theory of "providential design" was popular among nineteenth-century mission-minded Christians, which taught that God had allowed Afro-Americans to be enslaved and "civilized" so that they could return and "redeem" Africa.

Black American missionaries, exposed to Western ideas about the "debased" nature of African society, traveled to Africa with the idea that they were contributing to the "uplift" of the continent. After observing local life and customs, however, these missionaries often came to respect African culture. Unfortunately, when they reported back to the United States or lectured to church or secular audiences in this country, they continued to perpetuate many of the stereotypes about Africa, obviously as a justification for continued missionary activity. Nevertheless, the missionizing activity of black Americans in the late nineteenth

and early twentieth centuries never had the imperialistic overtones of that of white missionaries, possibly because of the realization that there was a similarity in the conditions of Africans as
a subjugated people and Afro-Americans as an oppressed people. Afro-Americans faced discrimination and exploitation in the
United States and were denied equality; but black American
missionaries in Africa were given some freedom and latitude in
their work in Africa, and perhaps unconsciously, or even consciously, volunteered to work in Africa to avoid racial problems
in America.

The Afro-American women who went to the Southern Presbyterian Congo Mission traveled to Africa for the purpose of aid-
ing in the "civilizing mission" there. Each was active in efforts
involving the women and children of Africa. Maria Fearing's work
in the Pantops Home for Girls at Luebo, Lillian Thomas De-
Yampert's efforts in the Luebo day school, Lucy Gantt Sheppard's
organization at Ibanche of the first women's society of the Congo
Mission, Althea Brown Edmiston's Bakuba *Grammar and Dictionary* and her many years of service, and Annie Katherine Taylor
Rochester's work in the Marie Carey Home at Ibanche stand out
as examples of dedication to the mission of helping to "Christianize and civilize" Africa. Although the accomplishments of
these women have been overlooked and somewhat overshad-
owed by the work of the male missionaries stationed in the
Congo, it is obvious that their work among the women and
children of the Congo had far-reaching effects. In the final analysis, these five women were representatives of the many black
Americans, both male and female, who during the nineteenth
and twentieth centuries saw their "special mission" in Africa.

Notes

1. I would like to thank Ms. Lannae Graham, archivist, and Dr.
Ruth D. See, research associate, at the Historical Foundation of the
Presbyterian and Reformed Churches, Montreat, North Carolina, for
their invaluable assistance in helping me to research this article.

2. Edwin S. Redkey, *The Meaning of Africa to Afro-Americans, 1890-1914*
(Buffalo, N.Y.: Council on International Studies, 1971), p. 18; Clifford

Haley Scott, "American Images of Sub-Sahara Africa, 1900-1939" (Ph.D. dissertation, University of Iowa, 1968), p. 164; and Julia Kellersberger, *Congo Crosses, A Study of Congo Womanhood* (Boston: Central Committee on the United Study of Foreign Missions, 1936), p. 173.

3. Julia Kellersberger, *A Life for the Congo, the Story of Althea Brown Edmiston* (New York: Fleming H. Revell Co., 1947), p. 140; and Ethel Taylor Wharton, *Led in Triumph* (Nashville, Tenn.: Board of World Missions, Presbyterian Church, U.S., 1952), p. 76.

4. Stanley Shaloff, *Reform in Leopold's Congo* (Richmond, Va.: John Knox Press, 1970), p. 40; and Althea Brown Edmiston, "Maria Fearing: A Mother to African Girls," in *Glorious Living, Informal Sketches of Seven Missionaries of the Presbyterian Church, U.S.,* ed. Sarah Lee Thomas (Atlanta, Ga.: Committee on Women's Work, Presbyterian Church, U.S., 1937), pp. 291-295.

5. Shaloff, *Reform in Leopold's Congo,* p. 40; Edmiston, "Maria Fearing," pp. 295-297; and Wharton, *Led in Triumph,* p. 75.

6. Edmiston, "Maria Fearing," pp. 301-303, 308; and William H. Sheppard, *Presbyterian Pioneers in Congo* (Richmond, Va.: Presbyterian Committee of Publications, 1917), pp. 151-152.

7. Shaloff, *Reform in Leopold's Congo,* p. 40; Edmiston, "Maria Fearing," p. 304; Wharton, *Led in Triumph,* p. 75; and Egbert W. Smith, "Alabama's Contribution to Foreign Missions During 100 Years, A Challenge to the Future," Address delivered at the Centennial of the Synod of Alabama of the Presbyterian Church, at Mobile, Alabama, October 9, 1935, in the Government Street Presbyterian Church, p. 12. This address can be found in the papers of the Historical Foundation of the Presbyterian and Reformed Churches (hereafter cited as Historical Foundation), Montreat, North Carolina.

8. Sheppard, *Pioneers in Congo,* p. 152; John Morrison, "Through a Rift to Clear Shining (Fifty Years in Africa)," in *Foundations of World Order, the Foreign Service of the Presbyterian Church, U.S.* (Richmond, Va.: John Knox Press, 1941), pp. 59-60; and Kellersberger, *A Life for the Congo,* pp. 11-12.

9. Edmiston, "Maria Fearing," pp. 304-305.

10. Marie Fearing, "Children's Page," *Kassai Herald,* April 1, 1904, p. 32. Most copies of the *Kassai Herald,* a journal devoted to the work of the American Presbyterian Congo Mission, published at Luebo, can be found in the Historical Foundation, Montreat, North Carolina. The discrepancy in the spelling of certain words throughout this article (for example, Kasai or Kassai, Bakuba or Bukuba, Baluba or Buluba) is not that of the author, but simply the preference of different missionaries.

Sheppard used the spelling Kasai, Bakuba, and Baluba. Other missionaries in their writings (such as Althea Brown Edmiston) used the spelling Bukuba. The mission journal, for example, was spelled Kassai, but the region was known as the Kasai. The original spelling has been maintained in direct quotations; otherwise, the commonly accepted spelling is used.

11. Sheppard, *Pioneers in Congo*, p. 156.

12. "A Letter from a Congo School Girl," *Missionary Survey* (April 1912): 423.

13. Edmiston, "Maria Fearing," pp. 308, 313-314.

14. *Kassai Herald*, July 1, 1901, p. 21.

15. *Kassai Herald*, January 1, 1902, p. 11.

16. Edmiston, "Maria Fearing," pp. 311, 313-318; *Annual Report of the Executive Committee of Foreign Missions of the Presbyterian Church in the U.S.* (1937), p. 9; Charles D. Fulton, *Now is the Time* (Richmond, Va.: John Knox Press, 1946), p. 165; and "Mission Reports Congo Mission, Africa," *The Missionary* 44 (May 1911): 219.

17. "Mrs. L. A. DeYampert," DeYampert Collection, Historical Foundation, Montreat, North Carolina. This article is taken from *The Missionary* (August 1930).

18. Ibid.; Edmiston, "Maria Fearing," p. 313; and Smith, "Alabama's Contribution to Foreign Missions," p. 17.

19. Lillian May Thomas, "Our School Children," *Kassai Herald*, March 1, 1901, p. 9; and "Our Schools," *Kassai Herald*, April 1, 1903, p. 19.

20. "Letter from Mrs. Lillian Thomas DeYampert," *The Missionary* 42 (June 1909): 308-309.

21. Ibid. and Edmiston, "Maria Fearing," pp. 313-314.

22. Smith, "Alabama's Contribution to Foreign Missions," p. 12; Julia Lake Kellersberger, "Lucy Gantt Sheppard, Shepherdess of His Sheep on Two Continents" (Atlanta, Ga.: Committee on Women's Work, Presbyterian Church in the United States, n.d.), pp. 5-10; and Lucien V. Rule, "A Daughter of the Morning," Unpublished typescript of interviews with Lucy Gantt Sheppard in 1940, William H. Sheppard Papers, Historical Foundation, Montreat, North Carolina.

23. Smith, "Alabama's Contribution to Foreign Missions," p. 12; and Kellersberger, "Lucy Gantt Sheppard," pp. 19-20.

24. Kellersberger, "Lucy Gantt Sheppard," pp. 18-20.

25. Ibid., pp. 16, 21, 23-24.

26. Lucy G. Sheppard, "Progress at Ibanj," *Kassai Herald*, July 1, 1901, pp. 16-17.

27. L. G. Sheppard, "The Girls' Homes," *Kassai Herald*, January 1, 1908, p. 17.

28. Kellersberger, "Lucy Gantt Sheppard," pp. 24-25.

29. Mrs. L. G. Sheppard, "A Sewing Class at Ibanj," *Kassai Herald*, April 1, 1902, p. 15.

30. Kellersberger, "Lucy Gantt Sheppard," pp. 25-28.

31. Of the five Afro-American women who went to the American Presbyterian Congo Mission before 1937, more information is available about Mrs. Althea Brown Edmiston. See Kellersberger, *A Life for the Congo*, pp. 23-24; and Robert Dabney Bedinger, "Althea Brown Edmiston, A Congo Crusader," in *Glorious Living*, pp. 263-264.

32. Kellersberger, *A Life for the Congo*, pp. 30, 33-35, 120; Bedinger, "Althea Brown Edmiston," pp. 264-266; and Smith, "Alabama's Contribution to Foreign Missions," p. 13.

33. Kellersberger, *A Life for the Congo*, pp. 38-39; and Bedinger, "Althea Brown Edmiston," p. 266.

34. Kellersberger, *A Life for the Congo*, pp. 10-12, 53-55; Bedinger, "Althea Brown Edmiston," p. 268; and Althea M. Brown, "Ibanj: Trip to and First Glimpses Of," *Kassai Herald*, April 1, 1903, pp. 15-16.

35. Kellersberger, *A Life for the Congo*, p. 58; and Bedinger, "Althea Brown Edmiston," pp. 269-270.

36. Kellersberger, *A Life for the Congo*, pp. 73, 76-77, 80-86, 88, 92; and Bedinger, "Althea Brown Edmiston," pp. 271-272.

37. Bedinger, "Althea Brown Edmiston," pp. 275-276.

38. Kellersberger, *A Life for the Congo*, pp. 119-122.

39. Ibid., pp. 138-139, 142-145; and Bedinger, "Althea Brown Edmiston," pp. 280-283.

40. Miss Althea M. Brown, "A Plea for the Women," *Kassai Herald*, October 1, 1904, p. 41.

41. Kellersberger, *A Life for the Congo*, pp. 113-114, 142; and Bedinger, "Althea Brown Edmiston," pp. 281-282, 284.

42. A copy of the grammar and dictionary can be viewed at the Historical Foundation, Montreat, North Carolina. See also Kellersberger, *A Life for the Congo*, pp. 129-133; and Bedinger, "Althea Brown Edmiston," pp. 276-280.

43. Kellersberger, *A Life for the Congo*, p. 135.

44. Ibid., pp. 147-148, 151, 154-156; and Bedinger, "Althea Brown Edmiston," p. 285.

45. Kellersberger, *A Life for the Congo*, p. 157; and Bedinger, "Althea Brown Edmiston," pp. 285-286.

46. Kellersberger, *A Life for the Congo*, pp. 167-171; and Bedinger, "Althea Brown Edmiston," p. 285.

47. Smith, "Alabama's Contribution to Foreign Missions," p. 17; and Note, *Kassai Herald*, January 1, 1908, p. 11.

48. Ibid.; Miss Annie Taylor, "News from the Marie Carey Home," *Kassai Herald*, January 1, 1909, pp. 11-12; and *Kassai Herald*, March 1, 1910, p. 14.

49. A. A. Rochester, *Missionary in the Congo: An Autobiography* (Atlanta, Ga.: Committee on Women's Work, Presbyterian Church in the United States, n.d.), p. 25.

50. Historical Foundation Files (130937) and (131182), Montreat, North Carolina; Rochester, *Missionary in the Congo*, p. 26; and Wharton, *Led in Triumph*, p. 90.

51. Charles L. Crane, Introduction, in Rochester's *Missionary in the Congo*, pp. 7-8.

52. Charles P. Groves, *The Planting of Christianity in Africa* 3, 1878-1914 (London: Lutterworth Press, 1955), p. 121.

Colonial Reaction to AME Missionaries in South Africa, 1898-1910

9

Carol A. Page

In 1898, Bishop Henry McNeal Turner made a five-week blitz through the Cape Colony, and the Transvaal and Orange Free State Republics, to formally organize the African Methodist Episcopal Church (AMEC) in that part of the African continent. The repercussions of his visit adversely colored subsequent twentieth-century European colonialist views on the black American presence in southern Africa and perhaps in sub-Saharan Africa as a whole.

The AME connection with South Africa began when the African-led Ethiopian Church, founded in 1893, merged with the AMEC in 1896.[1] Until 1897, the Ethiopian Church confined its activities to the Transvaal and Orange Free State Republics, Boer territories, where the church was recognized and its ministers were permitted to solemnize marriages. However, when the Ethiopian Church dispatched an emissary to the United States to effect a union with the AMEC and expanded its operations into the Cape Colony, rumblings about the mischievous purposes of the AMEC began within ecclesiastical circles.

European clergymen viewed the AMEC move into the Cape Colony as unduly ambitious and unnecessary, since in their opinion the field to the south was well represented denominationally and was in fact overcrowded. The European churchmen feared that the color of AME ministers would place them at an advantage in the competitive Cape field. And in their view,

AME missionaries could only garner converts through pilferage from the established churches. In their view, AME ministers were in effect, "missionary raiders." Hence, there were misgivings about the AMEC from the beginning of its merger with the South African independent church, but concerted opposition to the AME presence did not begin until after the 1898 visit of the church's senior bishop, Henry McNeal Turner.

To be sure, Bishop Turner was not the first Afro-American to visit South Africa.[2] Black Americans had gone to the southern tip of the continent during the gold rush in the 1880s and it is not unlikely that some had trickled in before the rush. A troupe of Hampton Institute (Virginia) singers made at least two visits to South Africa before the bishop's visit and several black Baptists had lived and worked there long before AME missionaries entered the field.[3] What made the Turner visit different from those of his predecessors was the notoriety that he left in his wake.

Turner was an arch-critic of U.S. imperialism and racism and an outspoken African emigrationist. He was the editor of perhaps the most combative black American newspaper then in existence, the *Voice of Missions*. Through the *Voice*, the bishop disseminated his views on the need for the international solidarity of blacks, the efficacy of assertive and concerted action to redress their common grievances, and the necessity for defensive violence. The *Voice*, which often contained graphic accounts of the outrages committed against blacks by whites, had been circulating in South Africa three years prior to Turner's visit. Among its subscribers were disgruntled indigenous leaders like Sigcau of Pondoland, Dalindyebo of Tembuland, and Lerotholi of Basutoland, as well as Cape activists like Walter Rubusana and A. Kirkland Soga.[4]

"Lovers of the race" were invited to attend the bishop's public lectures, one of which was entitled, "The Unity of the Race." During his travels, the bishop ordained a sizable number of deacons and ministers. He bought land on which to erect an AME college in the Cape Colony, and he had private audiences with the two republican presidents, Paul Kruger of the Transvaal and M. T. Steyn of the Orange Free State, all for the purpose of disclaiming any mischief on the part of AME ministers. Moreover, the bishop traveled, lived, and ate where he wished without incident.[5]

Press reaction to the Turner visit, particularly from the religious press, was decidedly hostile. Tengo Jabavu, the preeminent spokesman at the time for black South Africans, accused the bishop of importing racialist doctrines into the country, and he intimated that Turner might lead an exodus of black Americans to South Africa, a view shared by some colonialists as well.[6]

The *Christian Express* reported that the bishop had "struck rather a false and discreditable note" in his public addresses because of his ill-mannered insistence on haranguing his audiences about the wrongs perpetrated by whites against blacks. In the editor's view, Turner's diatribes on the horrors of the slave trade had little to do with establishing a church and more to do with fostering racial hatred. The editor dubbed Turner the "Archmischiefmaker" whose speeches had "poison[ed] the minds of the natives against the whites, fomenting disruption, and encouraging suspicion and discontent."[7]

Racialism aside, colonial missionary hostility toward the AMEC was in the main attributable to sheer fear of competition. Particularly toward the end of the nineteenth century, mission churches were racked with dissension over the lack of African ministerial advancement and the general color bar in the established churches. This difference culminated in a spate of secessions from virtually all the European denominations. Dissident African ministers either organized their own churches or flocked to the AMEC or the American black Baptists. They established their own schools as well, and they attempted to compete with European denominations for the few government subsidies that were made available to mission schools in the Cape.

It is clear from the early correspondence between the AMEC and their African correspondents that the magnet that most attracted them to the Americans was not so much doctrinal considerations as it was the large number of educational facilities operated by the church. Because the European mission societies controlled access to the educational facilities open to Africans, the secessionists had cut themselves off from the few institutions open to them. Therefore, a predominant theme in the correspondence between the black South Africans and Afro-Americans was the establishment of schools and, especially, a college. As one South African put it: "Give us . . . a college or an educational institute that will enable us . . . to stand upon the same platform as the white race . . . the same as the Negro is doing in America."[8] Indeed, African traditional leaders were much more amenable to proselytism if the establishment of a local school was part of the package.

Most certainly the AME educational goal of "the rudiments of an education for all, industrial training for the many and a college education for the talented few," was far in advance of any goal put forth by the mission societies for blacks, or for whites for that matter.[9] Given the fact that the Cape Colony subsidy for African education was minimal, which was far better than what was obtained in the northern republics where perhaps one in a hundred Africans was literate, the African churchmen who joined the AMEC were filled with high expectations about the educational promises held out by Afro-Americans.

It was on the issue of the black American influence on the education of Africans that the AMEC was savaged by one of its most unrelenting critics, the United Free Church of Scotland. The United Free Church operated Lovedale Institute, the foremost liberal educational institution in southern Africa open to Africans. It was a Hampton/Tuskegee type institution, albeit with a mixed European and African student body (though they ate and slept separately), and it was the first school to offer a teacher-training course for Africans.[10] In any case, shortly after Bishop Turner's visit, one of Lovedale's most dedicated African ministers, P. J. Mzimba, broke with the Presbyterians and formed an independent body of his own. The editor of the *Christian Express*, the United Free Church's mission organ, accused Turner of triggering the secession. From that point onward, the *Christian Express* dogged the AMEC and its missionaries' every move.

In addition to the institutional threat that the AMEC was perceived to pose to the established churches, European missionaries reacted with outrage and indignation toward the church for some very personal reasons. African churchmen were at odds with their former missionary overseers and their criticisms were published in the *Voice of Missions*. European missionaries were accused of pitting one African leader or ethnic group against the other. They were accused of living "in luxury off the sweat" of blacks, of "betraying" Africans because they stifled their aspirations for higher education for fear it would "spoil" them. And they were accused of maintaining a social distance between themselves and their parishioners.[11]

European churchmen also took issue with the AMEC's seeming territoriality regarding the African continent. They were incensed by the suggestion of the AMEC's secretary of missions that European churchmen relinquish the entire African field to black American missionaries. Having established AME societies in Pondoland, Basutoland, and Bechuanaland shortly after Turner's visit, the church's South African leaders envisioned moving out of southern Africa into Ethiopia and the Sudan and eventually belting the continent with AMEism. For AME churchmen, the promotion of Christianity was also the vehicle by which they could spread continental unity among Africans.[12]

Initially, the various government reactions to the AMEC were far less emotional than those of the missionary community. Prior to 1899, the Cape Colony government had recognized the AMEC as a legitimate church, as had the republican governments. Thus, AME ministers were permitted to solemnize marriages. However, following the Turner visit and the subsequent hostile reaction of European churchmen to the visit and to the expansion of the church into the Cape, the church began to attract the attention of colony government officials. In addition to the rather frequent criticisms leveled against the church in the various mission organs and in letters written to government officials, the AMEC attracted the attention of the authorities through its applications for church and school sites and through the marriage forms registered by AME ministers. In particular, the site applications captured the government's attention because the proposed sites were often located on crown lands and in districts where European mission societies were already in operation.

Faced with competition for adherents and in theory for government subsidies, European churchmen reacted angrily when local magistrates reconnoitered proposed sites before asking them for recommendations as to whether they should be approved. Unfortunately for church independents the magistrates frequently relied on local missionaries for information about the site and about AME activity in the area. Given the source of their information, it is predictable that in rendering their reports, the magistrates would label AME schools "opposition" schools and they would accuse the people who supervised them of being anti- white or of holding views that were antithetical to imperial ones.

As the negative reports reached the Native Affairs Department or the prime minister with increasing frequency, the Cape Colony government adopted a cautionary policy toward the AMEC. The secretary for Native Affairs, W. E. Stanford, was aware that if he denied all AME site applications, he ran the risk of being accused of discriminatory practices and thus would drive sympathetic recruits into the AME fold. Therefore, rather than deny AME site requests, the Native Affairs Department resorted to a policy of processing the applications in an intentionally dilatory manner and on completion of the process, more often than not the requests were denied. Colony officials resorted to these stymieing tactics in order to retard the growth of the AMEC, which they viewed as the "parent" of the South African independent church movement, or as they called it, "Ethiopianism." It was their contention that once the AMEC became isolated, the entire movement would collapse.

Even though several magistrates charged that the independents were manipulated behind the scenes by anti-imperialist Boers, the Colony government ministers took a less conspiratorial view of the situation. Though Prime Minister W. P. Schreiner felt "uneasy" about the movement, he nonetheless believed it was inevitable given the "intolerance" of European ministers and he pointed to the utterances contained in the *Christian Express* as a manifestation of this intolerance. Schreiner considered it important to contain the growth of the movement and not to martyr the proponents of church independence. His position was that his government should steer clear of a repressive course in dealing with the AMEs. While the secretary for native affairs concurred that the AMEs did not constitute a menace to state security, he insisted that the movement be monitored and its growth restricted through a denial of church and school sites and the issuance of marriage forms.[13] It was unfortunate for the AMEC that the Native Affairs Department's containment policy was instituted at a time when the church was rent by some internal troubles that gave the government the excuse to deny recognition of the church as a "legitimate" church and thereby deny acceptance of its ministers as marriage officers. Recognition was withheld from 1899 to 1901, when Levi J. Coppin arrived in Cape Town as the first resident bishop of the church.

By 1901, the AME American community in South Africa had grown to include Coppin; A. Henry Attaway, an educator who had been dispatched to run Bethel Institute, a high school and precursor to the proposed AME college; Conrad Rideout, a Seattle lawyer and educator who counseled Sigcau and Lerotholi, among others; and Harry Dean, an eccentric sea captain who had gone to South Africa in quest of an "Ethiopian Empire."

With the arrival of Attaway to run the educational program of the church, and with the increasing number of South Africans journeying to the United States to study in black institutions like Wilberforce and Lincoln universities, the European clergy alerted the government to the serious consequences of this African/American connection. The *Christian Express* warned that Africans educated in black American schools returned indoctrinated with the "dangerous poison" of race hatred which they spread to their gullible and uneducated brethren.[14]

Indeed, as early as 1897, a Cape Colony assemblyman warned that the African/Afro-American connection was potentially disruptive to South African race relations. He maintained that under AMEC influence, the African had begun to look to his black American counterpart rather than to his traditional liberal white allies for guidance and inspiration. He went on to say that since America's former slaves had risen to positions of achievement and influence, Africans looked to them as examples to emulate. He warned that should Africans follow suit, the colonial legislation which negated African rights would be hard to justify.[15]

Closely allied to this idea was the theory that black American notions of democracy, liberty, education, equality, and self-government would make the African difficult to control.[16] Africans had to be protected from "foreign political agitation in the guise of religion."[17] At all costs, then, Africans had to be kept away from black American schools.

James Stewart, Lovedale's principal, attributed an even more sinister plot to the African/Afro-American connection. Ironically, during his 1894 visit to Hampton Institute, he had suggested to some of its students that they should journey to Africa to help "uplift" their African brethren. However, in 1901, when it looked as though some black Americans were following his suggestion, Stewart told a government official that Europeans neither wanted nor needed American blacks in South Africa. He hinted at Boer collusion in the independent church movement and he waved the red flag of African enfranchisement. Stewart alleged that Africans in South Africa were in actuality agitating in behalf of southern blacks, who having failed during the post-Reconstruction period in America, were anxious to gain a foothold in the colony, after which they and their African allies would all vote together and presumably take over the reins of government.[18]

There was some reason for South African colonialists to believe a conspiracy was afoot for American blacks to emigrate to South Africa. Bishop Turner was after all an avowed emigrationist. He frequently published letters in the *Voice* written by African churchmen who called for skilled and professional blacks to emigrate to South Africa. They were exhorted to come to Africa in order to reclaim their "birthright" before Europeans had plundered all.[19]

Moreover, in the wake of Turner's visit, the call for American blacks to emigrate to South Africa reached a peak. Africans were joined in their invitation by black Americans already living in southern Africa. Stateside blacks were advised to come hurriedly to the continent before the "enemy" locked him out for good. By so doing, black Americans could compete with Europeans for land and cattle (no mention was made of their competition with Africans), and would therefore "enter honest competition for business and so enter the land to possess it."[20] Thus, between 1901 and 1904 when the American AMEs entered the Colony and a number of black American visitors passed through the

Colony, it looked to paranoid colonialists as if hordes of American blacks were flooding the Cape, and the charges of political agitation and incitement were leveled against the AMEC with increasing frequency and vehemence.

To be sure, many motives were attributed to the American AMEs for being in South Africa, but what exactly did the AME missionaries view as their rationale for being there? The first AME missionaries went to South Africa with the express purpose of bringing its millions out of "ignorance, and degradation and barbarism," as one of the church's bishops so colorfully described it. Therefore, their mission was not unlike that of European missionaries of the day. But the first AME emissaries also viewed their involvement in missions as a means of vindicating the race and of combating the notion of African "savagery" with which they were identified by virtue of their color. These men felt duty bound to work among black people scattered around the globe.

Although they were said to be racists and segregationists, Coppin and his men represented a church that was integrationist. Its slogan, "God our Father, Christ our Redeemer, and Man our Brother," attested to this fact. Moreover, the South African church counted among its members several Europeans.[21] Central to the character of the AME missionaries was their almost reverential respect for business acumen, which they viewed as the key to economic advancement. Business expertise was said to be the "watchword" of the AMEC, and so a number of the early AMEs went to South Africa with half-baked speculative schemes which more often than not ended badly for the African participants.

No less interested than their white counterparts in the breakdown of African "tribal" rule as a precondition for ushering in the millennium of "civilization and enlightenment," AME missionaries viewed British imperialism as essential to their missions' major goal. Therefore, they had an appreciation and respect for Great Britain and its alleged sense of "fair play." Thus, to a man, AME missionaries were pro-British regarding the Anglo-Boer War in which the country was then embroiled.

AME missionaries believed that the African had to prove himself worthy of being paced on a par with "civilized" peoples by improving himself morally, intellectually, and financially. Thus, they were willing to concede to a social division between blacks and whites. They also believed in a social division between the "raw" African from the rural areas and the educated one from the urban areas, but then so did the African leaders of the church. In addition, these black Americans believed themselves to be more culturally and intellectually advanced than the people they went out to Christianize. There was about them an overt and covert sense of cultural chauvinism that went to an extreme in someone like Attaway but that was more subtle in Coppin and Rideout.[22]

The first AME missionaries were basically self-made individuals who had risen to prominence in their respective communities by dint of hard work. They were relatively educated and well-to-do financially. To the extent that any of them could be described as political, Rideout seems to have been the only one who left the United States for any reason approaching a political one.[23] In short, these men were cautious, conservative in temperament, and petit bourgeois in orientation and outlook. They were supremely confident in the justness of their mission, which was not to be endangered by some reckless act or statement on their part or on the part of their subordinates. These men were not the zealots, the incendiaries envisioned and projected by their colonialist detractors.

Both African and Afro-American AMEs were almost naively loyal to the British crown. The AMEC viewed the advent of British suzerainty over the two republics of the Transvaal and Orange Free State as the precondition for racial justice and equality throughout South Africa. There were a number of African propagandists in the United States who wrote articles that were printed in AME newspapers and who gave speeches that were delivered from AME podiums, all extolling the superiority of British over Boer rule. AME prelates, particularly those who were colonial-born like Bishops W. B. Derrick and Charles S. Smith (both of whom served in South Africa), were adamantly British in their sympathies. Derrick went so far as to push through a church resolution supporting the British against the "misguided" Boers.[24]

Even though the AME's credentials as loyalists to the British crown were flawless, the Native Affairs Department continued to receive letters from Europeans impugning the AMEC as a front for Boer rebels, or accusing the church's ministers of teaching their followers that Africans were the rightful owners of Africa and were therefore entitled to be treated as the owners of the land. Predictably, the initial cries of sedition emanated from Natal. With its miniscule European population surrounded by the recently subdued Zulu, the establishment of the independent churches was envisioned as the precursor to the overthrow of European control.

The Natal governor was determined that the "American agitators shall not play the deuce with our natives under the guise of religion." And so, black American missionaries were banned from his colony.[25] A magistrate in the Transkeian territories charged that American blacks were planning to acquire large tracts of land in central South Africa for the purpose of establishing a nation governed exclusively by men of color.[26] Defiantly, the *Cape Telegraph* declared that the European was in South Africa to stay, the American-induced cries of "Africa for the African" notwithstanding. Europeans had not "the faintest intention of giving it up to please American Ethiopians."[27]

To counter the bad press the church received, Attaway circulated a pamphlet in which he denied that he or his fellow missionaries were "adventurers, . . . theorists, . . . [or] politicians." "Our policy," he said, "has been everywhere to gracefully adjust ourselves to the prevailing political, economic and social exegencies [*sic*]."[28] To negate Attaway's disclaimer of any seditious intent on the part of the AMEC, the *Christian Express* reprinted from the *Voice of Missions* a letter (published nine months earlier) from a Haitian domestic. In the letter, she predicted that ultimately the Africans would "whip" the British back to the Thames as the Haitians had repelled the French.[29]

In the wake of the *Christian Express* exposé, the *Cape Times* called for an official inquiry into the independent church movement and a proscription of any organization supporting the views expressed in the letter.[30] And the *Eastern Province Herald* viewed the letter as proof of a planned Afro-American seizure of the African continent and the overthrow of the imperialist governments.[31]

As a result of the hysteria generated by the Haitian letter and in anticipation of a Parliamentary inquiry, Alfred Milner, high commissioner for South Africa, called for an official inquiry into the Ethiopian movement. In mid-1902, the Native Affairs Department solicited reports from the district magistrates on the activities of the independent churches. When it is recalled that many of these magistrates were colonial-born and held all the views of the colonialists, and that they interpreted their role to be that of reconciling Boer and Briton, it is not surprising that the reports on the AMEC and other independent churches were on the whole uncomplimentary. As with similar inquiries, the magistrates relied on rival European missionaries, white traders, or African informants for their information.

Despite the Native Affairs Department's official inquiry into the independent churches and despite the mischievous motives attributed to them, the government was unable to collect any concrete evidence against the AMEC with which to prosecute the church for sedition. The only thing that could be proved was that Africans were indeed leaving the established missions to join independent churches. In the absence of concrete proof that the AMEC was a seditious organization, even during the "Black Peril" scare of 1904, the Cape government continued to view the AMEC and other independent churches as more annoying than dangerous. This was particularly true after 1906 when the AMEC was cleared of any involvement in the Bambata (Zulu) Rebellion and after the South African Native Affairs Commission absolved the church of any political mischief.

Although after Coppin's successful lobbying efforts the Cape government renewed its recognition of the AMEC as a legiti-, mate church and licensed a limited number of AME ministers as marriage officers, it continued to grant AME school and church site requests sparingly. Taking advantage of wartime travel restrictions, the government refused American AMEs travel permits to visit the northern republics. These restrictions were maintained long after the war ceased. The travel restrictions sorely hampered centralized control over the church's ministers. As a result, the bishops of the church began to send a number of declarations to the Colonial Office wherein they affirmed their loyalty to the British crown, their respect for the law, and their obedience to constituted authority. They reiterated that much of the trouble said to be caused by their African ministers was beyond their control because they were prevented from traveling to the northern colonies to supervise the ministers.

The church twice sent one of its colonial-born bishops, W. B. Derrick, to the Colonial Office to get the travel ban on Afro-Americans to the northern colonies lifted. His second attempt was successful, but the lift was short-lived. Because of the "very strong and unanimous feeling" among Europeans in South Africa about the "disturbing effects" of the AMEC, which was expressed at the Johannesburg Missionary Conference held in 1904, Milner once again placed the travel ban into effect.[32]

Undaunted, the AMEC appealed to President Theodore Roosevelt to intercede in its behalf with the British government.[33] The U.S. ambassador in London went through the motions of presenting the AME case to the Foreign Office, but it is clear that he was not inclined to press the matter. Hence, black Americans continued to be denied entry to the Transvaal and Orange Free State colonies.

Clearly, certain disabilities and limitations were placed on the expansion of the church in the Cape Colony during the post-Anglo-Boer War period. Nonetheless, African church members of the Cape continued in an optimistic and certainly aggressive way to procure church and school sites and to press for recognition of additional ministers as marriage officers. They inundated the Native Affairs Department and the Department of Education with site and education subsidy applications. When these requests were not honored, they occasionally built churches and schools on unauthorized plots. The AMEs sent countless delegations to interview the secretary of native affairs or the prime minister concerning church grievances. They wrote scores of petitions and letters of protest to local newspapers, the colonial secretary, and the Cape Parliament. Because they often bypassed the local magistrates, the antagonism between the AMEs and the local officials intensified. In addition African AMEs became embroiled in local political issues such as location removals and discriminatory inoculation ordinances whose constitutionality they threatened to test in the supreme court. Some AMEs went so far as to threaten to withhold their votes from Cape Assembly members who would not aid them in their religious and secular struggles.[34]

Fellow AME members in the Transvaal and Orange Free State colonies had a different and more difficult struggle, and they did not fare nearly as well. Milner had appointed as his Transvaal commissioner for native affairs Godfrey Lagden, who had a poor opinion of Africans in general but was exceedingly intolerant of so-called nontribal, educated Africans. Lagden consistently made the lot of AME ministers a difficult one by refusing to pay the slightest attention to their requests or by refusing to meet their delegations on the grounds that organized groups did not represent "legitimate" African interests.

The AME experience with the Transvaal and Orange Free State government officials in the postwar period demonstrates quite well that contrary to AME expectations, British control did not loosen the chains that bound Africans socially and politically in the former Boer republics but rather tightened them. Under British suzerainty, no black man in the former republics was recognized as a marriage officer, no recognition was given to independent churches, and no grants-in-aid were allocated to African independent schools. The Transvaal caretaker government was exceedingly vigilant concerning schools that operated independent of British control. It looked to the Boer Christian National Education schools for evidence of the potential that these independent institutions held for fostering nationalism. Transvaal AME ministers were, as a matter of course, denied exemption to the pass laws, a situation that prompted AMEs to defy the laws. Unlike the Republican days, AMEs were no longer recognized as ministers; and therefore, they were denied rail concession tickets, which were crucial to struggling, impoverished ministers.

What is clear from the AMEC requests for fair and impartial treatment in the Transvaal, Orange Free State, and Cape colonies is that neither the Africans nor their Anglophile Afro-American missionaries realized that the British plan for South Africa did not include a change in the pattern of race relations. In reality, African aspirations ran counter to imperial aims. Milner conceded that to reconcile the Boer to British rule would mean sacrificing the African.[35] And this he did. Furthermore, it should be borne in mind that some of the most stridently vocal and influential critics of the AMEC were the old, British settler supremacist groups like the "Rand Pioneers."

In conclusion, AME missionaries entered South Africa at a time when black American missionaries viewed Africa as their special domain. The AMEC, which was the best organized and most aggressive of the black churches involved in mission activities, took a leading role in what one scholar has called the Evangelical Pan-Africanist movement.[36] Although accused by the colonial authorities of being the "parent of Ethiopianism" and of importing racialist doctrines into the country, the fact is that the AMEC entered South Africa more than two decades after South Africans began their exodus from the established churches. The AMEC's first emissaries were "impeccably gradualist,"[37] as one historian has described them. What they imported into the country was Booker T. Washington's philosophy of thrift, capital accumulation, and character-building, in short, all the middle-class values inherent in the AMEC.

To the extent that the AMEC was involved in South African "politics," the impetus came from its African, not its American, members. It was Africans who organized along interethnic lines. They led the delegations and wrote the countless petitions; they confronted the Cape Town Parliament and the Transvaal commissioner for native affairs much to the consternation of the Americans resident in the Cape. The AMEs' reputation for "insolent" behavior in part sprang from the African resolve to constantly and persistently approach the imperial authorities when they felt aggrieved. Indeed, in the colonialist view, the African AMEs were so obstreperous in their approach that Coppin was repeatedly requested by the authorities to clamp down on the activities and behavior of his ministers. The government placed him in the untenable position of being the conduit through which his African ministers were told to communicate with the government. On more than one occasion, Coppin was forced to repudiate the actions and utterances of his ministers. In spite of this ploy, the African AMEs no less than their secular counterparts—the African Political Organization, the various congresses, the myriad vigilance societies that claimed as members a number of AMEs—continued to organize and agitate to secure and protect their limited rights as citizens in the newly constituted British South Africa.

European clergymen raised the initial cries of rebellion and revolt. They did so out of jealousy and fear of competition. Settler colonies are always rife with rumors of a "native" uprising and so these clergymen were joined in their alarm by some secular authorities as well. Although the imperial government never seriously considered the AMEC a threat to state security, during the war years it certainly feared an African revolt. Having failed to keep its wartime promises to better the lot of its African loyalists, during the reconstruction period, the government could not totally discount the possibility that the church independents could lead an uprising. When it became clear that the independent church movement was not the nucleus of a "native" uprising, the Cape Colony government sought to contain its growth by limiting the access of black Americans to their African charges in the north, by sparingly allocating crown lands for its churches and schools, by denying its schools government subsidies, and by limiting the number of men it authorized as marriage officers.

Order had to be reestablished within the European missions, for mission schools and churches were crucial to British political and economic interests and to the maintenance of the status quo. The hard-liner Transvaal and Orange Free State caretaker governments refused to recognize the church in any way. They neither granted the AMEC school sites on crown lands nor allocated government subsidies to the church's schools. Natal, on the other hand, categorically refused to allow AMEs, whether American or African, to enter the colony.

As a result of real and imagined AME activities in South Africa, the black American, and the black American missionary in particular, became *persona non grata* in colonial southern Africa. In 1912, at the International Conference of the Negro, representatives from the various American black churches involved in African missions appealed to Booker T. Washington to journey to South Africa and to apprise the authorities of the good intentions of black American missionaries. In fact, as late as 1926, at the International Conference on the Christian Mission in Africa at Le Zoute, Belgium, black American missionaries were still unsuccessfully trying to convince white mission societies and colonial governments that they were responsible churchmen and as such should be allowed unfettered entry into Africa.

Notes

1. For a detailed account of the AMEC and the Ethiopian Church merger, see Josephus R. Coan's classic study of the early history of the AMEC in South Africa: "The Expansion of the Missions of the African Methodist Episcopal Church in South Africa, 1896-1908" (Ph.D. dissertation, Hartford Seminary Foundation, 1961).

2. There was, of course, no "South Africa" before the union in 1910, but for the sake of simplicity, in this essay the republics of the Transvaal and the Orange Free State, as well as the Cape and Natal colonies, are referred to as South Africa.

3. Lewis G. Jordan, *Up the Ladder in Foreign Missions* (Nashville, Tenn.: National Baptist Publishing Board, 1901), pp. 21, 127-128.

4. Letter, J. Z. Tantsi to H. M. Turner, *Voice Of Missions*, September 1897 and July 1898.

5. For more on the allowances made for black Americans in South Africa, see E. De Waal, "American Black Residents and Visitors in the S. A. R. Before 1899," *South African Historical Journal* 6 (November 1974): 52-55.

6. *Imvo Zabantsundu*, April 20, 1898. Jabavu apparently followed the activities of the AMEC rather closely, reporting at one point that Bishop Turner had instructed blacks to shoot whites. (*Voice of Missions*, September 1897, Letter J. Z. Tantsi to Turner.) It should be recalled that Jabavu was a committed Wesleyan who felt beholden to the church. Therefore, it is predictable that he would take an anti-independent church stand. Moreover, Jabavu resented any threat to his position as spokesman for the "native." Another member of the educated elite placed in a similar position was the United Free Church's Elijah Makiwane. He described the independent churches as "intensely anti-white" and accused its leaders of using coercive tactics to recruit members. See

Letter, Elijah Makiwane to the Department of Education, November 12, 1901, Republic of South Africa Government Archives, Cape Town, NA 498. Hereafter cited with letter and Native Affairs Department file number (NA).

7. *Christian Express*, July 1, 1898, and March 7, 1899.

8. Letter, Edward Gow to H. M. Turner, *Voice of Missions*, June 1900.

9. Ibid., May 1900.

10. R. H. W. Shepherd, *Lovedale, South Africa, 1841-1941* (Cape Province: Lovedale Press, 1941), p. 98.

11. See for example the letter from J. Tule to the AMEC: *Voice of Missions*, March 1896. See also, M. Mokone to W. H. Councill, *Voice of Missions*, April 1896; and Edward Gow to H. Turner, *Voice of Missions*, November 1900.

12. In point of fact, some colonialists believed that the southern Africa independent church movement was a component of the Pan-African movement launched at the 1900 London Conference. See Dwane's report before the AME Council of Bishops, February 1899 in B. W. Arnett's *Episcopal Handbook for 1900*, pp. 39-40.

13. Letter, A. W. Preston to the Secretary for Native Affairs, March 15, 1898; Letter, P. J. Mavavana et al., to the Commissioner of Land and Public Works, November 19, 1898; Letter, H. C. Elliott to Secretary for Native Affairs, February 24, 1898, NA 498.

14. *Christian Express*, December 1, 1901.

15. *Christian Express*, September 6, 1897, and October 6, 1897.

16. Letter, Reverend T. R. Curnick to Resident Magistrate Butterworth, September 1, 1902, NA 447.

17. Letter, Resident Magistrate Bedford to the Native Affairs Department, September 1, 1902, NA 498.

18. Letter, James Stewart to Colonel Hutchinson, September 10, 1901, NA 497.

19. Letter, M. Mokone to H. Turner, *Voice of Missions*, July 1897.

20. Letter, R. A. Jackson to Turner, *Voice of Missions*, April 1898; and Letter, H. Scott to Turner, *Voice of Missions*, October 1899.

21. Levi J. Coppin, *Observations of Persons and Things in South Africa* (n.p., n.d.), pp. 32, 37.

22. See especially Attaway's essay "The Part The Twentieth Century Negro Will Play in the World's Civilization" in *Voice of Missions*, February 1901. See also the lecture he delivered at Cape Town's Metropolitan Hall reproduced in *Voice of Missions*, January 1902.

23. *Voice of Missions*, August 1899. Rideout's activities as legal advisor to Basutoland's Lerotholi and Sigcau of Pondoland raised the ire of colonial officials. See "Correspondence of the High Commissioner" S5/22 in the Lesotho Government Archives.

24. *A. M. E. Christian Recorder*, May 10, 1900.

25. H. E. McCallum to Chamberlain, April 23, 1902, Public Record Office, London, CO 179-224. Hereafter cited with letter and Public Record Office file number (CO).

26. Letter, H. C. Ellliot to the Secretary of Native Affairs, December 24, 1901. There was talk of such a scheme in the February 1901 issue of *Voice of the People*, which also circulated in South Africa. This newspaper was the official organ of the Colored National Emigration Association and was edited by Bishop Turner. It should be recalled that J. Albert Thorne was actively engaged in his Central African emigration project which was publicized in the *Voice of Missions*.

27. *Cape Daily Telegraph*, May 30, 1902.

28. Pamphlet found in CO 48-559. See also his letter to the *Cape Times*, reprinted in the *A. M. E. Christian Recorder*, August 7, 1902.

29. *Christian Express*, August 1, 1902.

30. *Cape Times Weekly Edition*, August 13, 1902. The word "Ethiopianism" was used to describe the breakaway movement of African churchmen who left the established churches to form independent ones. See George Shepperson, "Ethopianism: Past and Present," in *Christianity in Tropical Africa*, ed. C. G. Baeta (London: Oxford University Press, 1968).

31. *Eastern Province Herald*, August 13, 1902.

32. Letter, Milner to Lyttelton, July 22, 1904, CO 297-71.

33. Letter, AME Bishops to Theodore Roosevelt, February 21, 1905, "Miscellaneous Letters of the Department of State," U. S. Government Archives, Washington, D.C., R. G. 59, M 179, Roll 124.

34. *South African News Edition*, March 13 and 20, 1901; April 1901.

35. G. H. L. LeMay, *British Supremacy in South Africa 1899-1907* (Oxford: Clarendon Press, 1965), p. 11.

36. Tony Martin, "Some Reflections on Evangelical Pan-Africanism" or "Black Missionaries, White Missionaries and the Struggle for African Souls 1890-1930," *Ufahamu* 1 (Winter 1971): 77-92. For more on the Afro-American involvement in the mission movement of the late nineteenth and early twentieth centuries, see Donald Franklin Roth, "'Grace Not Race': Southern Negro Church Leaders, Black Identity, and Missions to West Africa, 1865-1919" (Ph.D. dissertation, University of Texas at Austin, 1975); and Walter Lee Williams, "Black American Attitudes Toward

Africa: The Missionary Movement, 1877-1900" (Ph.D. dissertation, University of North Carolina at Chapel Hill, 1974).

37. Donald Denoon, *A Grand Illusion: The Failure of Imperial Policy in the Transvaal Colony During the Period of Reconstruction, 1900-1905* (London: Longman, 1973), p. 107.

Missionary-Government Relations: Black Americans in British and Portuguese Colonies

10

Lillie M. Johnson

This essay was inspired by a desire to attack the myth of African colonialism which says: "First the Bible, then the sword." The intent of the research is not merely to defend missionary work. It is an effort to analyze the historical relationship of missions and government during the colonial period. This analysis is based on the assumption that foreign missions and colonial governments existed primarily as autonomous, self-seeking entities. However, in any study of political and social structures, there are overlapping concerns, religion being one of the more powerful and ambiguous. It is worthwhile, therefore, to give the missionary effort a fair chance to show what lay beneath the "Go Ye Therefore" impulse of Christianity as it worked its way through the colonial system.

Another assumption, not directly discussed in this essay but a part of its rationale, concerns the African role in missionary work. The missionary myth not only implies that Africans were subdued by Christianity, but also that they were indiscriminately receptive to missionary teachings. Any knowledge of African religions, the religious content of African rebellions, or European Christian traditions, reveals that Christianity has been reinterpreted, misinterpreted, and syncretized into various bodies with various practices. Christianity for Africans, even within colonialism, was no different. It is not, necessarily, the opiate of the people.[1]

The position of black American missionaries in colonial Africa was unique. They represented a complex combination of an oppressed, educated, middle-class racial group in America, exercising cultural authority and expressing paternalistic superiority over Africans, yet working within the European colonial system. The complex nature of their work encompasses the interests of students of African history, Afro-American history, and religious history, as well as those who believed in the Christian ideals of the missionary effort.

The problem for both colonial governments and black American missions was to find a niche within the colonial system for a foreign, black, philanthropic organization. As far as the black missionaries were concerned, there were several motives and goals in entering the African mission field. Their basic desire, not differing from that of white mission workers, was to Christianize Africans.[2] Their motives, however, included a keen feeling of brotherhood for Africans. At the 1902 Negro Young People's Christian and Educational Congress in Atlanta, the following sentiments were expressed:

African natives can best be reached by the American Negro. First because he is identified with him; this identification gives him a true knowledge of those whom he would help. This is one of the essentials to the success of all missionary effort.

The Negro, in the second place, is in sympathy with his race. It is his own and not another's. The American Negro is the bone and sinew of the African Negro, and he can not separate himself from nor refuse to feel an interest in and a love for the members of his own family that no other race can feel.[3]

Nevertheless, this racial identification did not end the black missionaries' feelings of superiority or check their opinions on African "backwardness," "heathenism," "paganism," and the like.[4] However, the social importance of the church as the focal point of the black community—as an autonomous organization for community power, status, and mobility—was transferred with these prejudicial attitudes. Otherwise, black American missionaries found a comfortable place in the colonial system. The existence of colonialism did not seem to bother them or to contradict the Christian tenets on which their work was based. In a 1924 letter to editor Robert S. Abbott of the *Chicago Defender*, Reverend Henry C. McDowell gave his opinion of colonialism by stating that he "takes no stock in any considerable portion of Africa passing wholly into the hands of colored people."[5] Later, in a 1926 letter to the Portuguese Chefe de Poste Manuel Antonio Broz of Angola, the black Congregationalist missionary, McDowell, stated that he did not want the missions to be considered "American" or "foreign," "but as an institution dedicated to the sound principles of government for which Portugal stands, and the progress and Christianization of the peoples of this region . . . to impart . . . to the native peoples . . . a real patriotism and high appreciation of the heroic nation that by discovery and historical connections they are now a part."[6] Although these statements suggest complete cooperation between black missions and government, the latter statement being overt flattery, the considerable degree of ambiguities within each group and problems between them require a closer investigation of the relationship.

Conflict and cooperation are not passive attitudes, but can be manifested through various forms, methods, and organized structures. The historical issue here concerns when conflict and cooperation existed, and how these situations were handled by missions and government. This essay examines the specific roles of black American missionaries[7] in Africa as an example of the general role of voluntary institutions in the colonial superstructure. It focuses on the degree to which black American missions could affect government policies on colonial development, and the attitudes and policies of the colonial government toward them. This approach adds to earlier research[8] by placing mission work within the broader historical perspective of colonial policies. It also extends black mission studies into the mid-twentieth century, the core of the colonial period Thus, the purpose of this essay is to survey the historical linkages between the black American missionary and the colonizing process. The basic assumption is that they were both constantly influencing or were influenced by political and economic decisions. Missions and colonial governments were not always collaborators and allies in imperialism.

This survey of black mission-government relations covers the period 1900-1940, concentrating on the interwar years. The years 1920-1940 were especially crucial for the development of new colonial and black American issues. For black Americans, the 1920s brought the political and economic ideology of the charismatic Marcus Garvey and his Universal Negro Improvement Association (UNIA). An earlier period saw the rise of the National Association for the Advancement of Colored People (NAACP) in 1910 and the first issue of its publication, *Crisis*. It was a stimulating period for the urban black intelligentsia and artists, known as the Harlem Renaissance.

For missionaries, the interwar years brought disillusionment over the destruction and immorality of World War I. The war had demonstrated that missionary work could be superseded by the political concerns of government. It presented the most poignant case of the extent to which mission difficulties could develop because of national prestige and military necessities of European governments. Discarding their pre-World War I apolitical policy, the missionaries adopted the role of helping to reconstruct colonial policy on African development and on missionary participation in that policy. The war not only stimulated a strong American missionary consciousness and new international role, but it also intensified the missionary's evangelical zeal because it had exposed the colonial world to European immorality. The issues of colonization and trusteeship, along with William E. B. Du Bois's Pan-African Congresses, focused attention on African and Asian peoples. Postwar strategy for missions, as discussed at the Foreign Missions Conference of North America in the early 1920s, included a continuing belief in the humanitarianism of British rule and in the unselfish role of America as an experienced third party that could best institute the philanthropic development of mandates and colonies.[9]

The problems of Africa during this period were based largely upon European fears of indigenous insubordination and rebellion, incited by independent religious activities. This is exemplified by the 1921 Kimbangu movement in the Belgian Congo, a separatist church movement led by Simon Kimbangu whose work was suppressed, with difficulty, by the Belgian government as a political threat. Such religious forms of African discontent were often manifestations of economic disorders and the difficulties of wartime. In such cases, religion served as an organizational tool or as a source of spiritual power.

The three major black denominations began mission work in Africa before the formal establishment of colonial rule.[10] The African Methodist Episcopal Church (AME), the African Methodist Episcopal Zion Church (AMEZ), and the National Baptist Convention (Baptist) initiated missions in Liberia in 1820, 1876, and 1883, respectively. AME missions were established in Sierra Leone in 1886 and in South Africa in 1892. The Baptists also had a South African Mission in 1895, and Nigerian work began in 1887. The AMEZ Church had a Gold Coast Mission by 1896.[11] Although church work in Liberia was the earliest and the most intensive that was established in Africa, much of this work was a denominational extension of services in order to maintain existing Christian communities. With resettled Christian slaves from the United States, southern Liberia was a successful case of colonization and church expansion. Thus, mission work with Liberians did not involve proselytizing to non-Christians as much as it involved the formal establishment of church congregations and the training of pastors for Liberian Christians.[12]

At first glance, after Liberia, British colonies would logically seem to be a primary area for black American mission work since there would have been no denominational, political, or language barriers. In spite of this logic, the British systematically blocked black American work in their African colonies. There is evidence of government measures taken against black Americans.[13]

Black Americans did work as missionaries in predominantly white denominations, the topic of Wilbur Christian Harr's 1945 dissertation. Harr concludes that, for a variety of reasons, predominantly white missions, even those that had used black missionaries in the nineteenth century, used them with rare exception in the twentieth century.[14] The most pertinent observation here is that one reason given for this change was the negative attitude of colonial governments in Africa against black Americans. For by the beginning of the twentieth century, colonial governments had begun to view black American missionaries as potential troublemakers and had encouraged churches to use only white missionaries.[15]

In examining the issues involved in government-black mission relations, it is necessary to examine the independent ambiguities of the values and methods of each side, and subsequently the varying patterns of ambiguity in their relationship to one another. The goals of any mission group appear to be most clearly stated in religious terms of their proselytizing efforts to Christianize as found in scripture: "Go ye therefore, and teach all nations, baptizing them in the name of the Father, and the Son, and of the Holy Ghost: Teaching them to observe all things whatsoever I have commanded you." (Saint Matthew, 28:19-20.)

However, mission rhetoric also professed to improve the "civilization" and culture of the dispossessed. Especially following World War I, missions were to compensate for the immorality of the industrial world by being the saviors of Africa and Asia. Such attitudes could at times take the form of upholding the myth of the innocent and "childlike noble savage" against the immoral and aggressive Western man. This dilemma brings into question the civilizing/Westernizing efforts of missionaries. Reverend Henry C. McDowell saw mission work as an aid in the development of the "civilizado."[16] At this stage, the original religious goals take on new social dimensions, some of which are inconsistent with the conservative nature of mission work or at other times conflict with mission efforts to effect change. The ambiguity of the missionary position lies in this dilemma of progressive versus conservative attitudes.

Likewise, in the case of European powers, Africa was partitioned and developed along rather unclear lines, or at least was regarded along several lines. There is a full range of historical debate on the motives and goals of colonial empires, illuminating the varieties of colonization between and within each European enclave.[17] In spite of the stereotype labels placed on the colonial powers—the benevolent, paternal British; the scientific Germans; the expansionist French; the cruel Belgians; and the exploitative Portuguese—each government tried to respond to various colonial situations in the most expedient way. This was done regardless of what was "on paper." This same flexibility

applied to mission workers. While "cooperation" with governments would be the natural position for foreign organizations in
the colonies, missions would ideally want to be considered independent of government. However, colonial attitudes and policies, official and unofficial, were not to be ignored.

Visa restrictions were the most frequently mentioned problem
between black missionaries and the British government, in particular. For West Africa, restriction ordinances against "alien
missionaries and teachers" provided additional barriers to entering British territories. A memo from the American consul, W. J.
Yerby, in Dakar, Senegal, revealed that, in addition to visa regulations, it was necessary for each missionary or teacher to secure
the permission of the governor of a colony before entering for
mission service.[18] This added regulation increased the difficulty
of entering British West Africa and increased the unpredictabil-
ity of decisions based on individual preferences.

Black mission difficulties with the British focus on South Africa, but not exclusively. One exceptional incident occurred in
South Africa in 1921 when Bishop William T. Vernon and family
were detained for three days upon their arrival at Cape Town,
by order of an official of the Immigration Department. Bishop
Vernon was the fifth bishop assigned to South Africa by the
AME Church since 1900. He was detained by the immigration
officer as an "undesirable alien," in spite of his visa, letters of
recommendation from prominent Americans, and his former
position in President Theodore Roosevelt's second administration. The portion of the 1913 Immigration Act of the Union of
South Africa (Act No. 22) which restricted "any person or class
or persons deemed by the Minister on economic grounds or on
account of standard and habits of life to be unsuited to the
requirements of the Union or any particular Province thereof"
was the basis of Bishop Vernon's detention, as well as the
general ministerial order prohibiting the entry of all "colored"
persons into the Union of South Africa.[19] With the aid of the
American consul general at Cape Town, Bishop Vernon and his
family eventually gained entrance into the Union of South Africa.

Later in the 1920s, articles on black American access to Africa
appeared in *The Foundation*, the publication of the Gammon Theo-

logical Seminary. A 1923 article stated that "an American Negro, however well prepared, to find access to the schools of Africa as a teacher, or to enter the continent as a preacher, Y.M.C.A. worker, or in any form of social uplift work has been understood as a difficult undertaking."[20] A longer 1927 article expressed the same sentiments in even greater detail.[21]

It is somewhat ironic that during this postwar period of British apprehension over a black American presence in its African colonies, plans were being discussed to establish the Tuskegee/Hampton model of education[22] in British Africa, particularly in Kenya, where there were no black American missions at that time. Part of this plan included sending African students to the United States to study, as well as sending black American students to work in Africa. The important factor here is that the American debate on liberal arts versus industrial/vocational education for black people was apparently known in international and colonial circles. With the encouragement of American philanthropy and its powerful representatives, for example, Thomas Jesse Jones of the Phelps-Stokes Fund, colonial governments favored the Tuskegee plan of vocational education as more beneficial to Africans than the liberal arts emphasis of the W. E. B. Du Bois school of thought.

In the British case, after 1919 as they solidified not only policies against "alien" missionaries, but also policies to control the education of Africans, black American missionaries were attacked. Black Americans remained the exception in the British open-door policy to missionaries, for that door was closed to them. Granted some black missionaries entered Nigeria, Sierra Leone, Gambia, and the Gold Coast, but those numbers were small.[23]

The black Congregational mission work in Angola challenges the usual barriers to black American missions in colonial Africa. This does not mean that problems did not exist, but that the problems were cushioned by diplomatic strategy on both sides. This Portuguese West African colony did have language and denominational barriers. Its official language was Portuguese, and its dominant religion was Catholicism. The Congregational Church and its established missions in Angola were probably aware of the extensive international publicity surrounding forced labor, slavery, and other atrocities of cocoa plantations. Since the investigation of these events took place between 1900 and 1910,[24] approximately ten years prior to black mission work, the Congregational Church would have had knowledge of these practices. It is probable that such problems would have encouraged rather than discouraged mission work in this particular colony, for missionaries are often drawn to sites of greatest moral challenge.

Actually, Angola was the easiest African colony to enter, with the exception of Liberia. Research by Dr. Cornelius H. Patton, one of the Mission Board secretaries, had shown that placement in southern Africa was impossible. The Rhodesian government had replied that "the Government does not view the introduction of these people for mission purposes, whether independently or under control, with favor."[25]

To offset some of the disadvantages of the Portuguese field, American missionaries were required to spend six months in Lisbon to learn the Portuguese language. In the case of black Americans, a one-year apprenticeship under white missionaries in Angola was also required.[26]

The selection of the first black missionary was of great concern to the all-white Mission Board. Prospective candidates were nominated by the Sustaining Committee, a group of black Congregationalists representing the "Supporters of the New Station or Stations in the West Central Africa Mission for American Negro Workers." At the October 1917 General Council Meeting in Columbus, Ohio, thirty to forty black delegates met with Dr. Patton. Reverend Henry C. McDowell was nominated and later appointed as one of the first black missionaries for the Congregational Church in Angola.

In spite of barriers of race and nationality, McDowell and his workers expressed a close affinity to "reputable houses" of established Portuguese families and for high-ranking officials. McDowell cultivated a congenial working relationship with the Portuguese through cordial visits to and from government officials. The mission attitude was one of respect for the position, rank, and authority of the government with a desire for reciprocal respect from Portuguese officials. The location of the new station at Galangue was an example of this cordiality. When the new station was formed in 1922, it was located on the main highway, partly to give the mission more contact with Portuguese officials.[27]

At the same time that McDowell and his colleagues were able to maintain amiable relations with government officials, conflict and subsequent complaints occurred over several issues: Portuguese traders, education, land purchases and property titles, and treatment of Africans. The earliest missionary complaints concerned land concessions. Although missions were allowed to settle freely on good agricultural land, cut timber, build houses and villages, develop irrigation, and use water power, they could not obtain titles to land.[28] In a letter dated October 5, 1920, McDowell complained of the hundreds of Europeans who had come to Angola and had bought large, choice areas of land. These immigrants and traders were the major group of Portuguese who came under frequent attack from McDowell. According to him, these sentiments were mutual because missionaries interfered with the Portuguese slave and liquor trade.[29]

Mission work was directly hindered in other ways. By September 1921, education requirements had become a major problem. The Portuguese government decreed that all school work had to be done in Portuguese. African languages were forbidden except for preaching.[30] What troubled the missionaries most was the extent of these new regulations. The missionaries were agreeable to the "civilizing mission" of teaching European languages, traditions, and history, but they did not want to eliminate the indigenous languages. In an effort to compromise, McDowell decided to conform to the Portuguese requirements and government regulations, while working toward keeping the vernacular for religious work. These efforts were not very well received as indicated by an editorial in the *Benguella Journal* which saw it as the reasonable duty of the mission to put forth a greater effort to teach the Portuguese language.[31]

The missionaries had ambiguous feelings about the success of their "civilizing mission." In 1922, when seventy-five out of seventy-eight school boys passed the government exam to teach school, McDowell viewed it as a "victory fraught with difficulties" because the students would be entitled to government salaries and Portuguese citizenship. McDowell was unclear as to why this situation was a "step into the dark."[32] The problem could have been the result of competition between government and missions for African workers and loyalty. Thus, McDowell may have felt a sense of loss when mission students entered into government service. In this same year, McDowell wrote to Dr. Alfred Lawless of the Sustaining Committee explaining that missions had to be careful because the government was suspicious of their harboring Africans. McDowell advocated faith in government friendliness to Africans and faith in the potential mobility of Africans. His major point here was that missions should not compete with government by taking too many people into their concession. These are, however, sentiments that conflict with the natural mission goal of increasing the number of Christians.[33]

Several areas of conflict directly involved the African population. In February 1921, McDowell wrote to a financial contributor to the mission, about a new government regulation concerning African taxation. Prior to this new regulation, there had been a "hut tax" for which the head of the family had paid taxes on his home. The new regulation instituted a poll tax (head tax) requiring every boy over fifteen or sixteen to pay. This financial burden forced some boys out of the Boys' Boarding School in order that they might earn money for their taxes.[34] This case is an example of indirect government interference with missions. This particular problem was settled by adjusting to regulations rather than protesting against the difficulties. To keep students from forced labor for tax payments, the mission paid the head tax for its students with a donation to the mission.

Other problems concerned the living and working conditions of the local populations. Forced labor was a major issue. In his January 1926 report entitled "Survey of Important Events and Conditions in Angola During 1925," American Consul Francis H. Styles included a report on African labor taken from a presentation by Professor Emory Ross at the League of Nations. The "anti-foreign element" in Angola was disturbed by Styles' report, as bitter feelings against the American missions in An-

gola grew with the belief that they had furnished the information. Even American trade was affected slightly by the report.

The missionaries, however, were timid in attacking these problems. Having some control in these situations involving Africans who were associated with the mission station, the missionaries made more of an effort to ease the labor situation. Their
overall answer to labor and other economic problems was education. This is not surprising since the same solution was the
major focus of black mobility in the United States. This solution
represented long-range mission goals. In a 1924 letter, McDowell encouraged more government support for African education
and African participation in that system. McDowell stated:

I covet the opportunity that is coming to some trained natives to head
up that system in a Christian way. [Speaking of one mission worker in
particular, he goes on to say]...I wonder if Jonas would not have a
future and opportunity to do a bigger thing and perhaps more effectively in connection with some such enterprise than as an employee of
the Mission. I think that if he could...go to Lisbon or Oporte for two or
three years, get the Portuguese point of view, Christianize and become
an enthusiastic, and loyal Portuguese—not an estranged one, he might
be able to...come to Angola and do great things for his people.[35]

Missionary apprehension over the Garvey movement provides
a good comparative measurement of colonial government attitudes. During a 1921 visit to the British Consulate, McDowell
was shown various communications that had been sent out by
the British Foreign Department with reference to the Garvey
movement and American blacks in general. In this situation,
McDowell's major concern was that these British sentiments
would not spread to the Portuguese.[36] McDowell was also careful not to subscribe to Garvey's literature, although the mission
did receive *Crisis*, the *Brownies' Book*, and the *Chicago Defender*.

Cooperation between missions and government was affected
by location. When the black workers moved from the Chileso
station to Galangue, they were further away from the Portuguese. The missionaries saw the Portuguese during the officials'
yearly travels for taxes, at which time the mission was used as
the seat of operation. This distance also made the Portuguese

more dependent upon McDowell in their relations with the local population.[37]

During the Depression, mission staffs were reduced and never recovered. The Congregational mission at Galangue lost its black identification because white missionaries wanted to serve there and new black missionaries came and did not want to work in a segregated mission. In the 1940s, Galangue entered into the general budget of West African missions and was no longer exclusively supported by black Congregationalists.[38]

Although the financial constraints of the Depression affected the missionary work of the major black denominations, another reason is given for the reduction in the African mission field. According to the present Mission Board secretary of the AME Church, Reverend John Collier, by the 1930s, most black missions had trained a local pastorate to minister to the needs of the Christian community.[39] Although white missions, especially those with boarding schools, also produced African Christian workers, these workers remained in a position subordinate to white missionaries. Black Americans, on the other hand, gave Africans positions of responsibility and decision-making.

The 1940s and following ushered in a new era of black American Christian involvement in Africa, which was mainly financial assistance from the predominantly black churches. This included funds for churches and educational funds for African students to study in church-affiliated schools in the United States. The continuing effect of missions throughout decolonization was the disproportionate placement of educated Christian Africans from mission localities in administrative and political positions. The goal for educated Africans was not church involvement. Mission education was the means to other forms of social mobility.

A Colonial Office reaction to black Americans can be used as a gauge, a reflection, of the bureaucracy's approach to educated Africans and their missionary role in African development. In the case of each government, the role of black American missionaries reveals or illuminates several characteristics of colonialism. First, the degree of development that could be instituted by any metropolitan government depended upon the political arrangement for governing foreign territories. Second, the scope of development depended upon the economic resources of the colonizing country as well as the economic potential of the colony.

The major role of black missionaries and all church organizations in the colonies was as educators. For black Americans in particular education had been (and continues to be) the tool for socioeconomic mobility. It is in the area of education that missions, the governing of colonies, and African development converge. When Africans were included in the political arrangement for a colony, their traditional or modern roles had to be outlined. Part of that outline included a knowledge of the colonial language. Black missionaries saw themselves as bearers of this means for social mobility for Africans. Especially in the Portuguese case, the position of "assimilado" was well defined in specific terms: education, job, and appearance. Social mobility in British colonies would involve these same factors.

The problem here centered on the colonial view of these former mission students. In the case of the Portuguese in Angola, McDowell stated that "the Portuguese were the least color conscious of any of the colonial powers." These sentiments were consistent with earlier reports by Dr. Cornelius Patton in 1913.[40] Thus, the problem for missionaries was the loss of their best students to opportunities in Loanda rather than work in the mission.

The British decision to follow the vocational/agricultural lines of the Phelps-Stokes Fund recommendations indicated a desire to control the educational path to socioeconomic mobility for Africans. Mission education was to have been part of this control. Black American missionaries, even though college-trained themselves, focused on getting their African pupils to the point of functional literacy. A crucial member of the Angola Mission was Samuel B. Coles, another black Congregationalist. He joined McDowell at Galangue in the 1920s as an agricultural missionary. It was his task to train students (boys) in a vocational curriculum—carpentry, brick masonry, and new agricultural techniques. The mission had two trade buildings for one hundred students and one hundred and fifty acres of cultivated land.[41] McDowell described African problems as "economic rather than political."[42] His position was similar to that of the Tuskegee idea of social uplift through hard work rather than through political action. Thus, much time was spent on the Protestant work ethic in making Africans "more industrious." These sentiments would have been compatible with those of colonial governments and the missionary ideals of American philanthropy.

In the Angola case, offenses against mission work were taken as personal confrontations with Portuguese officials which could be diplomatically solved through compromise. Problems concerning languages, visas, or land concessions would have been in this category. Offenses against Africans seemed to have been handled as political issues in colonialism, regardless of whether missionaries recognized this role. Labor and taxes were central to many indigenous problems. They essentially did not interfere with the work of missions, but labor and taxes did upset the social fabric of local communities. The Congregational mission especially seemed to handle African problems with as much diplomatic skill as mission problems. In fact, labor demands and the injustice of taxes involved moral issues that contradicted Christian ideals, whereas visa, land, and language problems involved no issues of "right and wrong" but were two areas in which missions could have some leverage in African development.

While it is easy to place the label of "politics" on the attitudes and actions of Africans or colonial authorities, it is more difficult to place that label on a missionary enterprise when the missionaries themselves stressed that religious work was apolitical and supranational. But political elements are implicit in missionary rhetoric, goals, and methods. Even though black American missionaries may have been unconscious of the politics of missions, they took political and diplomatic measures when circumstances required them.

The importance of this essay, then, extends beyond the boundaries of the church history of colonial Africa. The analytical framework of the study begins with the inherent political nature of religion which for the Afro-American included Pan-African and international concerns. By extending the race issue to include Africa and Europe, black Americans made discrimination an international problem, not merely for Africans, but also for themselves.

Notes

1. For further discussion of the sociopolitical functions of religion, see Eugene D. Genovese, *Roll, Jordan, Roll: The World the Slaves Made* (New York: Random House, 1972), pp. 159-284; and Robert I. Rotberg, ed., *Rebellion in Black Africa* (London: Oxford University Press, 1971). Portions of this article are taken from my dissertation, "Black American Missionaries in Colonial Africa, 1900-1940: A Study of Missionary-Government Relations" (Ph.D. dissertation, University of Chicago, 1981).

2. Leon Spencer interview with Reverend Henry C. McDowell, June 12-13, 1975, Talladega College Historical Collections, Oral History Program (Talladega, Alabama). References from this collection will hereafter be cited with the file number, and other pertinent data when available, and the abbreviation M/HC. See also Elder Vann, "The Centennial of Modern Missions," a sermon delivered before the American National Baptist Convention and the Baptist Foreign Mission Convention, U.S.A., September 17, 1893, in Washington, D.C.; and Reverend L. G. Jordan, "The Responsibility of the American Negro for the Evangelization of Africa" in *The United Negro: His Problems and His Progress*, eds. I. Garland Penn and J. W. E. Owen (Atlanta, Ga.: D. E. Luther Publishing Co., 1902), pp. 308-210.

3. Penn and Bowen, eds., *The United Negro*, p. 300.

4. Ibid., passim; and Reverend J. W. Rankin, D.D., "Methods of Missionary Work," *A.M.E. Church Review* 31 (January 1915):278-286.

5. File Number 2/9/2, Henry C. McDowell Papers, Talladega College. References from this collection will hereafter be cited with the file number, and other pertinent data when available, and the abbreviation, HCM.

6. April 15, 1926, 2/1/6, HCM.

7. References to black missionaries are frequently used in this essay to mean Afro-American missionaries, not indigenous African workers.

8. C.S.J. Francine Ann Dempsey, "Afro-American Perspectives on Africa: The Images of Africa Among Afro-American Leaders, Artists and Scholars, 1915-1940" (Ph.D. dissertation, University of Minnesota, 1976); Milfred C. Fierce, "African-American Interest in Africa and Interaction with West Africa: The Origins of the Pan-African Idea in the United States, 1900-1919" (Ph.D. dissertation, Columbia University, 1976); Wilbur Christian Harr, "The Negro As an American Protestant Missionary in Africa" (Ph.D. dissertation, University of Chicago, 1946); Sylvia Marie Jacobs, "Black American Perspectives on European Imperialism in Africa, 1870-1920" (Ph.D. dissertation, Howard University,

1975); and Donald Franklin Roth, " 'Grace Not Race': Southern Negro Church Leaders, Black Identity, and Missions to West Africa, 1865-1919" (Ph.D. dissertation, University of Texas at Austin, 1975).

9. Lillie M. Johnson, "American Missions, the War, and German Colonies," Unpublished paper, University of Chicago, May 11, 1977; and *Presbyterian Church Bulletin*, 1919, p. 142.

10. European and African historians use the signing of the Treaty of Berlin in 1885 as the beginning of formal empires in Africa, although the informal empires had existed in coastal enclaves since the height of the African slave trade in the eighteenth century. The end of the colonial period began with Ghanaian independence in 1957 and continued through the 1970s. However, 1945 and the postwar years are categorized as the decolonization stage of European rule in Africa and can therefore be viewed as the end of the empire-building phase, especially for British and French territories.

11. C. C. Adams and Marshall A. Talley, *Negro Baptists and Foreign Missions* (Philadelphia: Foreign Mission Board of the National Baptist Convention, U.S.A, 1944); Lewellyn L. Berry, *A Century of Missions of the African Methodist Episcopal Church, 1840-1940* (New York: Gutenberg Printing Co., 1942), passim; and Letter from William J. Harvey, Corresponding Secretary, National Baptist Convention, U.S.A., to Lillie M. Johnson, October 11, 1977.

12. Walter Lee Williams, "Black American Attitudes Toward Africa: The Missionary Movement, 1877-1900" (Ph.D. dissertation, University of North Carolina at Chapel Hill, 1974), pp. 124, 132, 155-156. This statement on Liberian missions does not include the work done with indigenous Africans in the hinterland who distrusted the church as political associates of their oppressors—the colonized former American slaves on the coast.

13. Harr, "Negro As an American Protestant Missionary," p. 62.

14. Ibid., passim.

15. Ibid., pp. 14-27, 39; Williams, "Black American Attitudes Toward Africa," pp. 94-95; and "Mission Minutes," *Presbyterian Board of Foreign Missions*, December 3, 1925, p. 32.

16. Ang., 2/5/2, HCM.

17. See Robert O. Collins, ed., *Problems in the History of Colonial Africa* (Englewood Cliffs, N.J.: Prentice-Hall, 1970), Chapter 1, for excerpts of various arguments on the partition of Africa.

18. Memo from Consul William J. Yerby, Dakar, Senegal, September 25, 1918, Document 848K, 111/1, National Archives, Washington, D.C.

19. Charles Spencer Smith, *A History of the African Methodist Episcopal Church* (Philadelphia: A.M.E. Book Concern, 1922), pp. 332, 334.

20. "The Open Door for American Negroes in Africa," *The Foundation* 13 (July-August 1923):7.

21. "American Negroes and Africa," *The Foundation* 17 (May 1927):19.

22. Kenneth James King, *Pan-Africanism and Education* (Oxford: Clarendon Press, 1971); Thomas Jesse Jones, *Education in Africa* (New York: Phelps-Stokes Fund, 1922); and Thomas Jesse Jones, *Education in East Africa* (New York: Phelps-Stokes Fund, 1925). Earlier, but similar, sentiments are expressed in quotes from Sir F. D. Lugard, then governor of Nigeria, in "Shall Education Anglicize the Negro?," *A. M. E. Church Review* 17 (January 1901):261-262.

23. Report by the Honorable W. G. A. Ormsby-Gore, Parliamentary Under-Secretary, on His Visit to West Africa, 1926, Record Group 59, Microfilm 583, p. 95, National Archives, Washington, D.C.

24. William A. Cadbury, *Labour in Portuguese West Africa* (London: George Routledge & Sons, Ltd., 1910; reprint ed., New York: Negro Universities Press, 1969).

25. File No. Afr., 3/4/1/1, pp. 66-68, Talladega College Papers, Talladega College. References from this collection will hereafter be cited with the file number, and other pertinent data when availble, and the abbreviation TC.

26. Afr., 3/4/1/2, TC.

27. August 21, 1922, Ang., 2/7/2, HCM.

28. Letter to Brother Flynn from Henry C. Mcdowell, October 5, 1920, Ang., 2/5/1, HCM.

29. Letter to Reverend Frank S. Brewer from Henry C. McDowell, April 19, 1920, Ang., 2/5/1, HCM.

30. September 22, 1921, Ang., 2/6/3, HCM. Decree No. 77 which outlines Portuguese regulations for missions was not officially issued until December 9, 1921.

31. Letter to Enoch Bell from Henry C. McDowell, April 30, 1921, Ang., 2/6/4, HCM.

32. Letter to Reverend G. J. Thomas from Henry C. McDowell, February 25, 1922, Ang., 2/7/2, HCM.

33. Letter to Dr. Lawless from Henry C. McDowell, February 24, 1922, Ang., 2/7/2, HCM.

34. Letter to Mrs. Holland from Henry C. McDowell, February 18, 1921, Ang., 2/6/2, HCM.

35. December 27, 1924, Ang., 2/9/2, HCM.

36. Letter to Reverend Johnson from Henry C. McDowell, August 21, 1922, Ang., 2/7/2, HCM.

37. Gen., 5/1/2, M/HC.

38. Gen., 5/1/3, Side 1, M/HC.

39. *A. M. E. Church Departmental Quadrennial Reports: 29th Annual Report: 1928-1932* (Philadelphia: A.M.E. Book Concern), p. 13.

40. Letter to Lillie M. Johnson from Henry C. McDowell, July 22, 1978, and Afr., 3/4/1/1, pp. 66-68, TC.

41. Ang., 2/12/2, HCM.

42. April 15, 1926, Ang., 2/11/6, HCM.

CONCLUSION:
THE MISSION MOVEMENT

IV

The Impact of Black American Missionaries in Africa

11

Sylvia M. Jacobs

This anthology attempts to survey black American participation in the American Protestant missionary movement in Africa in the nineteenth and twentieth centuries. Although Afro-Americans were dispatched as missionaries to many parts of the world, Africa was seen as their "special" field. Both white and black churches in the United States commissioned a large number of blacks to Africa as missionaries; the exact number awaits further research. Among the major white denominations that sent black missionaries to the continent were the Congregationalist, Baptist, Methodist, Episcopalian, and Presbyterian. Black mission boards prominent in Africa were the African Methodist Episcopal Church, the African Methodist Episcopal Zion Church, the National Baptist Convention, and the Lott Carey Baptist Home and Foreign Mission Convention of the United States. The essays that comprise this study discuss the foundation of the missionary ideology that resulted in the use of blacks as missionaries in Africa and the activity of these Afro-American representatives from the major American Protestant churches with African missions.

Both the mission and the missionary were affected by the prevailing contemporary image of Africa as a "dark" un-Christian continent in need of "civilizing." The initial goal of missions on the continent was the evangelization of the "uncivilized" and "debauched" African. Later, the mission objective shifted from a solely religious one to one that encompassed the transformation of "civilization."

The first section in this anthology, "Introduction: Mission Ideology," presents the background on the rise and development of a Protestant mission ideology in the late eighteenth and early nineteenth centuries, one that continued to prevail throughout the remainder of the nineteenth century and first half of the twentieth. The American mission movement was essentially an outgrowth of the European impulse for worldwide conversion. In the first decades of the nineteenth century, American church boards accepted Africa as an important area for mission work and encouraged black Americans to return to the land of their forefathers with the "light" of "civilization" and Christianity.

In the mission movement, the relationship of Afro-American missionaries with Africa and Africans was both ambivalent and contradictory. Black Americans felt that the African mission field was a special "black man's burden," a duty or obligation that they owed to the homeland because of their exposure in a Christian and Western society. Yet, American Christian civilization regarded all blacks as inferior. In fact, by 1900 white mission boards began to discourage and openly oppose the use of black Americans as missionaries in Africa. By this date, stimulated by denominationalism, missionary paternalism, and imperialism, missionary goals in Africa had shifted from the "three-self" formula of a "self-governing," "self-supporting," and "self-propagating" church to the development of Christian colonial outposts. After 1920, white boards withdrew black Americans from missionary work on the continent, and for almost forty years few were stationed there. Thus, racism eventually undermined the effectiveness of black participation in the African mission movement. Black American missionaries in Africa were forced to develop a mission philosophy different and distinct from the widespread white Christian one.

The Afro-American evangelization movement in Africa suffered from lack of financing and racial prejudice. Despite these shortcomings, black American missionaries were able to maintain a continuous interest in the homeland. Africa, as homeland and mission field, became a source of identity for Afro-Americans, and they were able to distinguish a mission ideology that emphasized African capabilities and accomplishments and not African "degradation" and "inferiority."

The second section, "The Mission: Motivations, Objectives, and Results," considers the incentives and influences of black Americans in the mission movement in Africa. The American missionary tradition, with its roots in the colonization movement, first focused on Liberia, and this country continued to be the center of Afro-American missionary efforts in Africa. Liberian colonization was the first stage of the black American missionary movement in Africa. The American Colonization Society, founded to transport Afro-Americans back to Liberia, perceived its efforts as an experiment in transmitting Christianity and Western "civilization." Among the first black emigrants carried to Liberia by the ACS were several who later served as missionaries. The nature of the colonization movement made all emigrants missionaries in the land of their forefathers and helped create a Christian society in Africa.

Throughout the nineteenth century, most of the missionary efforts and activities in Liberia, whether carried out by black or white missionaries, were directed toward and more successful among the colonists rather than among indigenous Africans. Afro-American migrants, with a feeling that their culture was superior, were understandably resented by indigenous Africans. Nevertheless, early Afro-American missionary activity in Liberia was influenced by the parallel development of a settler society.

Nineteenth-century black American missionary concern with African societal "uplift" and development culminated in twentieth-century interest in education as a means of bringing about these improvements. Tuskegee Institute, first under Booker T. Washington and later under his successor, Robert R. Moton, played a significant, though ambiguous, "missionary" role as a model for black educational systems throughout colonial Africa, thereby making a definite contribution to African educational philosophy.

Moton, consistently reporting on African education, culture, and politics, became a spokesperson on African affairs. Thus, Tuskegee received an endless stream of educators, politicians, philanthropists, and missionaries from around the world who wanted to discover the secrets of the Tuskegee ideal. Tuskegee students visited and worked in different parts of colonial Africa, with Moton playing a significant role in Liberian affairs. By 1935, when Moton resigned, the scale and scope of Afro-American missionary contact with Africa had grown, but the underlying motivations remained constant, the idea of religious regeneration and modernization along Western lines.

It was in the area of education that the work of black American missionaries took an unusual turn. One of the least recognized and most fascinating consequences of the black American missionary presence in Africa was the impetus it gave to generations of young Africans to study in the United States, and later to the development of higher education on the continent. An AMEZ missionary sponsored the American education of James Aggrey, later a prominent African educator, and Aggrey encouraged still another youth to travel to America, Nnamdi Azikiwe.

Azikiwe became a successful academic entrepreneur by presiding over the founding of an American-style university in Nigeria, the University of Nigeria at Nsukka. But despite Azikiwe's sincere desire to create a noncolonial, Tuskegee-style university, in the end the Nigerians, arguing over a British- or American-style education, institutionalized a system of education that proved to be inappropriate for their needs. This experiment went beyond the aspirations, and was a somewhat curious and distorted legacy, of early black American missonaries who encouraged and fostered educational development at all levels in Africa.

The next section, "The Missionary: Methods, Interests, and Activities," includes a group of essays that describe the life and work of a representative number of black American missionaries who served in Africa. The black missionaries' common activities and problems tell much about their motives and the results of their involvement in Africa. Although Afro-Americans who volunteered as missionaries had many of the same motivations as missionaries in general, they did differ in a number of respects. The idea of a special duty and moral obligation was particularly prominent in the minds of these Afro-American missionaries. Some volunteered for mission work to gain the respect of whites and blacks in America. Still others hoped to escape white oppression in America since Afro-American missionaries were given more freedom and latitude in their work in Africa than they could have received working in the United States.

One of the most influential and well-known Afro-American missionaries during the period of the "civilizing mission" in Africa was William H. Sheppard. Sheppard was sponsored by the white Southern Presbyterian Church and saw Africa as the land of his forefathers. He traveled to the Congo to aid in the uplift of the continent. Sheppard identified himself with Africans, even if he was sometimes paternalistic, and he was well liked by them.

After the death of his co-worker, Samuel Lapsley, Sheppard concentrated his mission efforts on the Bakuba people. He lived among the Bakuba for four months. While the Bakuba liked him, they were satisfied with their own religion and were not interested in conversion. Sheppard's concern for the Congolese was most clearly demonstrated by his thoroughness and persistence in exposing atrocities of the Leopoldian government in the Congo. He was later acquitted in a libel trial that resulted from his allegations, but because of the litigation and a loss of independence in mission work as whites established more control, Sheppard retired from the Congo in 1910. Although he condemned aspects of their culture, Sheppard presented Africans in a favorable light and was less moralistic than most nineteenth-century missionaries in Africa.

The most direct evidence of Sheppard's influence on black Americans, besides their monetary contributions, was seen in those blacks who volunteered as missionaries to the Congo. Between 1890 and 1941, nine Afro-Americans from the Southern Presbyterian Church were appointed to work in the Congo. Five of them were women. Maria Fearing, Lillian Thomas DeYampert, Lucy Gantt Sheppard, Althea Brown Edmiston, and Annie Katherine Taylor Rochester variously served in the Congo from 1894 to 1937. They learned the languages, taught religious lessons, supervised girls' homes, taught domestic science, began schools, and worked in the surrounding villages. All of these women missionaries believed that their major duty in Africa was to improve the lives of the women and children, and their accomplishments had far-reaching effects on Congolese society.

In South Africa, Afro-American missionaries, particularly AMEs, were viewed with suspicion because it was feared that they would encourage Africans to become politically active. The AME connection with South Africa began with its merger in 1896 with the African-led Ethiopian Church. The magnet that attracted Africans was the large number of educational facilities operated by the church. Black South Africans hoped that the AME Church would be able to aid them in the establishment of schools, especially a college.

In spite of white South African fears that black American missionaries were political agitators and incendiaries determined to destroy race relations in the country, early AME missionaries went to South Africa solely to uplift the people and combat the notion of African inferiority. AME missionaries were cautious, conservative, and petit bourgeois in outlook. They were not the zealots envisioned by the white colonialists. What AME missionaries imported into South Africa was Booker T. Washington's philosophy of thrift, capital accumulation, and character-building—in short, all the middle-class values that were inherent in the AME Church. Yet, as a result of real and imagined AME activities in South Africa, the black American missionary became an unwanted element in colonial Africa. Thus, during the period after 1920 few new black American missionaries were stationed in Africa by white church boards.

The one notable exception was the establishment of the ABCFM Galangue black-manned station in Angola in the early 1920s. The experiences and circumstances of black American missionaries in British and Portuguese colonies, and the response of these colonial governments, were similar to those in South Africa. But, interestingly, in spite of the additional problems of language and denominational barriers, Portuguese Angola between 1920 and 1940 was the easiest African country for an Afro-American missionary to enter, with the exception of Liberia.

The Galangue station was opened in 1922, with Reverend Henry C. McDowell appointed as a missionary for the Congregational Church in Angola. He, too, followed the Tuskegee principle of education. Black American missionaries, like whites, supported industrial education for Africans, but they were more concerned with the social mobility of their adherents and gave them positions of responsibility and decision-making within the church. The Congregational mission in Angola, despite often diverging purposes, handled problems with the colonial government with diplomacy and compromise.

A number of themes are discussed in this volume. The overall thesis of the anthology is that the "special" relationship that Afro-Americans felt they had with Africa and Africans was a significant factor both in their motivations for African mission work and in their activities on the continent. Because of the small number of American missionaries in Africa before 1945, the impact of black American missionaries was severely limited. Afro-American missionaries were an insignificant percentage of the total American missionaries stationed in Africa before 1960, and they were restricted to certain areas of the continent.

While the impact of black American missionary efforts in Africa cannot be easily measured, they did make several notable contributions to the continent. Probably the most rewarding for future generations was the tremendous amount of information about traditional African society that black American missionaries recorded in their autobiographies, diaries, and letters written back to America, and that was displayed in the artifacts they brought back with them. Black American missionaries also helped to dispel some of the myths and negative stereotypes about Africa, its people, and its culture by projecting a more positive image about the continent. This resulted in a greater Pan-African alliance between Afro-Americans and Africa. In addition, these missionaries brought about some social and political reforms in African society. There were also the educational contributions which black American missionaries made both directly and indirectly to Africa and Africans. In the final analysis, the singular impact of black American missionaries on the continent of Africa is somewhat illusive. Yet, it is certain that their presence resulted in positive developments for continental Africans and for Afro-Americans.

BIBLIOGRAPHICAL ESSAY

V

Black Americans and the Missionary Movement in Africa: A Bibliography

12

Sylvia M. Jacobs

The field of general Christian missiology has been well documented. Kenneth Scott Latourette has written the most thorough guide on Christian mission activities. In the seven-volume work, *A History of the Expansion of Christianity* (1937-1945), he surveys the spread of Roman Catholic, Protestant, and Orthodox churches throughout the world up to about 1940. In this multivolume study, the continent of Africa is discussed in three chapters, one of these exclusively on Madagascar and another on the northern shores of Africa, neither of which Latourette considers "truly" African. Christianity in Africa south of the Sahara is summarized in yet another chapter in Volume 5; in this chapter, black American missionaries are rarely identified as such, although they may be briefly mentioned.

In his five-volume work, *Christianity in a Revolutionary Age, A History of Christianity in the Nineteenth and Twentieth Centuries* (1958-1962), Latourette capsulizes Christian events in Africa (both North and sub-Saharan) in the nineteenth and twentieth centuries into two chapters in Volume 3 and two chapters in Volume 5. In both of these publications, North African activity is separated from that of Africa south of the Sahara.

For a more specific treatment of missionary activity solely on the continent of Africa, the four-volume work of Charles P. Groves, *The Planting of Christianity in Africa* (1948-1958) continues to be the major source. This study takes the continent as a whole and presents a chronological account, beginning with the early church in Egypt and North Africa and ending with the Christian church in Africa in the post-World War II era. (Madagascar is not included.) The magnitude of this careful and reliable investigation is astounding, but it is still lacking in its interpretation of the role of black American missionaries in Africa, although they are cited with a brief description of their activities.

Finally, in surveying missionary ideology that led to mission activity in Africa, several other sources may be helpful. The *American Journal of Sociology* devoted a whole issue (November 1944) to mission philosophy and doctrine. The symposium, on "Culture and Missions," consisted of six papers that had been read at the Fifteenth Annual Festival of Music and the Fine Arts, held at Fisk University (Nashville, Tennessee) in April 1944. Those articles that would be useful in understanding mission attitudes as they related to Africa include Robert E. Park, "Missions and the Modern World"; Hugh Stuntz, "Christian Missions and Social Cohesion"; Ako Adjei, "Imperialism and Spiritual Freedom: An African View"; and G. Gordon Brown, "Missions and Cultural Diffusion." Similarly, William H. P. Faunce, in *The Social Aspects of Foreign Missions* (1914), discussed the social functions and achievements of missionaries in foreign fields.

General material on American missionary activity can be found in Clarence Clendenen and Peter Duignan, *Americans in Black Africa Up to 1865* (1964) and Clarence Clendenen, Robert Collins, and Peter Duignan, *Americans in Africa, 1865-1900* (1966). Both books have sections on missions and missionary activity. Black American missionaries are discussed briefly in the second study. Although a followup survey after 1900 has been promised, none has as yet been published.

In researching this topic, after the general reference materials, which give some leads to Afro-American missionaries, primary sources become the most beneficial, including church archives and historical libraries, autobiographical and eyewitness accounts, and missionary publications such as newspapers or journals. The best place to begin this investigation is with two books on missionary holdings in libraries and church archives. These are Robert Collins and Peter Duignan, *Americans in Africa: A Prelimi-*

nary Guide to American Missionary Archives and Library Manuscript Collections on Africa (1963) and Peter Duignan, *Handbook of American Resources for African Studies* (1967). Both of these references are good guides for the location of missionary holdings in the United States. *Americans in Africa* describes fifty-two missionary archives and forty-seven library manuscript collections of sources dealing with American mission-sending societies to Africa. The *Handbook* has a section entitled "Church and Missionary Libraries and Archives."

A few black American missionaries wrote autobiographical sketches of their experiences in Africa. After the manuscript collections and letters of Afro-American missionaries in church archives and libraries, these autobiographies are important, although they are few and do not necessarily represent a continental survey or a composite picture of all the American Protestant societies sponsoring missions. The most well-known and easily accessible autobiographies of black missionaries who served in Africa before 1960 include Clinton C. Boone, *Congo As I Saw It* (1927) and his *Liberia As I Know It* (1929); Alexander Priestly Camphor, *Missionary Story Sketches* (1909); Daniel Coker, *Journal of Daniel Coker* (1820); John J. Coles, *Africa in Brief* (1886); Samuel B. Coles, *Preacher with a Plow* (1957); Levi Jenkins Coppin, *Observations of Persons and Things in South Africa, 1900-1904: Letters from Africa* (n.d.); William H. Heard, *From Slavery to the Bishopric in the A. M. E. Church, an Autobiography* (1924); Thomas L. Johnson, *Africa for Christ, Twenty-eight Years a Slave* (1892) and his *Twenty-eight Years a Slave; or the Story of My Life in Three Continents* (1909); Lewis Garnett Jordan, *Pebbles from An African Beach* (1918) and his *On Two Hemispheres: Bits from the Life of Lewis G. Jordan, As Told By Himself* [1935]; William H. Sheppard, *Presbyterian Pioneers in Congo* (1917); Amanda Berry Smith, *An Autobiography* (1893); Charlotte Crogman Wright, *Beneath the Southern Cross* (1955); and Richard Robert Wright, Jr., *87 Years Behind the Black Curtain: An Autobiography* (1965).

All religious denominations have some type of history of their church. Several also have specific studies on mission activity, while others include this type of information in the general church history. For an investigation of the role of black American missionaries in the major Protestant churches, general church histories and church mission histories are a good starting point. Diligent and careful research of this material is required since black missionaries, when discussed at all, are rarely identified as such.

The best source on early ABCFM activities continues to be William E. Strong's *The Story of the American Board, An Account of the First Hundred Years of the American Board of Commissioners for Foreign Missions* (1910). The American Board's mission periodical, the *Missionary Herald*, is valuable and contains letters from black American missionaries stationed in Africa. Two doctoral dissertations would also be useful: "Protestant America and the Pagan World: The First Half Century of the American Board of Commissioners for Foreign Missions," by Clifton Jackson Phillips (Harvard University, 1954) and "A History of the American Board Mission in Angola, 1800-1940," by Fola Soremekun (Northwestern University, 1965).

Baptist mission activity is well documented. Northern Baptist mission history (the American Baptist Churches in the U.S.A.) is discussed in George Winfred Hervey, *The Story of Baptist Missions in Foreign Lands* (1884); Edmund F. Merriam, *A History of American Baptist Missions* (1913); Robert G. Torbet, *Venture of Faith: The Story of the American Baptist Foreign Mission Society and the Woman's American Baptist Foreign Mission Society, 1814-1954* (1955); and Henry C. Vedder, *A Short History of Baptist Missions* (1927). A history of Southern Baptist Convention missions is documented in Henry Allen Tupper's *Foreign Missions of the Southern Baptist Convention* (1880) and in his updated *A Decade of Foreign Missions, 1880-1890* (1891). A more recent account is Baker J. Cauthen, *Advance: A History of Southern Baptist Foreign Missions* (1970). Also helpful would be Davis Lee Saunder's doctoral dissertation, "A History of Baptists in Central and Southern Africa" (Southern Baptist Theological Seminary, 1973).

The history of the work of the foreign mission board of the black National Baptist Convention in Africa can be found in Lewis Garnett Jordan, *Up the Ladder in Foreign Missions* (1901) and his *Negro Baptist History, U.S.A., 1750-1930* [1930]; C. C. Adams and Marshall A. Talley, *Negro Baptists and Foreign Missions* (1944); Edward A. Freeman, *The Epoch of Negro Baptists and the Foreign Mission Board* (1953); and Owen D. Pelt and Ralph Lee Smith, *The Story of National Baptists* (1960). The activities of another black Baptist group, the Lott Carey Baptist Home and Foreign Mission Convention of the United States, is chronicled in Leroy Fitt's *Lott Carey: First Black Missionary to Africa* (1978).

Of all church mission histories, the missions of the Methodist Church have been the most documented. An early endeavor was Thomas B. Neely's *The Methodist Episcopal Church and Its Foreign Missions* (1923). The first extensive survey of this church's mission activities is recorded in the three-volume edited work of Emory Stevens Bucke, *The History of American Methodism* (1964) and the four-volume study, *History of Methodist Missions* (1949-1973). Volumes 1, 2, and 3 are by Wade Crawford Barclay and Volume 4 is by J. Tremayne Copplestone. Missions of the Methodist Church from 1769 to 1939 are discussed. The African missions of the Methodist Episcopal Church, South, are presented in Chapter 7 of James Cannon III, *History of the Southern Methodist Missions* (1926).

The histories of the two major black Methodist churches with missions in Africa are described in Lewellyn L. Berry, *A Century of Missions of the African Methodist Episcopal Church, 1840-1940* (1942); Artishia Wilkerson Jordan, *The African Methodist Episcopal Church in Africa* (n.d.); George A. Singleton, *The Romance of African Methodism* (1952); and David Henry Bradley, *A History of the African Methodist Episcopal Zion Church* (1970). For an extensive discussion of AME mission work in South Africa, see Josephus R. Coan's doctoral dissertation, "The Expansion of the Missions of the African Methodist Episcopal Church in South Africa, 1896-1908" (Hartford Seminary Foundation, 1961). Obviously, these sources are extremely valuable because all the missionaries sent to Africa by these boards were black, and this considerably reduces the amount of time spent cross-checking and identifying Afro-American missionaries.

Organization of the Domestic and Foreign Missionary Society and mission activity of the Protestant Episcopal Church (today the Episcopal Church) is reported in S. D. Denison, *A History of the Foreign Missionary Work of the Protestant Episcopal Church* (1871). For a survey of the first hundred years of the Domestic and

Foreign Missionary Society of the Protestant Episcopal Church, see Julia C. Emery's *A Century of Endeavor, 1821-1921* (1921). The reports of the Department of Foreign Missions in the church's *Annual Report of the National Council* and the mission periodical, *The Spirit of Missions*, could also be useful. A discussion of the role of black Americans in the Episcopal Church is given in George F. Bragg, *History of the Afro-American Group of the Episcopal Church* (1922).

A summary of Northern Presbyterian missions can be found in Robert E. Speer, *Presbyterian Foreign Missions* (1901) and Arthur J. Brown, *One Hundred Years, a History of the Foreign Missionary Work of the Presbyterian Church in the U.S.A.* (1936). A general survey of Southern Presbyterian missions is presented in *Our Church Faces Foreign Missions* [1931] by the Presbyterian Church in the U.S. Executive Committee on Foreign Missions. An examination of the Southern Presbyterian Church and its relations to blacks, with one section on missionaries in Africa, is noted in A. L. Phillips, *The Presbyterian Church in the United States ("the Southern Presbyterian Church") and the Colored People* [189?]. Finally, the best study of the Southern Presbyterian mission in the Congo is Stanley Shaloff's *Reform in Leopold's Congo* (1970).

Of course, most American Protestant churches have published individual annual reports of foreign mission activity, but sometimes foreign mission department reports are included in the annual convention proceedings. In addition, larger church organizations had their own mission journals.

The Missionary Review of the World, which was published monthly from 1878 to 1939, sometimes contained articles by or about black American missionaries, but here again the researcher must know the name of the specific missionary. (For example, this periodical had many articles written by and about William Sheppard of the Southern Presbyterian Congo Mission.) The researcher must also go through each volume individually. One interesting article on Afro-American missionaries can be found in the December 1903 issue of the *Review*, entitled "The Negro As a Missionary."

Harlan P. Beach's *A Geography and Atlas of Protestant Missions* (1903) contains an alphabetical list of Protestant missionary societies and statistics on Protestant missions in Africa. James S. Dennis, Harlan P. Beach, and Charles H. Fahs, editors, in *World Atlas of Christian Missions* (1911) is equally helpful in identifying the numerical strength of American missionaries in Africa. The *Atlas* contains a directory of missionary societies, including American, and statistics on societies with African missions, with information such as the year of the first work, ordained missionaries (men and women), and the number of mission stations. The *World Missionary Atlas* (1925), Harlan P. Beach and Charles H. Fahs, editors, contains a directory of missionary societies, statistics of Protestant missions, maps showing the location of Protestant mission stations, and descriptive notes on Protestant missionary work throughout the world.

Beginning in the late nineteenth century through the mid-twentieth century, a number of conferences were called which considered the role black Americans should play in the "civilizing mission" in Africa. At the World's Congress on Africa, convened on August 14, 1893, in Chicago, Illinois, over one hundred papers were read by explorers, scientists, anthropologists, statesmen, and missionaries. The conference, sponsored by the American Missionary Association, was held in conjunction with the Chicago World's Fair, and the organizers hoped to create a sentiment for African development. Frederick Perry Noble discussed the Congress in two articles: "Africa at the Columbian Exposition," *Our Day*, November 1892, and "The Chicago Congress of Africa," *Our Day*, October 1893.

A second meeting, the Congress on Africa, was convened in Atlanta, Georgia, December 13-15, 1895, under the auspices of the Stewart Missionary Foundation for Africa of the Northern Methodist Church's Gammon Theological Seminary. The general purpose of the conference was to promote interest among American blacks in missionary work in Africa. *Africa and the American Negro* (1896), edited by J. W. E. Bowen, is a collection of the speeches made at this meeting.

The International Conference of the Negro was held at Tuskegee Institute in Tuskegee, Alabama, April 17-19, 1912. Most of the participants were missionaries and theologians. Among the questions considered was how Afro-American missionaries could best serve Africa within the framework of European colonial rule. The best account of this meeting can be found in "The Negro Conference at Tuskegee Institute," *African Times and Orient Review* (July 1912).

Edwin William Smith in *The Christian Mission in Africa* (1926) chronicles the work of the International Conference on the Christian Mission in Africa at Le Zoute, Belgium, held during September 14-21, 1926. Resolutions were passed relating to the lifting of restrictions on Afro-American missionaries in Africa and the need for greater participation by these blacks in the evangelization of their homeland.

Finally, of significance to the study of black American missionaries in Africa was the convening of the Church Conference on African Affairs, held at Otterbein College (Westerville, Ohio), June 19-25, 1942. One session of the meeting was concerned with "The Contribution of the American Negro to Africa." The conference recommended that black Americans be provided a larger role in American missionary service. The proceedings can be found in *Christian Action in Africa* (1942).

A wealth of information on black American missionaries can also be found in a number of unpublished dissertations completed at American universities. They have only limited use, however, because most discuss only one religious denomination, a specific region in Africa, or a narrow time period. These studies include Wilbur C. Harr, "The Negro As an American Protestant Missionary in Africa" (University of Chicago, 1946); Walter L. Williams, "Black American Attitudes Toward Africa: The Missionary Movement, 1877-1900" (University of North Carolina at Chapel Hill, 1974); Donald F. Roth, " 'Grace Not Race': Southern Negro Church Leaders, Black Identity, and Missions to West Africa, 1865-1919" (University of Texas at Austin, 1975); Sandy Dwayne Martin, "The Growth of Christian Missionary Interest in West Africa Among Southeastern Black Baptists, 1880-1915" (Columbia University-Union Theological Seminary, 1981); and Lillie M. Johnson, "Black American Missionaries in Colonial Africa, 1900-1940: A Study of Missionary-Government Relations" (University of Chicago, 1981).

In conclusion, the contribution of black Americans to the total missionary movement in Africa has not as yet been documented in one general book-length study. However, a recent publication, *Black Americans and the Evangelization of Africa, 1877-1900* (1982) by Walter L. Williams, discusses the activities of black Americans in Africa during the years of the height of missionary fervor.

Several articles written in the 1970s on this aspect of African mission work are also available. Kenneth J. King in "The American Negro As Missionary to East Africa: A Critical Aspect of African Evangelism," published in *African Historical Studies* (1970), considers black American missionaries in Africa only in the broadest sense. Most of the discussion centers around Max Yergan and the International Committee on the Young Men's Christian Association in East Africa. Tony Martin in "Some Reflections on Evangelical Pan-Africanism" or "Black Missionaries, White Missionaries and the Struggle for African Souls, 1890-1930," published in *Ufahamu* (Winter 1971), briefly discusses the role of black Americans in the missionary movement in Africa. Finally, the article by William Seraile, "Black American Missionaries in Africa, 1821-1925," *Social Studies* (October 1972), is the best source for a terse review of this phenomenon.

The Protestant American missionary undertaking in Africa before 1960, though limited, was significant. American missionaries in Africa became involved in African society. Before the 1950s, most schools and hospitals in Africa were run by missions, and not by the European colonial governments. Black American missionaries in particular were significant in the modern nationalist movements that gained momentum in Africa in the early twentieth century. Although missionaries have been accused of only disrupting African traditional society, some positive impacts are now being realized. The long-term effect of the missionary movement in Africa has not as yet been assessed. This study elucidates the continuities and discontinuities relative to determining the impact of black American missionaries on African society and perhaps presents new information. Hence, more analytical deliberations can begin, which can then initiate a paradigm for understanding how to appraise the contributions of Afro-American missionaries to the African continent.

Index

33, 107, 132, 142, 146-47, 148,
205, 207-8, 221. *See also*
Afro-American missionaries
"Africa for the Africans," 21, 86,
187
African: children, 133, 139, 155,
157, 158-59, 161, 163, 164, 166,
168, 170, 171, 172, 223;
education, 21, 22, 23, 42, 43,
44, 71, 77, 78, 79, 81, 82,
83, 84, 90, 95, 96-99, 101-4,
105-18, 133, 134, 161,
179-80, 181, 190, 204, 206, 208,
209, 210, 221, 222, 224;
evangelists, 19, 209; independence, 23, 36, 42, 90, 108, 111,
112, 184; independent
church movement, 133, 178,
179, 180, 182, 184, 187,
188, 190, 191, 192, 200, 201;
indigenous church, 13,
15, 16, 141, 178; nationalism,
43, 44, 95, 96, 99, 109,
134, 137, 190, 237; psychological
self-assurance, 146; rebellions,
20, 192, 197, 200, 201;
religious disunity, 23, 51, 52,
54; resentment of colonial
rule, 70; self-determination,
108; self-redemption, 43;
survivals, 72; traditional culture,
7, 23, 34, 35, 36, 43, 45,
47, 132, 141, 148, 171, 180, 206,
210, 211; women, 133,
155, 157, 161, 163, 164, 166,
168, 170, 171, 172, 223
African ethnic groups: Bakete,
139, 140; Bakuba, 139-40, 141,
142, 143, 145, 148, 163,
165, 166, 168, 170, 172, 223;
Baluba-Lulua, 157, 159,

161, 163, 165, 169; Bassa, 71;
Glebo, 56-57; Kasai, 147,
149; Sesotho, 81; Zappo-Zap,
143, 147; Zula, 187
"Africanization," 97, 113, 115
African Letters (Turner), 34
African Methodist Episcopal
Church, 10, 17, 21, 32, 34,
35, 42, 49, 73, 132, 177, 178,
179, 180, 181, 182, 183,
185, 186, 187, 188, 189, 190,
191, 192, 201, 203, 209,
219, 224, 233
African Methodist Episcopal Zion
Church, 10, 35, 43, 95, 118,
201, 219, 222, 233
African Morning Post, 104
African National Congress, 87
African Political Organization (South
Africa), 192
African students at Lincoln
University (Pennsylvania):
Liberia, 101; South Africa, 101
African students at Tuskegee
Institute (Alabama), 84
Africa's Luminary, 53
Afro-American: churches, 32-33,
36, 74, 135-36, 193, 198;
educational institutions, 18, 42,
78, 83, 100, 171, 182, 183,
184, 209, 224
Afro-American missionaries: African
education and, 43, 96, 99, 118,
225; European colonialism
and, 133-34, 198-99, 201, 203,
211, 224, 236; European
opposition to, 20, 21-22, 178,
182, 187, 192-93, 201, 202,
203-4, 207, 220, 224; immunity
to African diseases of, 16-17,
53, 56, 135, 136; the "special

About the Contributors

THOMAS C. HOWARD, Associate Professor of History, Virginia Polytechnic Institute and State University, received the Ph.D. degree in American history from Florida State University. His work has been on various aspects of the Western impact on Third World societies. His publications include articles on intellectual linkages between Africa and the United States.

SYLVIA M. JACOBS, Professor of History, North Carolina Central University, received the Ph.D. degree in African history from Howard University. She has given papers before historical organizations and has had articles published on the relationship between Afro-Americans and Africa. Her first book, *The African Nexus: Black American Perspectives on the European Partitioning of Africa, 1880-1920*, was published in 1981.

LILLIE M. JOHNSON, Assistant Professor of History and Coordinator of African/African-American Studies, Earlham College, received the Ph.D. degree in African history from the University of Chicago. Her dissertation title was "Black American Missionaries in Colonial Africa, 1900-1940: A Study of Missionary-Government Relations." She has had a study packet published on "Black American Missionaries in Colonial Africa" (1978).

MANNING MARABLE, Associate Professor of Political Economy and History, Africana Studies and Research Center, Cornell University, received the Ph.D. degree in American history from the University of Maryland. He has written articles on Pan-Africanism and has had several books published on Afro-American political history, including *From the Grassroots: Social and Political Essays Toward Afro-American Liberation* (1980) and *Blackwater: Historical Studies in Race, Class Consciousness, and Revolution* (1981).

SANDY DWAYNE MARTIN, Assistant Professor of Religion, University of North Carolina at Wilmington, received the Ph.D. degree from Columbia University-Union Theological Seminary. His dissertation topic was "The Growth of Christian Missionary Interest in West Africa Among Southeastern Black Baptists, 1880-1915." He has delivered papers at conferences on black Baptists and foreign missions.

CAROL A. PAGE, Assistant Professor of History, Howard University, received the Ph.D. degree in African history from the University of Edinburgh, Scotland, with a dissertation entitled "Black America in White South Africa: Church and State Reaction to the A.M.E. Church in Cape Colony and Transvaal, 1896-1910." She has delivered papers and has had articles published on mission efforts of the AME Church in southern Africa.

DONALD F. ROTH, Managing Director, Hartford Symphony Orchestra, in Hartford, Connecticut, received the Ph.D. degree in American history from the University of Texas at Austin. His dissertation topic was " 'Grace Not Race': Southern Negro Church Leaders, Black Identity, and Missions to West Africa, 1865-1919." He has delivered papers at historical conferences on black church interests in Africa.

TOM W. SHICK, Associate Professor, Afro-American Studies Department, University of Wisconsin at Madison, received the Ph.D. degree in African history from the University of Wisconsin at Madison. He has delivered papers at professional meetings and has had articles published on Liberian emigration. His first book, *Behold the Promised Land: A History of Afro-American Settlers in Nineteenth-Century Liberia*, was published in 1980.

WALTER L. WILLIAMS, Associate Professor of History, University of Cincinnati, received the Ph.D. degree in American history from the University of North Carolina at Chapel Hill. He specializes in the history of interethnic relations and has had more than a dozen articles published on this topic. His other publications include an edited collection, *Southeastern Indians Since the Removal Era* (1979) and *Black Americans and the Evangelization of Africa, 1877-1900* (1982).